How to be Happy Though Human

W. BERAN WOLFE

TO ALFRED ADLER My friend and teacher

2016 by McAllister Editions (MCALLISTEREDITIONS@GMAIL.COM). This book is a classic, and a product of its time. It does not reflect the same views on race, gender, sexuality, ethnicity, and interpersonal relations as it would if it was written today.

CONTENIDOS

- PREFACE 7
- CHAPTER ONE: OF BASIC PRINCIPLES: LIVING AS A FINE ART 10
  - *Definition of Happiness* 11
  - *Creative Self-sculpture* 12
  - *Some Sources of Unhappiness* 14
  - *The Case of Robert* 16
  - *Can we Change Human Nature?* 17
  - *The Law of Psychic Inertia* 19
  - *How to Know Yourself* 20
  - *Twelve Laws of Personality Evolution* 21
- CHAPTER TWO. OF MATERIALS: THE INFERIORITY COMPLEX 27
  - *Universality of the Inferiority Feeling* 28
  - *Social Life as a Compensation* 30
  - *Isolation: The Basis of the Inferiority Complex* 33
  - *Symptoms of the Inferiority Complex* 35
  - *The 'Organ Jargon' of the Inferiority Complex* 38
  - *Sex and the Inferiority Complex* 40
  - *Negative Patterns of Life* 41
- CHAPTER THREE: OF OBSTACLES: FEAR AND INFERIORITY 44
  - I. OF PHYSICAL DISABILITIES 44
  - *'Left-Handedness* 46
  - *Beauty and Ugliness* 48
  - 2. THE FAMILY CONSTELLATION 49
  - 3. SEX 52
  - 4. SOCIAL, ECONOMIC, AND RACIAL DETERMINANTS 54
  - 5. EMOTIONAL ATTITUDES OF PARENTS AND TEACHERS 56
  - *Parental Mistakes* 58
  - 6. FALLACIES OF FORMAL EDUCATION 60
  - 7. SUBJECTIVE SOURCES OF INFERIORITY FEELING 63
  - *The Role of Sexual Trauma* 64
- CHAPTER FOUR. OF CRAFTSMANSHIP: COMPENSATION, AND OVERCOMPENSATION 67
  - *Four Methods of Compensation* 69
  - *Compensation as A Function of the Total Personality* 72
  - *Social Channels of Compensation* 73
  - *How to Compensate for Being Pampered* 75
  - *'Plus Gestures, And The Superiority Complex* 76

Valid Uses of 'Plus Gestures' *78*
Fundamental Techniques of Compensation *79*
Hobbies as Old Age Insurance *82*
Neuroses as False Compensations *83*
Two Patterns of Life *85*
The Substitution of Techniques for Goals *86*
Money as A Fiction of Power *88*
Recapitulation *89*

CHAPTER FIVE. OF TOOLS: CHARACTER AND PERSONALITY 91
The Dynamic Concept of Character *94*
Introversion and Extra-Version *95*
'Good, And 'Bad' Characters *96*
The 'Ideal' Character *98*
The Evolution of a Personality *100*
The 'Evolution of a Neurotic Character *103*
How to Analyse a Character *106*

CHAPTER SIX. MORE ABOUT TOOLS: CONFLICT AND EMOTION 110
Vanity and Egoism *112*
Ambition: Its Use and Misuse *114*
The Meaning of Conflict and Doubt *115*
Some 'Psychoanalytic Bogeys' *118*
The Dynamics of Evasion *119*
Make-Believe Superiorities *122*
The Misuse of Mind *123*
Fundamental Attitudes of The Good Life *124*
The Profession of Worry *125*
The Purpose of Worry *128*
Analysis of Jealousy *129*
The Relation of Jealousy to Love *131*

CHAPTER SEVEN. OF TRAINING: DREAMS, HUMOUR, AND PHILOSOPHY 133
Psychic Selectivity and Experience *134*
How We 'Make' Our Experience *135*
Procrustes and the Scheme of Apperception *137*
The Training Formula *138*
The Function of Memory *141*
The Importance of Childhood Memories *142*
About Dreams *144*
Of Wit and Humour *147*

The Psycho-Dynamics of a Joke *148*
The Value of Sport *150*
Of Basic Philosophies *151*
Mysticism, Fatalism, and Hedonism *153*
CHAPTER EIGHT. OF GOALS: THE THREE RING CIRCUS 156
The Importance of Useful Work *157*
The Social and Sexual Tasks *159*
The Battle-front of Life *160*
The Concept of 'Distance' *162*
About 'Nervous Breakdowns' *163*
The Holiday Neurosis *165*
About Idlers *166*
Of Sexual Virtuosity *168*
Emergency Exits of the Soul *169*
Normal Sex Relationships *170*
The Inter-relation of Human Problems *172*
Catalogue of Side-show *173*
Why 'Normality Pays *174*
CHAPTER NINE. OF FALSE GOALS: THE SIDE-SHOWS 177
How the Family Inhibits Mental Maturity *178*
The Necessity of Educating Young Children Outside the Family *180*
The Normal Uses of Individualism *181*
The Evasion of Work *182*
The Sexual Side-show *183*
The Bogey of Masturbation *185*
The Cure of Masturbation *187*
Homosexuality *189*
Why Homosexuality Can Be Cured *190*
Sexual Athletics and the Double Standard *192*
Prostitution *194*
Minor Conversions of Sex *195*
The Problem of Narcotics *196*
Psychological Aspects of Alcoholism *197*
The Cost of Flight from Reality *199*
CHAPTER TEN: PATTERNS OF FAILURE: ABOUT NEUROSES 202
The Neurotic Decalogue *204*
Types of Neuroses *210*
Fallacies of Freudian Psychoanalysis *212*

Adler and the Hormic Point of View *213*
Fundamental Dynamics of Neurotic Behaviour *214*
Techniques of Evasion *216*
The Flight from Reality *219*
Split Personality: A Neurotic Fiction *220*
Suicide *222*
The High Cost of Neuroses *223*
Psychological 'Rackets' and the 'Cure' of Neuroses *225*
How a Neurosis is Cured *228*
Who Shall Treat the Neurotic? *229*

CHAPTER ELEVEN. PATTERNS OF COOPERATION: LOVE AND MARRIAGE 232
Ignorance as it Cause of Marital Disaster *236*
Marriage as a Task *237*
The Socialisation of Sex *239*
The Vital Role of Contraception *240*
The Curse of Sexual Competition *241*
Historic Origins of our Sexual Morality *244*
Syzygiology v. the Old Psychology *245*
Androtropism and Gynetropism *246*
Sex Appeal and the Dangerous Age *247*
Tragedies of Sexual Competition *248*
The Cancer of Romantic Infantilism *250*
The Romantic Fallacy *251*
Romantic Hocus-pocus: Falling in Love *253*
The Aftermath of Love at First Sight *254*
'Practical Suggestions *257*

CHAPTER TWELVE. OF TECHNIQUES: THE TRIUMPH OF MATURITY 260
The Technique of Empathy *262*
The Dynamics of Friendship *263*
How to Start a Friendship *265*
Hints on Social Success *266*
The Fine Art of Making Presents *268*
How to Widen your Social Horizons *269*
The Vital Need for Hobbies *270*
'Either... or' v. 'Both... and' *272*
Some Useful Hints on Controversy *273*
Of Deferred Living *274*
How to Grow Old Gracefully *275*

The Uses of Leisure and Adversity 278
L'Envoi 280
THE END. 281

PREFACE

Mental hygiene Is the science of the hour. In its twenty-five years of existence this infant among the sciences has already contributed a distinctive flavour to the twentieth century. The vast literature of dynamic psychiatry has touched such diverse phases of human conduct, and illumined so many hitherto mysterious corners of the human soul, that no truly civilized adult dare remain ignorant of its basic principles any longer. The twentieth century, indeed, is characterized by its tendency to seek for meanings, not in the superficialities of overt behaviour, but in the unconscious depths of human motivation. Never before have men known so much about the human spirit, and never before have they been more eager to discover the quintessentials of the human personality.

The science and art of psychiatry are established to-day as valid disciplines of human thought, but the literature of psychiatry is shrouded in the mysteries of abstruse technical terms. The most worth-while contributions to the understanding of human conduct have been written by psychiatrists for psychiatrists, and in terms generally unintelligible to untrained lay readers. The. best psychiatric literature, moreover, is not only complex in its terminology, but is so inaccessible that it is practically unavailable to any but the most specialized students.

On the other hand, a veritable Niagara of pseudo-psychological literature has been poured upon the lay reader. We are living in an age of self-appointed psychological messiahs. Champions of pseudoscientific panaceas can be found on every street corner. Otherwise decent and self-respecting people go about 'analysing' the 'complexes' of their dinner partners as if the practice of psychoanalysis were a new parlour game. Scientific terms which appeared only in the most technical journals ten years ago have invaded the popular press and misused psychological jargon peppers the text of nearly every new so-called psychological novel and drama. It is the open season for self-styled 'psychologists'.

Intelligent, 'normal' adults have a right to demand a common- sense treatise on the science of human relations. If modern psychiatry has a valid message, that message can be given in terms intelligible to educated readers. It is an auspicious portent that the intelligent layman is interested in the newer developments of modern science as part of his spiritual orientation. The crisis of modern civilization has turned men to the consideration of their own basic personality problems. They want to know the whys and the wherefores of human behaviour, as never before in history, and they want to know how, moreover, they can avoid the personality disasters that strike their fellows with alarming frequency on every side. It is to meet this need that the author has essayed the task of writing a Baedeker of the soul,

The present volume was undertaken to fill the gap between scientific but technical texts on psychopathology, and existing, oversimplified, and frequently unsound primers of psychological information. In preparing the text, the author has attempted to avoid writing 'just another theoretical book on psychology', and at the same time, to escape the accusation of being totally devoid of a sense of humour by adding to the existing over-supply of 'tabloid' psychology.

The idea of writing a book which would attempt to steer the difficult course between the Scylla of psychiatric obscurantism and the Charybdis of pre-digested psychology, was relegated to the limbo of vague agenda until the author's belief in the desirability of such a book' was echoed by a variety of requests from the most diverse sources. In the beginning these requests came chiefly from patients who wished to supplement the work of their own analyses with a book which would present the scope and meaning of psychological re-education. Further requests originated from those who, having been enlightened and liberated by their own adventures in the reconstruction of their vital attitudes and the re-direction of their vital patterns, desired a book to place in the hands of friends 'who needed psychological readjustment but were either ignorant of their own difficulties or fearful of the implications of psychiatric treatment.

An additional stimulus to prepare this book came from colleagues who desired a trenchant outline of the scope of individual psychology together with a guide of 'what to do' and 'how to treat' the problems that arose in the everyday practice of medicine. Students who attended the author's courses and lectures contributed an additional impetus by requesting the author to put the material of these lectures - which were of necessity the merest outlines of the subject - into book form. The actual writing of the book, finally, was undertaken because of the author's growing realisation that a practical treatise on psychotherapy could be of value to the large number of essentially normal men and women who suffer some unpleasant neurotic episode from time to time, or realize that their efficiency is impaired by some vaguely recognized neurotic conduct. These men and women are intelligent enough to apply the general principles of rational psychotherapy to their own cases as soon as they are acquainted with the true meaning of the facts. In many instances these temporary or potential neurotics can obviate and correct their own mistakes after appropriate orientation in the meaning of their own difficulties and after the application of the practical hints which the author has incorporated into the text for the use of just such readers.

The purpose of this book, which might be sub-titled: 'A catalogue of instigations for those who would walk with courage', may be stated thus: to sketch, in the barest outlines, certain basic principles of the good life; to stimulate the reader to further self-training and self-clarification; and finally, to suggest certain practical measures for the extension of the reader's vital horizons. The book contains no magical formula for the attainment of happiness, nor does it purport to present a panacea for all conceivable human disappointments and chagrins. It offers no guarantee, not does it advance any claim to completeness. It is written for men and women who are not afraid of ideas, for those who believe Shat many tragedies may be avoided, for those fighting optimists who believe that human happiness is attainable, and for those who prefer to live in the conscious knowledge of life's implications rather than to 'muddle through' it by a process of unconscious vegetation.

Countless ideas derived from the works of other writers have in-. evitably been incorporated in a treatise of this scope. To acknowledge these copious borrowings in detail would necessitate so extensive a bibliography that, for purely practical reasons, the writer must forego the adequate acknowledgement of many valuable sources of his information. The author wishes, however, to acknowledge specifically his profound debt to his friend and teacher, Di: Alfred Adler, and to his colleague, Dr Erwin Wexberg, in the translation of whose book he has derived so much valuable knowledge and insight-. Special acknowledgement, also, is due to Miss Nannine Joseph for her generous help in the preparation of the manuscript.

The cases cited in the text have been drawn from the author's private and clinical practice. Needless to say, names, dates, and places, together with all personal data which would lead to identification of the individuals concerned, have been altered to preclude all possibility of recognition. The author must express his deep appreciation to these patients for the Insight they have vouchsafed him into the dynamics of human conduct. Without their help he could not have written this volume, nor would he have presumed to offer his counsel to others had not they demonstrated its validity in the conduct of their lives. The author can ask no better reward for his labours than that an occasional reader will be encouraged to essay the task of psychological self-education, or be helped by these pages towards a new insight into his own nature, or a better understanding of his fellow-men.

CHAPTER ONE:
Of Basic Principles: Living as a Fine Art

Definition of Happiness - Creating Self-sculpture - Some Sources of Unhappiness - The Case of Robert - Can We Change Human Nature? - The Law of Psychic Inertia - How to Know Yourself - Twelve Laws of Personality 'Evolution

As a human being you have the choice of three basic attitudes toward life. You may approach life with the philosophy of the turnip, in which case your life will consist in being born, eating, drinking, sleeping, maturing, mating, growing old, and dying. Of human turnips there are no end, and theirs is a calm contentment undisturbed by the problems of this world. They require neither books nor teaching, since vegetation is the be-all and end-all of the human turnip's life. The same Providence that protects puppy dogs and earthworms watches over their destiny and provides their simple wants in life. They vegetate at the lowest level consistent with humanity, and as they never read books, we need not disturb their placid existences by useless instruction in the art of living.

The second basic attitude is to look at life as if it were a business. A great many so-called successful men and women believe that life is a business, and they arrange their conduct and behaviour accordingly. If you believe that life is a business your first question of life, naturally, is 'What do I get out of it?' and your first reaction to any new experience is, 'How much is this worth to me?' In a world based on this attitude, happiness becomes a matter of successful competition, and this is the method of choice in the animal world. The stronger eats the weaker. The fittest, in point of personal power, survives at the expense of the weaker. Life becomes a matter of aggressive offence and successful defence. Every animal shifts for himself* and living alternates between savage victory and abject defeat.

The great majority of human beings to-day look at life as if it were a business. Their basic philosophy is one of aggressive competition and personal efficiency. Our skyscrapers, our 'rush hours', our super-motor-cars and our 'high-pressure' salesmanship are all the laudable results of personal competition. So also are slavery, war, class conflicts, despotism, serfdom, and the exploitation of smaller nations by their more powerful neighbours. The belief that might is right is the direct result of a 'strictly business' attitude towards life. The aggressive egoism of the 'might is right' school leads to a variety of 'nervous breakdowns' which preclude happiness, and anyone who has watched the struggle for personal prestige and power in a family or in a business office knows how disastrous the business attitude is in the private lives of men and women. And anyone who has read the history of the world must likewise be impressed with the failure of the 'What do we get out of it?' school of national politics.

We are too prone to overlook the terrific costs of the wrecks of the competitive system to individual and to State. The competitive system in life does not kill outright, as in the 'animal world,' where its success is greater. Applied to Human life it maims, it cripples, it makes dependent. It breeds crime, perversion, and insanity, the costs of which weigh heavily on victor and victim alike. Any attitude toward life which has such an impressive list of titanic failures to its credit in the history of the world, is hardly likely to load to individual happiness when applied to the lives of individuals. If we would be happy in being human, we must look at our lives neither with the placid eyes of the human turnip nor with the greedy eyes of the aggressive, self-seeking business man.

The third attitude toward life is the approach of the artist. Here the underlying philosophy is 'What can I put into it?' and the basic relation of the individual to his fellow-men, one of cooperation and common sense. If we have recourse to history again as a test of the validity of this attitude we find as confirmation of this point of view that history remembers best

those who have contributed most richly to the welfare of their fellow-men* And when we examine the lives of these great contributors we find that their genius was never one of aggressive self-seeking, but one of contribution to the welfare of their fellows. The more we investigate and the more we learn about living the more we become convinced that the artistic attitude is the only one which is consistent with human happiness. Our book, therefore, will be devoted to the investigation of living as a fine art, and our thesis will be that happiness is a quality of successful artistry in living.

Definition of Happiness

But what is happiness? We ought to define our terms in the very first sentence lest misunderstandings arise from the very beginning. But we are going to evade the challenge and leave the definition of human happiness to metaphysicians and undergraduates, because happiness is not a thing that can be defined by mathematical formulas. Happiness is no apple that you can peel and eat. Happiness is a quality and an attribute of the good life. The more you try to define it the less you know about it. It is as ineluctable as electricity, as evanescent as melody, as indefinable as health, as variable as speed, time* matter, and the other fictions on which life itself is built. Happiness knows no standard and no limits. If we want to know what happiness is we must seek it, therefore, not as if it were a pot of gold at the end of the rainbow, but among human beings who are living, richly and fully, the good life.

Nearly every human being is looking for happiness, but' very few know what happiness is. Nevertheless, if you observe a really happy man you will find him building a boat, writing a symphony, educating his son, growing double dahlias in his garden, or looking for dinosaur eggs in the Gobi Desert. He will not be searching for happiness, as if it were a collar stud that has rolled under the dressing-table. He will not be striving for it as a goal in itself, nor will he be seeking it among the nebulous wastes of metaphysics. He. will have become aware that he is happy in the course of living twenty-four crowded hours of the day. If you have taken up this book in the hope that you will find some magical formula for attaining happiness, some panacea to cure all human ills, you will be disappointed in your quest. But if you are searching for knowledge, if you desire a better understanding of human nature, if you are seeking for a significant goal in living, or a better technique of attaining the goal you have set yourself, let us encourage you to read on. For it is our thesis that living happily is a fine art that nearly everyone who possesses an iota of intelligence, courage, and a sense of humour can learn.

Creative Self-sculpture

The art of being a complete, and happy, human being may be likened to a process of creative self-sculpture. This term best describes the art of attaining poise and satisfaction, of gaining the courageous hopefulness and sense of freedom, the objective self-esteem that are the essential premises of happiness. Our heritage as human beings is the raw material of the fine art of being human. Every man must take this rock and hew out a design for himself. If he succeeds in this task within the time limit set by nature, he may well consider himself a happy human being. And success in the process of creative self-sculpture is open to all human beings with the exception of those unfortunates whose cases must be described in books devoted to the gross pathology of mind and body. If you have read as far as this paragraph you are equipped with adequate material and sufficient tools to make yourself a happy and efficient human being.

There may be men and women involved in a mesh of circumstances so inexorable that their happiness on this earth is definitely precluded, but we have seldom seen such a case. Hardly any human situation is irremediable, most of the very bad ones can be ameliorated, and nearly all men and women can, with courage and understanding, become happier than they are. Those who have attained complete happiness will hardly read these pages, except perhaps to find confirmation and corroboration of their own technique of living, while those so inadequately endowed by nature as to be Incapable of happiness in the larger human sense, will not turn to this book for solace. Happiness lies within the scope of all others.

The object of this book is to acquaint the reader with the principles and practice of the art of living well. It is not designed as a training course for saints and angels. Its principal thesis is that a tremendous artistic and creative satisfaction awaits any man, or woman, who devotes himself to the task of self-sculpture, providing he Is modest enough to play the game according to the rules, and confident enough in his powers to believe that the final product, while not perfect, may well be good. Our first premise is that nearly every human being's lot may be changed for the better. Over two thousand years ago Socrates taught' his pupils that Virtue may be learned'. Surely the major chagrins and disappointments of life may be avoided. Most of the torturing conflicts and much of the mental pain we experience are unnecessary and avoidable. There is hardly an intolerable anguish that cannot be replaced by some reasonable peace of mind. Most of the major personality disasters can be ameliorated if not entirely prevented. Some can be cured, many can be solaced, all can be consoled. Happiness is the interest that is paid men by nature for investments in the good life. It is not the reward of perfection. It begins as a dividend on the first step in the right direction, and it accrues by compound interest.

We shall proceed, therefore, to examine the problem of human happiness not as if it were an isolated goal of human life, but as if it were an attribute and an accompaniment of the good life. And the good life, as we have seen, is a fine art which can be learned. Consequently, our first concern is to know more about the artistic processes involved in creative self- sculpture, and our book will be devoted to research as to the goals of the good life, its problems, its tools, its techniques, and finally to the major satisfactions which it holds for the average, intelligent, adult human being.

When we examine the artistic process, whether in music, sculpture, painting, drama, or in creative self-sculpture, we find that the artist must master four fundamental wisdoms.

The first wisdom is knowledge of his material. As the painter must know his pigments, so the artist in living must understand human nature. The second wisdom is craftsmanship. Craftsmanship consists in the art of modifying raw material into a meaningful design. The writer must know how to mould his words so that they convey his meaning to the reader. The sculptor must know how to chisel granite, carve wood, or mould the plastic clay to his design. The artist in living must know how to modify human nature. He must begin by self-education, and he must be capable of influencing his fellow-men in such a way that the human community will be a better place in which to live. The third wisdom is again knowledge, this time knowledge of the purpose and goal of art. If you know human nature, and know how to change your own conduct or influence the lives of your employees, your child, or your housemaid, and have no plan or design for your own life, you cannot be very happy in being human. The fourth and most intangible of these necessary wisdoms is courage. Every art interposes obstacles in the way of the artist. Many a newspaper man has dreamed of writing a great novel only to shrink timidly from his task when faced with the impudence of half a dozen sheets of white paper. Many a would-be sculptor has dreamed his heroic figures only to falter at the persistent obstinacy of cold granite. And so also many a man, knowing his potentialities, sure of his technique, aware of his goal in life, has hesitated and been lost because the obstacles of age, of sex, of time, of money, of geography, climate, mothers-in-law, public prejudice, hay-fever or religious belief have discouraged him from carrying on.

Some Sources of Unhappiness

A great deal of human unhappiness is due to the fact that people are for ever trying to carve wood with tools designed to chisel granite, while others, driven by the spurs of egoistic ambition, attempt to cut marble monoliths out of a handful of clay. Many are unhappy because they are discouraged by first attempts at self-sculpture; others are unhappy because they have lost sight of their final design in the process of working out details. Because time is an element in human life, there are people unhappy because they have set themselves an impossible task, while others, having chosen too simple a design, finish too soon, and are unhappy because they have nothing more to do.

We once saw a young woman polishing her finger-nails at a football match. It was a smashingly dramatic moment A centre had caught a long forward pass. He stumbled, wavered, regained his feet and was racing for the opposing goal posts. One lone half-back stood between him and victory. Seventy thousand people were on their feet, frantically cheering, half of them pushing one way, half of them pulling the other in fierce identification with that bounding dynamo of muscle and desire. Hardly lifting her eyes from her finger-nails the young woman asked her escort, "What are all those people shouting for?" It is amazing to see how many human beings regard the spectacle of life with the bored indifference of this young woman. They suffer from an acute stricture of their mental horizon. They are unaware of the breathless drama that moves on the stage of the world all about them. They sit in the wings, twiddling their thumbs, while the sublimest tragedy of all time stalks the boards. Others, again, while waiting patiently for Santa Claus, go on suffering civilization instead of enjoying it. Others still defer their lives to some ideal psychological moment when they promise themselves they will begin to live.

You, as an individual citizen of this world, cannot be happy if jot do not know why your neighbour is neurotic, why the stockbroker's daughter Steals trinkets from Woolworth's, why your, niece has temper tantrums. And you, as an individual, cannot be happy unless you are interested in the why and wherefore of college suicides, prostitution, homosexuality, racketeering, war, prohibition, child labour, or religious persecution. Finally, you cannot be happy unless you know why you want to be a millionaire, why you like to be the first off the train, why you procrastinate, why you hate responsibilities, why you are always so over-punctual for appointments, why you cannot sleep at night, and why you are afraid of growing old. Not to answer these questions is to limit your mental horizons to an arc so narrow as to be inconsistent with human happiness.

Much of our unhappiness is directly due to discouragement, and most human discouragement is due to ignorance. Just as ignorance of the law is no valid excuse in committing a crime, so ignorance of life can no longer be considered an excuse for unhappiness. The cultivation of awareness and interest in all that concerns humanity, and the development of your sensitivity to new stimuli is the first step in the fine art of being a complete human being. Discouragement is the common denominator of all unhappy lives. Unfortunately, discouragement and ignorance stalk us in our youth, when it would be most advantageous to be wise and courageous. We begin our self-sculpture at a time when our critical faculties and our physical powers are at their lowest level. The ideal picture which we use as a design is distorted by false values. We grow, we learn, we become more capable, but the false ideal remains fixed as a pattern in our unconscious life, just as our technique of attaining that ideal is also fixed. Both our goal and our technique may be completely out of harmony with reality. We are unhappy. We redouble our efforts, still in the old false patterns, and still with the old false goals before us. Unhappiness is heaped on unhappiness, and false ideals and poor craftsmanship follow each other in a vicious and endless circle. This is the tragedy of ignorance.

The Case of Robert

Let us take an example to illustrate the role of ignorance in the production of unhappiness. Robert, aged four, was the oldest son of a magistrate. When Robert was a child, his father was already a relatively great man. He stood for law and order in his community. Robert saw other great men coming to consult with his father. He knew that the entire life of his family was subordinated to his father when his father was in art important conference. If his father was in his study writing a decision, everyone had to walk very quietly and talk in a whisper, Robert believed that to be a man one must be a great man like his father. But when Robert was four, he could not even read. In fact, he could not even ride a bicycle like Julian, his five-year-old neighbour. Robert was depressed by a secret and unconscious discouragement. He had already begun to doubt the validity of his material for self-sculpture, Robert began to play 'robbers' with the other boys in the street. He knew that his father had great powers over the police. Then he made a great, if mistaken, discovery. If he could fool the 'bobbies' he would be smarter than his father. He began to play the idle of robber passionately in the street, in a discouraged attempt to compensate for his sense of weakness. We adults know this is a mistake, but this four-year-old boy did not understand the objective relationships between authority and crime. Robert also began to tease and torture his younger sister Marian at this time. He vaunted his power over her. He refused to play with her friends. 'What good are girls, anyhow!' he said, 'They can't even climb!'

A wise and knowing parent would have considered this statement very significant as an expression of deep discouragement. At that time Robert already had a false design which could have been formulated in the phrase: I must be greater than my father. If I find that I cannot compete with him in his own way, I will destroy his power. If I can raise myself at the expense of anyone else, that's all in my favour!' Of course Robert really does not say these things. But he acts as if he were already hopeless. We see him in the meshes of a competitive struggle for power and authority with his father.

We see Robert next in hospital. He is now nineteen years old. He has unsuccessfully attempted to commit suicide during his first year at the university. Has his pattern changed? Hot at all. Robert wanted to be popular with his fellow-undergraduates. He was not. Robert wanted the love of his tutor's daughter, and she 'turned him down'. He considered these two achievements essential to his happiness, and when he failed, his self-esteem, always based on false subjective values, was shattered. He knew only one way out - suicide. And you must remember that suicide not only seemed to solve Robert's problem, but pointed an accusing finger at his father, his fellow-undergraduates, and his girl, as if he were saying, "You see what you have done to me?' - thus shifting the responsibility from his own shoulders to those of society. It is a general human tendency to avoid responsibility for our failures, and this tendency is inordinately exaggerated in those who have too ambitious a goal, or those who are discouraged by the obstacles in their way.

Perhaps the fact that Robert did not succeed in his attempt was part of his unconscious plan. It served as a warning, as though he were announcing to the whole world, "Now you must take care of me lest I commit suicide." And in a cheap, useless way Robert attained his goal of superiority by attempting suicide, because it brought his whole family to his bedside, concerned every member of his college, and no doubt wrenched the heart of his tutor's daughter.

Can we Change Human Nature?

Hardly anyone will consider Robert's life a happy one, but many will shrug their shoulders and counter with that worn-out cliché, "You can't change human nature!' Now there is a great deal of truth in that cliché. Really, no one wants to change human nature. But we should know a great deal more about it. The people who usually tell you about the difficulties of changing human nature really mean, "You cannot change human conduct" And deep down in their hearts they mean, "I am afraid to change my own pattern of life even though I am unhappy in it. Therefore, I will screen my fear by calling on this accepted and time-worn old motto to rid me of the responsibility of looking into the matter" This fallacy, like so many others, is based on ignorance and fear, the two greatest enemies of human happiness.

Why does human conduct seem to resist change so stubbornly? Let us go back to our analogy of self-sculpture. We come into the world with a shapeless mass of material from which we must carve out our lives. Our idea of the design is almost universally bad because it is formed when we are ignorant of the world of design, of material, of technique, and of tools. Nevertheless, we choose some design, depending on the circumstances of our childhood situation, pick the most likely tools, and chisel away, in some instances blind to the activities of our fellows who are busily hammering out their destinies at our side, in other instances equally blinded by an aggressive ambition, an early discouragement, or a crippling competition with a parent or brother.

As an example let us take the case of Ruth, who is the youngest child in a family of four. She is also the only girl in that family. Her father is the golf champion in his town and once played football for his university. He wants his boys to grow up into '100 per cent he-men' and he feels that it would be just as well to educate his daughter exactly as he does his boys. Little Ruth, now five years old, climbs, rides a small bicycle, swims, and has already begun to play golf. She has no use for dolls, small tea-sets, or the other toys that girls in her neighbourhood play with. She wants to be a boy, and she has already shown that she can beat her younger brother in swimming. She is not very dear as to the physical differences between boys and girls. Her mother is an unimportant member of the household. Masculine ideals of sport and courage and fair play rule the household. Golf is the chief topic of conversation at the table. Her ideal in life is to 'hole out in one'.

Ruth is a strong healthy girl, and at the present nothing stands between her and her ideal to be 'a boy among the boys'. She is innately ashamed of other members of her own sex, and year by year she has less contact with them. At the age of fourteen Ruth begins to menstruate. This is a calamitous occasion in. her life. Her mother tells her timidly about sex. Ruth is not very encouraged. She calls her menstrual period 'the curse'. She regards her femininity as a distinct drawback in the attainment of her ideal. She is not allowed to swim at her menstrual period which is accompanied by a great deal of pain. This pain and the attendant unhappiness are the indicators of a very unhappy future. Ruth is attempting to use the

material given her by nature, being a girl, to a false end. This leads to conflicts with nature and society. She cannot make a confidante of her mother because her mother does not share her ideals. Her mother suffers her femininity in silence. Ruth is determined that she will be a 'modern' woman. She wants to be a physical instructor at college, and at the age of seventeen she has already definitely made up her mind that she will never marry and never have children. 'It plays havoc with your figure and your strength, you know" she adds by way of explanation.

In this case we see a very common, and tragically mistaken, pattern of life. Here is a woman who has tried to make a man of herself. Life does not teach her the fallacy of her actions, for she stuffs every new experience into the old trunk of her childhood pattern. She rationalizes her failures; she overlooks her mistakes. She considers herself a very emancipated young lady, but the chief attributes of her pattern of conduct are ignorance and persistence. She can never attain happiness, because a woman can no more find happiness in trying to subvert nature by acting 'as if' she were a man, than a rabbit can achieve happiness acting 'as if' he were a lion.

The Law of Psychic Inertia

As a first step in the understanding of human conduct, let us formulate the law of psychic inertia. Human beings tend to maintain a fixed pattern of conduct, determined by the dynamic forces of early childhood, unless some profound experience, or a systematic psychological analysis and re-education diverts that pattern into a new channel. In other words if a human being were to perceive and evaluate himself as a huge block of marble in early childhood, and would pick out the drills and chisels necessary to hew that marble into the heroic statue he wanted to be, that man would tend to continue hacking away at the resistant stone despite all criticism and proof that he was dealing with a small block of wood, unless some distressing accident such as a grave self-injury, or a systematic and friendly review of the pattern of his activities from early childhood, an analysis of his early childhood misconceptions, and a re-education in the use of new and more appropriate tools, were instituted.

Under such circumstances our man would learn to be objective about himself, and not subjective. By objective we mean that he would know that he was hewing at a block of wood, and finding joy in carving it into a fine, if small, statue. (The subjective man hacks at a block of wood with chisels designed for marble, because he is afraid to look at reality, and acts 'as if' it were marble. To do this, naturally, he must exclude the opinions of his fellows to a large extent, and if he becomes so subjective that he excludes all common sense and lives according to a private system of logic and reason, we call that man insane, and his ideas hallucinations or delusions.) It is very difficult to be really objective about yourself unless you have learned to look at yourself with the eyes of another. Many people still believe there is something slightly disgraceful about a psychological analysis and re-education, as if consulting a psychiatrist about a problem of conduct wire an admission of mental incompetence. Nothing could be farther from the truth, for the merit of any system of psychological re-education lies chiefly in the fact that a good psychiatrist helps the patient to get an objective bird's-eye view of his own pattern of conduct. When the patient sees himself and the unconscious processes of his behaviour with the psychiatrist's objective eye, the patient must finally do something about it himself. All the psychiatrist can do is point the way toward mental maturity, and encourage his pupil, for he is more a pupil than a patient, to go on by himself.

But it is very difficult to get the average man to admit that his pattern of conduct is hot mature and even more difficult to make him see that he knows little about his inner self despite the fact that he has been living with himself all his life. "But doctor, I know myself like a book! I know myself much better than anyone else does!' is the common retort when a psychiatrist questions the motives and purposes of an individual's conduct. Most people believe that they know themselves extremely well, and it is difficult indeed to get a man to admit he is not a good judge of human nature. As a matter of fact, it is the rarest of human beings who knows more than a few superficial and unconnected data about himself. Most of us are complete strangers to our deeper selves. A man may know that he likes to play golf, and that he is irritated by snobs, and that he prefers blue neckties, but he can seldom give you a psychologically valid reason for his actions and reactions.

A woman may know why she does not eat bread and potatoes, but she would resent the imputation that her desire to remain slender was actuated by a deep unconscious desire to remain a child and to avoid responsibilities, and she would be amazed to know that her diet and her disinterestedness in the world of business and politics, her coyness, her cult of a perfect complexion, her choice of filmy and fluttery dresses were all related, all tools for the sculpture of the same figure of a grown-up baby-doll. And even if she knew all these things she would not know why she had chosen the ideal of being a baby-doll from the whole host of other available designs, nor why she persisted in pursuing this ideal in the face of all common-sense data about the unattainability of that goal in reality.

How to Know Yourself

A worm in a peach may know the inside of his peach with a precise and 'scientific' knowledge, but it requires another worm, perhaps no better or more knowing, to tell the first worm where his peach hangs on the tree. Every individual knows something about himself within the fixed pattern of his personality, but usually he is unaware of the design of that pattern, that is, its goal, its significant form, its tempo of progression, and the material of the design. And what he knows least of all is the relationship of his design to the designs of other members of his family and to other members of his social group. The mere collection of data about ourselves is an interesting, but rather useless pastime. This is the so-called 'scientific' method.

To follow the Socratic dictum fully, you must 'know yourself' with the eyes of another person. This requires this distinctly artistic processes - identification and interpretation. Just as being a human being is a fine art, so knowing human nature is an artistic process. That is why poets, novelists, painters, generals, salesmen, and office-boys have usually known more about human nature than so-called 'scientists*.

Because we are all human beings, because we are all similar in our design and structure, because we grow according to the same general plan, and because, finally, we are inherently heir to certain weaknesses - and really, the similarities between human beings, despite the paradoxic dissimilarity of individual conduct, are far more numerous than their differences - the scope of our self-sculpture, and the craft of working out our lives into a happy design are limited by nature to certain broad channels and to certain natural goals. Before we go into the discussion of individual patterns of life, we should clarify these innate similarities, so that we can trace the general pattern through the maze of individual differences. Indeed, this general pattern of growth and personality evolution will be our guide to the understanding of the most bizarre differences in individual conduct. There are twelve psychological laws that govern human conduct and development. We shall merely sketch these laws here, for we shall have the opportunity of developing each one separately in later chapters.

Twelve Laws of Personality Evolution

I. Every human being experiences his incompleteness as a child. He cannot talk and he cannot walk and he cannot satisfy his hunger, but he can see that his parents and other adults are capable of all these mysterious actions. Thus there arises a sense of incompleteness or inadequacy. The physiological basis of this law is the fact that the brain and apperceptive powers of the child develop out of all proportion to his motor ability to satisfy his wants. Also, the dependence of the human infant is relatively greater than the dependence of the young of any other species.

II. All human beings grow toward a goal of completeness and totality. The design which is sketched in in infancy is filled out in maturity. This goal is fixed in our unconscious because it is formulated before the advent of complete speech and full consciousness. The goal of totality may often be concretized in a vague formula: 'I want to be a millionaire' or 'I want to be a big man', or I want to travel and see everything in the world'. This tendency to develop toward a goal of totality is a phenomenon common both to living and to dead matter. A drop of oil suspended in a solution of water tends to assume a spherical form regardless of its shape on being introduced into the solution. The acorn grows into an oak by a fixed and unchanging evolution. The acorn is the microcosm of the oak, just as the child-personality is the microcosm or prototype of the adult-personality.

The tadpole and the larva develop in a straight line of evolution into frog and bee in much the same fashion that 'the child is father to the man'.

3. The goal of an individual's life usually represents the complete compensation or over-compensation of his own inadequacies. In early childhood the goal-idea is usually concretized in some one person who, to the child, seems a perfect, all-powerful being. Thus the small boy who suffers from rickets and cannot coordinate his muscles properly wants to be a motor-cycle policeman because the motor-cycle policeman seems to embody all the strengths which he lacks. The poor boy wants to be rich. The ugly duckling finds its ideal in the stately swan. The child with poor digestion dreams of himself as a fat banker with great wealth, the social compensation of his interest in food. The short-sighted child wants to study the stars. Nature fills in defects with a lavish hand. If a tubercle bacillus lodges in our lung, nature throws up a more than adequate defence of fibrous tissue. The callous formation about a fracture in a bone is always larger and stronger than the bone itself. A boil represents the overwhelming defence of the body against invasion of germs. The child seeks an over-plus of activity in adult life to compensate him for the inadequacies of his childhood.

4. The goal of an individual's life-pattern is fixed when his critical faculties are still undeveloped. If may therefore represent the compensation for defects which only seem to exist, and it may he concretised in a goal-ideal which, to adults, seems very inadequate. (Our goal in life, therefore, depends upon our interpretation of our own inferiority situation and our idea of superiority and totality, and not on the facts as they are.) An example is the vary undernourished child who stated that she wanted to be the fat lady in the circus. Another is the son of a railway magnate who wanted to be a porter at St Pancras Station.

Any individual life is a pattern from a situation believed and considered a 'minus' toward a goal believed and considered a 'plus' Once the goal idea and the goal situation has been fixed in the unconscious, it acts as a magnet which directs all human activities towards itself The small boy wants to be a fireman because he is dissatisfied with 'small-boyishness', and sees in the glamour of the clanging fire engines a situation of 'plus'. He does not *say* he is dissatisfied with being a small boy, but he acts *as if* he felt dissatisfied. Dwarfs aspire to be giants - giants never want to be dwarfs. A young boy wants to be a doctor 'So I can stick the needles in people's arms'. To this boy the hypodermic syringe is the symbol of complete power. All human lives are a pattern from an imagined weakness to an imagined strength, from impotence to power, from insignificance to significance.

6. A human being cannot do anything outside his pattern. This is true all through the world of nature. Elephants do not grow humming-bird wings nor do oaks suddenly produce pomegranates. Elephants and oaks must be elephants and oaks from start to finish. The complete unity of any individual pattern is one of the most important laws of psychology. Everything we do, think, desire, fear, avoid, cherish, love, or hate, fits into our unit pattern. That is why dreams, early childhood recollections, our favourite film actors, our favourite sports, our antipathies, the clothes we wear, the way we shake hands, our gait, our habits, our handwriting, our physiognomy, our choice of foods, friends, recreations, hobbies and wives must fit into the same pattern. Fortune tellers, who are shrewd judges of human nature, detectives, artists, playwrights, all make use of this fact of the unity of the personality. If we go to a play in which a character has appeared as a good man for the first two and a half acts, only to be unmasked as the villain in the last scene, we think it a bad play because it outrages this unity of the personality.

If you are sure of five or six important facts about a man's life, you can practically fill in the rest of the pattern. Good psychiatrists can sometimes tell a patient ail his symptoms before he has said a word, from watching him enter the room and sit down. Good salesmen seize on one aspect of a prospective customer, add modify their sales talk to fit into his pattern. The whole art of character interpretation by graphology depends on this unity of the personality. For this reason, we can almost chart the life of an individual from five or six knows facts.

The tedious and unnecessarily long analyses of the psychoanalytical school are false and dangerous for this reason. They tend to involve the patient in a useless research into the past when the pattern of the personality can be determined after a few weeks of conferences - even if the patient lies. People have learned to lie with words, but they cannot lie with their gestures, their dreams, or their handwriting - and if their words are a contradiction of their unconscious acts, the unconscious acts are always the true basis of their personality.

7. The goal of life is fixed in early childhood, and tends to persist, according to the previously announced law of psychological inertia, unless it is modified both from without and from within. The goal- idea may experience many modifications, however, with the growth of the individual, without suffering an essential change. Thus, a psychiatrist of our acquaintance began life with the ambition to be an animal trainer. Later, as his knowledge of the world grew, he desired to be the conductor of an orchestra. He studied medicine because he wanted to be a 'leader' in his community, and finally, after an analysis of his own personality pattern by his teacher in psychiatry* he became a psychiatrist Psychiatry represents the final stage in the evolution of his goal-ideal from its beginning in a desire for purely personal power to the same sense of power through activity on a high plane of social usefulness

8. *Human beings have always lived and must always live in groups.* This is mankind's compensation for the individual weakness of its members. It is the basic law of human psychology. Any personality goal, and any personality pattern, which leaves the social connectedness of human beings out of account, runs counter to nature, and must end in personal disaster. During the early part of an individual's life he is a parasite on his family, the unit of most social groups. During this period of individuation, he is supported by his group while he trains and grows, and thus obviates the greater inferiorities of childhood in the 'normal' way. He transforms his childhood 'minus' into a 'plus' by physical and mental growth and evolution. Thereafter he must contribute the commonweal; and the 'normal' human being socializes his childhood goal of power and totality at this time by working out his personal deficiencies in terms of social usefulness. It is the duty of parents, to initiate their child into the fellowship of human beings and give Mm a sense of the dignity of work, which is the individual's dividend to society for society's original investment of protection, nutrition, and education during the period of his individuation.

9. *Every man fits his experiences into his pattern of life.* As we grow we meet many obstacles to our fixed pattern of conduct. Some of these obstacles deflect us from our course, some of them are surmounted or destroyed by us. What we call experience is the impression that Is left on us by the interaction between ourselves and the world in which we live. Most of us do not learn from experience, because we have a definite standard of evaluation with which we approach the world about us. This standard of evaluation is called a 'psychic scheme of apperception'. It is determined by our goal in life, and because this goal is based on subjective interpretations ' our reaction to any experience Is seldom objective. We view 'things in terms of their usefulness or uselessness to us in attaining our goal. Three men pass a huge oak in a forest One says, 'I could build a fine mast for my boat out of that trunk ' The second says, 'I could tan hundreds of shoes with the bark of that tree!" The third says, 'The acorns of that tree would feed all my pigs!" Each has had the same' experience but each has valued it in terms of his own goal and his own personality pattern.

24

10. There are three great groups of problems which every individual must solve in the course of his life. These problems are the problems of society, of work, and of sex. They may be likened to the three great rings of a huge circus, in which everyone of us must do his act. Because of the close interconnection of all human life it is no private matter whether we solve these problems. Every time we fail to solve a problem our fellow-men must assume a heavier burden; every time we make a mistaken solution, our neighbours or our children suffer. If we refuse to cooperate, and evade the obligations of humanity, we are denied the fruits of being human by the workings of an inexorable natural law. Those who are afraid to do their act, in the main three rings of life are usually to be found in the side-shows of life, rationalizing their conduct to themselves and attempting to deceive the world by shifting their responsibility to some scapegoat. Such self-deception and evasion of responsibilities is usually the product of fear and ignorance of the meaning of life.

11. The sum total of the tools and techniques an individual uses in the pursuit of his unconscious goal in life constitutes his character and personality. Character traits are always relative, and must be interpreted in relation to the individual pattern of conduct, never as absolute entities. Apparent contradictions in character or changes in personality may signify either a change of goal, or the pursuit of the same goal in a different environment.

The well-adjusted man or woman is honourable, sincere, optimistic, sympathetic, friendly, self-confident, generous, unafraid, because these are the best tools to gain the goal of human happiness. The thief, never having been initiated into the fellowship of mankind, considers every man his born enemy. He believes that the world owes him a living, and that those who have more worldly goods than he, possess them by virtue of undue discrimination in their favour. He develops the traits of stealth, treachery, dishonesty, false honour, slyness, and cruelty not because he was born with these traits, but because these are the best tools of thievery. It is impossible to evaluate a character by a single trait, just as it is impossible to know a melody when you know but a single- note. As in every art, and as in mathematics, you must have several points to establish a curve or a design.

If James, aged six, is a little destructive devil at home, and neat and orderly in school, it is not a paradoxical contradiction, nor yet evidence of the unpredictability of human traits. It means that James gains his end, to be the centre of attention, by being destructive at home, whereas in his classroom, where no nonsense is tolerated, he chooses a different tool.

When two individuals exhibit the same trait, that trait usually signifies two entirely different tools. Eloise, aged eight, and Marjorie, aged nine, are both very timid. Eloise is timid because she has been a spoiled, only child, and has never learned to make contacts with the world. Her timidity represents a strengthening of the bond between her and her mother. Eloise's timidity enslaves her mother. Marjorie, on the contrary, has very good contacts with the world, but she has been teased and ridiculed so often by her three elder brothers, that she fears to make a step lest she arouses their jibes. Her timidity represents a defence mechanism of a very different sort.

12. *Happiness is the attribute of being completely and successfully human.* This means that every individual who works out his private pattern from his situation of 'minus' to a position of 'plus' in terms of socially useful behaviour attains happiness. Happiness is not a matter of chance or of destiny. To be a successful human being means to affirm the laws of human solidarity, to contribute to the commonweal in terms of useful work, to solve the sexual problem in terms of social responsibility. It consists in transmuting the imagined or real inferiorities of childhood into objective superiorities of social value in adulthood. Its quintessential elements are courage and knowledge. Its tools are common sense, work, love and imagination, and a sense of humour, the rarest and most precious of human qualities.

Armed with these laws of human conduct which are universal in their application, we are prepared to consider the individual problems of human behaviour. We have purposely stated the fundamental principles that govern the fine art of being human briefly, in order that the reader might proceed as rapidly as possible to the practical and more interesting labour of creative self-sculpture. Yet, without a knowledge of these basic principles, the reader could not build wisely. Life, like art, demands the discipline of natural law, to be good.

To build without knowledge of these basic principles would be comparable to attempting to write a symphony without a knowledge of harmony. A child banging on a piano is a spontaneous and creative artist, but mature art, whether in music or in living, demands discipline and design to be meaningful The fine art of living is not acquired by 'muddling through. If you would be successful in the art of creative self-sculpture it would be well to keep the fundamental biological and psychological laws of human conduct constantly in mind. They are the structural framework on whose strength and soundness the integrity of every individual life depends.

CHAPTER TWO.
Of Materials: The Inferiority Complex

Universality of the Inferiority Feeling - Social Life as a Compensation - Isolation: The Basis of the Inferiority Complex - Symptoms of the Inferiority Complex - The 'Organ Jargon' of the Inferiority Complex ~ Sex and the Inferiority Complex - Negative Patterns of Life

Our first chapter has led to the conclusion that human happiness is attainable only when we scrap the philosophy of the turnip and the business man, and approach life as artists, with the' motto, 'What can we put into living?? In outlining the basic principles underlying the fine art of living the good life, and in the statement of the twelve psychological principles that govern human conduct, we build the structural framework of the art of creative self-sculpture. We are now prepared to examine the material which is available for use in the process of making something of ourselves. It must be apparent to the reader that this knowledge is of prime importance, because without a full awareness of the unique data of human life and living, the most perfect craftsmanship and the most exquisite conceptions of design would be futile.

Because of the limitations of the scope of this book the present chapter most be limited to the discussion of purely psychological data. An encyclopaedia of anatomy and physiology, of anthropology and ethnology, of history, sociology, economics, medicine, art, politics, religion, literature, and logic would really be in place as the second chapter of this book. We are aware of the manifest defects that result from this artificial limitation of scope, and submit only a pragmatic sanction as an excuse. Those readers who wish to pursue their self-sculpture will, it is hoped, be stimulated by their insight into the purely psychological problems outlined here, to continue their studies in the correlated fields of human culture. In 1907, Dr Alfred Adler, a Viennese physician, published a small book called A Study of Organ Inferiority which demonstrated, for the first time in history, how nature compensates for certain physical defects in an organ of the body by increased activity or by changes in structure which enable that damaged or inferior organ to more than carry on its usual work. An example of this compensatory activity may be seen in the formation of callous bone at the site of a fracture, the new bone acting as an additional supporting framework, or in the formation of scar tissue which fills in the defect when skin or muscle are cut. Adler also showed that when certain sense organs, such as the eyes or ears, were defective or injured, other sense organs occasionally became more active and thus helped to restore the injured individual to a greater measure of human efficiency.

This discovery led almost immediately to the realization that nature was very much concerned in keeping any organism, whether plant, animal, or man, at a high level of efficiency, and made provision to nullify any existing defects with a lavish hand. Further researches showed that when nature compensated for a defect, either in structure, such as a broken bone, or in function, such as in a heart whose valves did not function correctly, the compensatory mechanism frequently more than filled in the defect. In other words, where nature found a 'minus' she was inclined to replace it with a 'double plus', the healed bone being stronger than the original fractured bone, the leaking heart, by virtue of an overgrowth of muscular tissue, becoming in some instances a better and larger pump than a normal heart.

From this discovery it was but a step for Adler to find that compensations were not confined to the structure and functions of single organs, but that the total organism reacted in a compensatory fashion to the existence of a defect. This discovery constitutes one of the most important laws of modern psychology because it is the basis of the belief, now proved beyond all peradventure, that the character of a human being is often the result of the existence of some defect or inadequacy of his body. Thus we find men and women who have suffered from defects, often very minor ones, of the eyes, whose entire lives seem to be directed toward translating the world about them into visual values, while children who have suffered in childhood from rickets, a disease which affects the development of the bones and muscles in such a way as to increase the difficulties of movement, become distinctly 'motor, characters in later life, bending every effort to increase the efficiency of their locomotion, either by athletic training or by the invention of motor appliances, from wheels to aeroplanes, to aid them in their efforts.

Universality of the Inferiority Feeling

The next step in the investigation of these interesting aspects of human behaviour was the discovery that the entire human race suffers from a feeling of inadequacy, and has, throughout the ages of man's existence, evolved its unique human character as a compensation for its weakness. To test this universal human sense of inferiority we need but recall our complete inability to master the fickle elements or to solve the problems of death, disease, and the degeneration of our bodies. It is only in the most recent years that we have learned to understand something of the physical world in which we live, and we are still at the mercy of lightning, floods, earthquakes, or capricious hurricanes. Primitive man, with his hairless body, his ignorance of hygiene, his imperfect sense organs, his relatively weak muscular development, was in a far more serious plight; and If we can allow our imaginations to recall those early days when some man-like ape first descended from the trees to the open plain because some fortuitous degeneration of his feet compelled him to relinquish a life of climbing, thereby leaving his forelegs completely free and forcing him to stand erect and become a 'man', we can well imagine that the entire human race might easily have gone the way of the ichthyosaurus but for the fact that nature had endowed us with a little bigger brain and the ability to compensate for our defects.

The dawn of mankind is shrouded in darkness, and our interpretations must, perforce, remain conjectures. No one knows how and when the transformation occurred. Yet, if some sceptic were to doubt the above deductions, we would still have very important biological data to demonstrate the existence of a universal sense of inferiority in all human beings. One of the most significant and unique characteristics of man is the fact that the growth of his mental faculties and the growth of his physical apparatus for accomplishing his purposes proceed at disproportionate speeds, the mental faculties being well developed long before the physical apparatus is capable of the required coordinations. This remarkable fact is due to the late development of man's brain, and its relative completeness at birth, and it is this phenomenon which distinguishes man from all other living animals, in whom the growth of mental faculties and motor apparatus proceeds in a nearly parallel curve.

The young robin which has grown old enough to distinguish a worm has likewise developed physically to the point where he can catch the worm and eat it. Kittens pass through a relatively short period of helplessness, but when they are old enough to know what a mouse is they are simultaneously capable of stalking it, catching it, and eating it. Young calves can distinguish poisonous from edible grasses at an early age. Young turtles are barely hatched from their eggs when they make unerringly for the sea, and begin life as independent organisms. Contrast the situation of the human baby! The baby can recognize its bottle long before it is old enough to reach for it and feed itself. The baby cry if it is uncomfortable, but the satisfaction of its wishes depends entirely upon the good will of a parent or a nurse. Long before the child can walk, it can realize that its parents move with comparative ease. The mysteries of speech remain unsolved long after the child realizes that adults in its environment communicate with each other by means of language.

The relative dependency of the human child is much greater than that of the young of any other species. Civilization and culture have increased this period of dependency to such an extent that to-day, in an urban civilization, a human being has frequently passed through childhood, adolescence, and early maturity before he can begin life as an independent member of society. The longer the period of dependency, the deeper the realization of the individual's inadequacy. This important biological fact, so frequently overlooked by psychologists of other schools, signifies precisely this: The human being is the only living organism that experiences a sense of its own inadequacy.

We have thus two important factors which determine a sense of inferiority in the human race: the relative weakness and unpreparedness of the race as a whole to fight for existence, and the individual experience of inadequacy because of the biological phenomenon of an unequal development of his brain and his motor abilities. If our thesis, that nature tends to replace a 'minus' with a 'double plus' of compensation is true, we might expect to find that man has made important compensations, both as a race and as an individual, for his sense of inferiority. This, indeed, is just what we find.

We know that every living organism makes a characteristic response to the challenge of existence in an attempt to maintain itself securely and attain that most important goal of all living things, the maintenance of life. The tortoise hides behind his carapace when danger threatens; the hare trusts to his heels; the chameleon adjusts his colour to his environment; the gorilla lives in solitary power, master of the jungle. Each in his own way works out an effective formula of behaviour in terms of his physical organization and the specific problems of his environment. It is impossible to conceive of a tortoise behaving like a hare; ludicrous to imagine a chameleon acting like a gorilla. Each has a unit pattern of adjustment which is characteristic and unchanging for the species.

Social Life as a Compensation

Man is no exception to the rule. Man's characteristic pattern of solving the difficulties of existence is the formation of social groups and communities. An isolated human being is as inconceivable as a thin-skinned rhinoceros. So far as we know from historical data and archaeological researches men have always lived in groups. A human child, isolated from the community of its parents, would die miserably in a few days. An isolated man could maintain his life only by virtue of knowledge gained from other human beings. The community, whether in the form of the family, clan, tribe, nation, or race, is an essential of human life. Society is man's first and last line of defence against the inexorable forces of nature.

It follows logically, therefore, that a successful human being must be a member of a group. The well-adjusted member of the social group as nearly attains complete security as any human being can. The converse is likewise true: the isolated human being - and it makes little difference whether he is isolated physically, mentally, or emotionally from his fellows - suffers man's sense of inferiority the more keenly because he has not availed himself of the protection of his group, the only device that man has found an unfailing bulwark against nature.

One of the first rules, therefore, in the art of being a complete human being, and thus attaining the sense of happiness which accompanies the good life, is to make yourself socially adjusted. Look around you, in your office, in your club, in your church, in your family circle, and count the number of people who are well-poised and happy in the companionship of their fellows. The majority of human failures make their first mistakes in this important human activity. As a matter of fact, loneliness is the most dangerous plague of civilization. Compared to the ravages of social isolation, cholera, bubonic plague, tuberculosis, and venereal diseases are insignificant annoyances.

The communal life of man has evolved a special technique of adjustment as varied and complex as the needs of human life itself. Nature, again with lavish hand, has bestowed on you the capacity for making a variety of bonds, with which you may effectively link yourself to your fellows. One of the most important of these bonds is speech. Common sense, whose very etymology connotes its social origin, is another of these fundamental bridges which serve to connect one human being to another. Love, sympathy, friendship, and pity are emotional links; music, painting, sculpture, and writing in all its forms, drama, play, sport, religion, ethical codes, social responsibility, honesty, laws, science, politics, philosophy, hygiene, clothes, commerce, the whole world of technique, are but further devices which nature has placed at the disposal of man for effecting his social solidarity. That human being who most completely utilizes these bonds is most secure in his humanity; and conversely, the more links any individual excludes from the practical conduct of his life, the less secure, the less effective, in a word, the less humanly happy he will be.

The need for social life is the paramount truth in human existence. Evidence for this statement may be adduced from the fact that biological instincts far older than man have become subordinated and modified by this social need. Such primitive urges as hunger and sex, common to all living things, are dominated and socialized by this need. Marriage, which exists in some form in all human communities, is the socialization of the sex instinct; the art of cooking, together with the various rituals of eating, is no more than the complex socialization of the instinct to keep alive by the ingestion of food. Other animals, better prepared for life, and therefore capable of living independent existences, have never developed plumbing, fashions, skyscrapers, newspapers, wireless, aeroplanes or the other appurtenances of civilized life.

Two special facets of the larger social problem require further explanation at this point. The first is the problem of work which exists only among those living organisms that have developed a communal life. We may well consider the lilies of the field, the tiger in his jungle, the robin in his apple tree - they work not, neither do they spin. But ants, wasps, and human beings - organisms that maintain their existence solely because of the efficacy of their communal organizations, must work. Among the insects the problem of work has been crystallized in the course of the ages, but among men, with their wider range of adjustments, the choice of occupation allows of greater latitude. Yet work is an essential of human life. Society exists for the protection of the individual, but demands of every individual a contribution toward the maintenance of the group. It is therefore not a private matter for any man to say whether he will work or not. Society allows a wide choice of occupations, but work in some form or other is as obligatory as common sense to any man who would call himself human. In a later chapter we shall deal with those who do not work - it will suffice here to indicate that work, far from being a curse, is one of the chief sources of personal salvation, as important as social adjustment for the attainment of happiness.

In the second place there is the case of marriage. Man is a bi-sexual animal. Bi-sexuality is a device of nature to insure the proper evolution and development of the species. The higher an organism stands in the scale of evolution, the more marked the differences between the sexes, and the more complete the division of labour between them. But the problem of the sexes is also a social problem, and human society therefore countenances only those forms of sexual union which contribute to the commonweal. Marriage, with its assumption of mutual responsibilities toward the State and toward the children by the contracting parties, is the most satisfactory solution of the problem of bi-sexuality.

The widely varying forms of marriage to be found in savage and civilised communities share a common denominator of social responsibility. Just as in the case of work, the sexual problem is a matter whose solution cannot be left to individual caprice. Every unsocial sexual relation affects not only the individuals involved but also their neighbours and their progeny. Were it not for this fact we should not have • such complicated mores respecting the sex relations. Incest, child-marriage, rape, and homosexuality would not bear the stigma of social taboo were it not for the fact that these forms of sexual union are subversive of the social good because they are socially irresponsible. Marriage and the foundation of the family and the assumption of its complicated obligations and responsibilities, or the preparation for this solution, remain, with work and social adjustment, fundamental techniques in the art of being human. And here too the converse is true - the unmarried individual, with rare exceptions, falls short of human security and happiness.

Let us review briefly the basic data of this chapter. You have seen that the human being is an organism especially weak and poorly adapted for life in this world. You have seen, furthermore, that the period of dependence of the human infant is relatively longer than that of the young of any other animal. You have learned that a child's brain grows faster than his body; and for this reason a child is the only living organism that experiences his own deficiencies. You have found that for these three important biological reasons every human being falls heir to a feeling of inferiority. This feeling of inferiority has been compensated for by nature by means of the complicated, and many-sided adjustments of social life, You have learned, moreover, that to be a complete and effective human being you must affirm the pattern of human compensations, that is, that you must accept as many of the bonds of human relationship as possible in order to be secure and happy in your humanity., We have shown that in order to gain this sense of security, totality, and happiness you must take a definite attitude toward the problems of work and of sex, and solve these problems not according to your individual caprice, but in terms of the social demands of the group in which you live. We have indicated again that there is but one solution of the individual's problems of existence, and that is the solution which conforms to the technique of living which the human race, through millions of years of trial and error, has found good,   ,

Isolation: The Basis of the Inferiority Complex

It now follows conversely that any individual who does not solve the problems of existence in a socially acceptable manner is liable to the same feelings of inferiority and inadequacy that threatened the primitive caveman who, being separated from his clan fire, was exposed to the ruthless dangers of an unfriendly world. We can well imagine this isolated caveman ancestor shivering with fear in the face of the lurking dangers about him, when by accident he became detached from his fellows. We can imagine him straining every fibre of his body to return to the magic circle of flame which stood between him and death. Proof of our contention that the race has solved its problems of inadequacy by social union, and evidence that the origin of society lay in primitive man's fear of isolation is found in the fact that every modern individual, isolated from his fellows, for one reason or another, shows the identical fear and trembling which is the inevitable accompaniment of the inferiority complex.

This brings us to one of the most important axioms in our book: The inferiority complex as it exists to-day in the individual, is an expression of his isolation from the body of mankind, either physical, mental, or emotional. The chief emotional accompaniments of the inferiority complex, fear, anxiety, hesitation, indecision, are linked together by a sense of personal inadequacy. We know that the individual in his development from a single cell to the complex billion-celled organization of the adult, recapitulates the evolutionary stages, which the race has experienced as a whole. This is one of the first laws of biology. It is equally true that the mental and emotional development of the individual recapitulates the broad patterns of the adjustment which mankind has made. Every child suffers and experiences the same torturing sentiments of inadequacy that his defenceless ancestors of the stone age experienced. It follows, moreover, that the identical path of attaining security which has proved valuable in the case of the race, is also open to the individual. The individual, like the race, must cute his inferiority complex by social adjustment.

The inferiority complex now unmasks itself as no more than the expression of a bad technique of fife. This is a very hopeful and important consideration to any individual who feels himself perplexed and tormented by the feeling that his own life is inadequate. If the inferiority complex is no more than evidence of bad craftsmanship in the process of self-sculpture, and if, as we have said, the path towards security and happiness may be found by learning new methods and new ways of attaining social adjustment, we come to the inevitable conclusion that you need not retain your inferiority complex, no matter what its origin, if you learn a better technique of living.

What the race has done to obviate its sense of inadequacy, the individual can do also. In our modern life, the individual who suffers from an inferiority complex does so, not because it is difficult to effect a social adjustment, but because he has not learned the technique of adjusting himself. When you suffer from an inferiority complex, it indicates that you have based your life upon a fallacy. This fallacy, in brief, is that it is easier to win security and happiness by building walls around yourself than by building bridges to your fellow-men. It is the old problem of armaments versus allies. Any man who stops to consider the lessons of history must recognize that allies have always prevailed over the most powerful armaments. The cure of every inferiority complex therefore consists simply and solely in the realization that social adjustment is not only the easiest but the best technique of being happy as a human being. The technique of the cure follows as a logical consequence: it lies in the art of building bridges to one's fellow- men, and in the courageous affirmation of life.

We have intimated that the need for security is the reason for the existence of society and civilisation. Very often, however, an individual becomes panic-stricken because he senses his insecurity so deeply. More often than not, he is ignorant of the natural and easy way to attain security -that is, by being a socially adjusted human being, and he looks to his private and uniquely individual defences to give him a greater plus of security. He proceeds to build walls about himself. The more walls he builds, the more anxious he becomes, and the more anxious he is, the higher he builds his walls. This is the vicious circle of isolation. The tragedy of these people is that they sometimes succeed in walling themselves in so completely that they not only keep out all danger, but also light, food, life, and love - the very things that could bring them happiness. If the defences are battered down by fortune (and they usually are), all is lost. If fate deals unkindly with an individual who has built his bridges according to the second diagram, he remains relatively secure and happy. The First World War proved conclusively that in the war between armaments and allies, the allies eventually win.

Symptoms of the Inferiority Complex

How can you recognize whether you have an inferiority complex? A whole volume might be written about the complicated manifestations of this almost universal phenomenon. The inferiority complex reveals itself in all human situations in which an individual is naturally placed in a position of greater danger, or in situations demanding a definitely social adjustment. Our assumption is indicated by the facts. One of the simplest situations in which an individual senses his isolation most keenly - in which therefore the experience of complete adjustment is necessary for security - is the situation of nightly sleep. Sleep is one of the few biological phenomena in which isolation is desirable. Here isolation enables the body to recuperate its powers for the arduous tasks of social adjustment during the day. To the individual who suffers from an inferiority complex, who is therefore already isolated, sleep presents a major danger because it intensifies this isolation to pathological proportions.

A man asleep may be likened to an army in camp. Only a few sentinels are posted for contact with reality. If the army is camped for summer manoeuvres only a few sentinels are necessary. The normal sleeping man is like an army in its summer camp. He sleeps soundly and securely in the realization of his value as a unit in the social organism. In the morning, he is wakened by the few sentinels, his eyes, his ears, his sense of passing time, which he has posted to keep him in touch with reality. The human being with an inferiority complex, however, is like an army on the battlefield. Here most of the army is on guard and only a few individuals are allowed to sleep at a time. The man with the inferiority complex lives like a stranger in a hostile country. To sleep under such circumstances would be fatal. He must remain awake in order to maintain his armed isolation. We find thus that one of the commonest types of the inferiority complex, insomnia, fits into our scheme and justifies the premises which we have drawn from biology.

What is commonly known as 'nervousness, is another expression of the inferiority complex. Here again we find' a counterpart of the fear which primitive man experienced when separated from his fellows. It is well known that fear is accompanied in man and animal by greater emotional tension and greater muscular activity. In situations where fear may be considered a normal expression, this greater tension and activity, with the chemical changes that take place in the body as a result of this emotion, are worth-while, useful activities designed to mobilize the individual's complete powers to escape from or to surmount danger. Nervousness, anxiety, worry, timidity, or actual fear where no real danger exists are therefore the manifestations which accompany an unconscious realization of danger and isolation. An individual who has effectively isolated himself feels -himself in constant danger in situations where normally social men and woman feel secure.

A third expression of the inferiority complex is egoism and all its associated concomitants. The egoist lives not by common sense but by a sort of 'private logic, which he seeks to superimpose upon the laws of communal living. At a certain stage of human development, during infancy and early childhood, egoism is a natural phenomenon, as desirable as isolation is in sleep, for during these periods the individual must really look to his personal growth in order to survive. Society demands little more of a child. But when a man or a woman has grown to maturity and persists in remaining an egoist, ills evidence of the fact that he still feels as dependent and inferior as a child and ha$ gained neither the courage to contribute to society nor the proper social feeling towards his fellows. In a later chapter, we shall be able to trace more in detail the life history of egoism as a technique of living. But here it must suffice to indicate that egoism, the cult of personal superiority, the desire for great personal power as expressed in an overweening ambition for riches, knowledge, and prestige, together with a feeling of uniqueness and individuality which may range from personal eccentricity in dress or manners to the cult of personal saintliness, are common manifestations of the lack of social adjustment, and certain signs of the presence of an inferiority complex.

Similarly, those states which are commonly called "the blues', melancholia, disinterestedness, apathy, and boredom, chronic hesitation, vacillation, indecision, and doubt are evidences of the inferiority complex. The well-adjusted person finds the world a very interesting place to live in. He finds that each day presents an opportunity to work out his personal inadequacies in terms of social service and social interest. The variety of his bonds to his fellow-men makes every minute of his existence interesting, and leaves his nights free for peaceful sleep. Those unfortunate individuals who have attained a misanthropic point of view, or have had isolation and the inferiority complex thrust upon them in any of the variety of ways that we shall describe in later chapters, find the work-a-day world dangerous or boring. It follows, therefore, that they are jealous and envious of their fellows, misanthropic in their point of view, uninterested in their work, afraid of the other sex, apathetic to the world of nature and of men, hesitant and indecisive in their approach to life. Frequently, in their despair, they seek the emergency exits of suicide, insanity, or crime, as an escape from their intolerable isolation.

Beyond these general manifestations of the inferiority complex, we can catalogue the manifestations of the inferiority complex under four headings and under a variety of unsocial techniques of life. The physical symptoms of the inferiority complex are among the most interesting because they are the least understood both by laymen and by doctors. From our description of the inferiority complex, it must be obvious that the individual with the inferiority complex is saying "No!" to life. One of the most significant contributions of Alfred Adler to medical and psychological science is the thesis that you can say "No!' to life in a variety of ways. Frequently the individual suffering from an inferiority complex is far too intelligent to say "No!' in so many words. He seeks rather to shift the responsibility - a favourite technique with all isolated individuals, who, because of their lack of social adjustment, have also failed to acquire social responsibility - to conditions seemingly beyond his control.

The 'Organ Jargon' of the Inferiority Complex

Alfred Adler was one of the first to call attention to the fact that while the entire individual takes up an attitude towards life, this attitude may be expressed by any single organ or organ system. When organic deficiencies sufficient to cause an inferiority complex exist, these very organ systems may become the loud-speakers, so to speak, of the total personality. The individual's 'No!' is expressed then in the unhealthy functioning of this defective organ system. This is clearly demonstrated in the case of a man, thirty-five years old, who has an inferiority complex because of various unfortunate conditioning factors in his childhood, whose most obvious expression is to be found in his fear of woman. This man, an intelligent lawyer, recognizes intellectually that he ought to be married. He comes to the psychiatrist complaining of impotence, bitterly protesting that he would like to be married if it were not for his unfortunate ailment. This man is saying 'No!' to the problem of sexual adjustment, not in so many words, but in an organic language, an 'organ-jargon' of his sexual organs, The differential diagnosis between a real physical ailment and an expression of the inferiority complex in bodily symptoms is often to be found in those little words, 'but' or 'if', which demonstrate to those who understand human nature that the individual has an underlying inclination to evade the problems of life and to shift the responsibility to phenomena which are seemingly beyond his control.

Other physical symptoms of the inferiority complex which are frequently encountered are headaches, migraine, 'nervous indigestion', asthma, palpitation of the heart; the vague fatigue, loss of appetite, and general malaise, which used to be called neurasthenia and psychasthenia. Impotence and premature ejaculation in men; frigidity, painful menstruation, and painful intercourse in women; vomiting, asthma, tics, grimaces, bed-wetting, and night terrors in children; insomnia, 'nerves' and panic, the fear of old age, death, cancer, tuberculosis, or syphilis, together with the profession of 'being healthy' or 'being sick' are additional symptoms of the inferiority complex in adults. To be sure, these symptoms may be the expression of organic disease, and it requires a psychiatrist well versed both in medicine and psychology to determine whether a given symptom is part of a physical ailment or whether, as in the case of pathological blushing, sweating, palpitation of the heart, tremors, and neuralgia, there is not some underlying psychological purpose which the patient attains by means of his symptoms.

Not infrequently, a real physical condition is developed into a psychological symptom, and many men and women burdened by an inferiority complex make a profession of some trivial or minor ailment because in gaining the attention and care of a capable, but psychologically unschooled, physician, they effectively attain the 'extenuating circumstances' with which they justify their evasion of life's problems. In recent years, with the rise of modern mental hygiene, not a few patients have been able to trick the best-intentioned psychiatrist by prolonging their psychological analyses from months into years, thus effectively removing themselves from the battlefront of life.

The second group of manifestations deals with the problems of social life. Here the inferiority complex manifests itself in some well-disguised or overt misanthropy. Few people realize that the criminal and the social snob have a common denominator of social maladjustment, jealously and envy, the cult of uniqueness, overzealous family pride, or its projection, professional patriotism, are manifestations of the inferiority complex. Uncouthness in manners, exotic dress, slovenliness in keeping appointments, inconsiderateness, apathy to the problems of human suffering, a dislike of children and animals, social isolation, whether in the form of a hermit life or in the artificial isolation of class and family consciousness which we usually term snobbishness, are further evidences of mental immaturity and social maladjustment. Here also belong shyness and timidity, arrogance, racial and religious bigotry, the 'will-to-be-first', chronic procrastination and doubt, extreme pride and saintly humility, belligerent argumentativeness, the 'will-to-be-right', and all the complex aspects of human vanity.

The third group of symptoms which betray the presence of an inferiority complex are those which deal with the work-a- day world. People who believe that work is a curse, and those others who do not work at all, show that they have not understood the fundamental logic of human life. The enslavement of other human beings either legally or illegally, whether in the sweatshop and the kitchen as it is practised in modern civilization, or in peonage and serfdom as practised in some countries, is an instance of inadequate social insight. There are some occupations which are almost frankly anti-social, such as the profession of soldiering. It seems hardly possible that anyone with a great love for humanity could be interested in learning the art of bayoneting a fellow human being. The prostitute and the pimp, the procurer, the pedlar of narcotics, and others of their kind, clearly demonstrate their lack of social feeling in their professions. Men and women who set impossible conditions before they will work show their inferiority complex. Others who are constantly changing their jobs say, in the language of psychology, that they do not want to work at all.

Sex and the Inferiority Complex

A fourth set of symptoms which betray the existence of the inferiority complex are those referable to the world of love and sex. The great frequency with which the inferiority complex manifests its existence in this sphere of human relations is due both to the exaggerated interest in sexual activity which is characteristic of our present-day civilization, and to the more important fact that the sexual problem is the one human problem which the individual may leave unsolved without bringing about his own death or complete isolation. The solution of the sexual problem demands a maximum of social adjustment, self-confidence, and socialized courage, together with a well-developed sense of personal responsibility spiced with a sense of humour. At the same time its solution is optional to the degree that a man or woman may practically evade the problem without becoming a social outcast. Sexual maladjustments are exceedingly common because of our inadequate sexual education, because of our cultural over-valuation of sex, and because the solution of the sexual problem requires the highest development of human responsibility. Some psychologists, notably the Freudian psychoanalysts, consequently have made the mistake of believing that all human problems derive from maladjustments of the sexual life, but sexual maladjustments are but seldom the sole basis of human inadequacy. The sexual problem is only one aspect of the general problem of human adjustment to the world in which we live.

The characteristic signs of the inferiority complex in the sphere of sex are expressed in the complete evasion of the sexual problem, evasion through the fiction of organic inability, evasion through perversion, and evasion through exaggeration of the importance of sex. In the first category we find those individuals who believe that sex is a sin and a curse, and thus lead a life of pseudo-saintly avoidance of all sexual adjustment. The misanthropic women and the misogynic men who maintain a position of arrogant superiority to sex, or tremble with an equally fallacious panicky fear of venereal disease, sexual unhappiness, or sexual disappointment, seek to cover their underlying fear of sexual adjustment with a thin veneer of rationalization. The puritan and the prude exhibit their inferiority complex as clearly as the critical male or the romantic woman whole search is for an 'ideal, mate. Few confirmed old bachelors and few siccant old maids are to be found among the leaders of human thought and action.

Comparable to these deserters from the sexual problem, and hardly more courageous, are those men who are impotent or suffer from premature ejaculation in the sexual act, and those women who say 'No!', to the sexual life in terms of the 'organ jargon, of frigidity, incompatibility, vaginismus, extreme dyspareunia or dysmenorthoea, Men and women who make sex a game or an arena of combat in which they strive for supremacy over the other sex, paradoxically signify a disinclination to make a courageous adjustment to sex. Don Juan and Casanova, patron saints of this type of male, are the virtuosos of sexual conquests who remain bunglers in the finer art of holding a woman's love for a reasonable period of time. Their feminine counterparts are to be found in women like Catherine the Great of Russia, Messalina, the famous French courtesans, and our modern flapper Vamps'.

A favoured evasion of sexual adjustment which bespeaks the inferiority complex is to be found in the perversions which consist in the elevation of some single aspect of the sexual relation to a role of supreme importance. We call this perversion of sex, fetishism. Hair, gloves, shoes, breasts, lingerie, the smell of the body, the sight of the beloved and similar substitutions of a part for the whole may be the objects of fetishistic love, capable of evoking ejaculation or orgasm. The circumscription of all sexual interest to thin women, fat women, blonde or brunette women, or even in some cases, to lame or cross-eyed women, is a variety of fetishism which bespeaks lessened courage and social adjustment.

Finally, the complex phenomena of homosexuality are expressions of the inferiority feeling. Contrary to common belief, homosexuality is never an inborn quality, but probably always the result of vicious conditioning influences in childhood reinforced by self-inflicted mental training. The examination of all homosexuals reveals a deep-seated, often entirely unconscious, fear of the opposite sex or of the responsibilities of marriage or pregnancy, but this fear is frequently so well masked by a specious superstructure of rationalization and tradition that the individual is completely unaware of its existence.

Negative Patterns of Life

When we have eliminated the above easily recognized indices of the existence of the inferiority complex we may still detect its presence in certain characteristic life-patterns which in their entirety reveal the absence of a courageous affirmation of life. The commonest of these negative, hesitating, or actively unsocial patterns is the neurosis. The neurosis is not a disease - it is a cowardly attitude toward the problems of life. The neurosis frequently expresses itself in painful symptoms. The common denominator of every neurosis, no matter how bizarre its structure, is the factor of social irresponsibility. A neurosis is a pattern of life in which painful alibis are substituted for the performance of the ordinary tasks and obligations of life which appear fantastically difficult to the miseducated neurotic. The fiction 'I cannot' is substituted for the admission 'I will not' in every case. The shibboleth of the neurosis may be detected in such neurotic phrases as 'I would marry, *but* for...' or I would have made a success of my job, if...' or I would go out in society, *but*...' and the like.

In the life pattern we call crime, the individual, for lack of proper initiation into the fellowship of mankind, feels himself a stranger in a hostile country. He misinterprets the realities of life as personal insults, and in consequence is aggressive against a society which he cannot understand. Any aggression against society, or its champions, the police and the courts, seems thoroughly justifiable to the criminal who has complete faith in his first premise that society has banded together in an offensive alliance against him. Punishment does not deter the criminal - it corroborates his belief that he is justified in using trickery, malice, stealth, against the hated individuals who are 'in' Here again a basic sense of inferiority and the inability to meet the demands of social life compel the criminal to make a short cut to power and security.

Alcoholism and drug addiction are the life-patterns of those discouraged individuals who escape into the spurious elation of intoxication or the quiet elysium of morphine dreams when faced with the bald realities of existence. Alcohol and morphine. are crutches for pessimistic disconsolates who feel inadequate to the task of living. The tramp evades the challenge of work, wandering aimlessly in his infantile fear of having to contribute to the commonweal; the spiritualist, the theosophist, the Christian Scientist, and other religious fanatics demonstrate their gnawing sense of inferiority by projecting their interests on an unknown and uncharted world. No well-adjusted, contributing member of human society needs the solace of a 'second chance' in a world of ghosts, fantasies, ectoplasm or nirvana, for the reason that life showers its rich satisfactions upon him with a lavish hand. The psychological examination of religious faddists, of philosophical nihilists, pessimists, and fatalists the world over, reveals that the basic fallacy of their lives lies in their frantic flight from reality.

Existence on this crust of earth may be likened to the operation of a slot machine: those who contribute their coin are rewarded by their bit of chocolate, and the satisfaction of a fair return on their investment. This simple relationship remains an ineluctable mystery to the individual burdened with the inferiority complex. He stands before the slot machine whining for a second chance in a future world; he curses the slot machine, or he boasts that he is too good for it; he parades vainly before the mirror, or gnashes his teeth in rage and vituperation; he covers himself with ashes, or bleats his remorse and guilt; he protests that the slot machine does not really exist, or deprecates the quality of the chocolate; he blames God, the perfidy of women, the weakness of his flesh, the Bolsheviks, his lack of education, or the malice of his parents: so long as he does not contribute his coin, he cannot gain his bit of chocolate!

What is to be done with the inferiority complex? What are its causes, and can it be cured? Can human nature be changed? Can the timid be made courageous, can the criminal be transformed into a philanthropist, can the tramp enjoy his day's work and the homosexual thrill to the love of a woman? The answer is yes! Mankind has said yes with civilization, Confucius, Isaiah, Christ, have said yes in their preachings. Demosthenes, Beethoven, Darwin, Edison have said yes in their work. Socrates with the keenest of psychological insight said: 'Virtue can be learned!' We shall endeavour to trace the why and the how of the inferiority complex in the subsequent chapters of this book. A knowledge of the special origins of

the inferiority complex in the individual is invaluable if you wish not only to proceed with your own self-sculpture, but also to understand the mistakes, the bogeys, the fallacies in your neighbour's life.

CHAPTER THREE:
Of Obstacles: Fear and Inferiority

Seven Sources of the Inferiority Complex - Of Physical Disabilities - Left-handedness - Beauty and Ugliness - The Family Constellation - Sex ~ Social, Economic, and Racial Determinants - Emotional Attitudes of Parents and Teachers - Parental Mistakes - Fallacies of Formal Education - Subjective Sources of Inferiority Feelings - The Role of Sexual Trauma

In our first two chapters we sketched the concept of living as a fine art and indicated some of the rules that govern the good life. In our second chapter we outlined the nature of the human material with which each individual is endowed, and specifically described man's weakness as one of the most important data in his life. And we came to the conclusion that fear, ignorance and discouragement were the chief enemies to successful self-sculpture. In. the present chapter we shall deal more intimately with people and their problems, and trace the evolution of fear and inferiority from their seven sources in physical disability and disease, in the dynamics of the family situation, in sex, in social, economic and racial disabilities, in the emotional mistakes of parents and teachers, in the fallacies of formal education, and finally in a group of purely subjective individual misinterpretations of life and its values which do not logically fit into the other categories.

I. OF PHYSICAL DISABILITIES

It must be apparent to any observer of modern life that profound physical disabilities or diseases are a severe handicap in the competitive struggle for existence. The child who grows up with weak eyes, or the child who is handicapped in his breathing by tonsils and adenoids, the deaf child, the lame child, or the child with a damaged heart, begins life with a severe handicap, which, added to his natural sense of inadequacy, may produce that exaggerated sense of helplessness which we call an inferiority complex. Because we cannot, in this brief text, cover the multitude of physical disabilities to which the human flesh is heir, we content ourselves with a sketch of the various types of physical disability.

We gain our knowledge of the world through our sense organs, and any defects, no matter how medically unimportant, of the eyes, the ears, the nose, the tongue, the finger tips, as well as aberrations of those less recognized but equally important senses of equilibrium and tone, make our lives more difficult because they distort our picture of the physical world in which we live, and therefore handicap us in our relations to our fellow-men.

The case of Marie R. is an example. Since childhood Marie has had a squint medically so unimportant that an operation was not advised. Nevertheless, Marie feels that her crossed eyes are so noticeable that she has withdrawn from the companionship of children and adults since she was a young girl. At college now, she is considered aloof and 'uppish', whereas in reality she is very self-conscious and timid. Marie's point of view is much more warped than her vision. Her isolation is compensated by a world of day-dreams in which she sees herself as a heroic but lonely actress. Her moods vary from fantastic exaltation in splendid loneliness to depression and blues when she finds that day-dreams are small comfort on a rainy Sunday afternoon. Marie was very unhappy until her misinterpretations of life were explained to her, 'The value of a human being" said the psychiatrist, 'does not lie in her looks, but in her contributions" Marie was told of a famous film actress who also suffered from a squint, and became a star despite her disability. Marie's tendency to self-dramatization was used as a basis of her cure. She was urged to join the dramatic society of her college where her histrionic ability, not in 'princess' roles, but in 'character' parts, finally brought her recognition and friends.

A second group of physical disabilities are those of single organs or organ systems. Alfred Adler long ago pointed out in his epoch-making book, Organ Inferiorities and their Psychic Compensations, that if you are burdened with a weak heart, an over-sensitive digestive system, a poorly functioning respiratory or urinary system, or if, as is so often the case where other organ inferiorities occur, the sexual organs are not adequately developed, you will have a tendency to meet the world in terms of this defective organ or organ system and evaluate all your experiences in terms of this point of least resistance. We might, indeed, classify human beings according to the sense organs which dominate their psychic point of view. Visual, auditory, tactile, respiratory, or sexual types are easily recognized by their likes and dislikes, as well as by their behaviour.

You can frequently understand people by observing the type of physical security they seek while travelling. Persons with digestive difficulties will tour Europe looking for the 'right' restaurants, others, with respiratory weaknesses, will always be on the look-out for badly ventilated rooms or railway carriages. A man, asked what he liked best in Europe, answered that he was most thrilled by the fact that he could fly from Vienna to Venice in six hours. He had suffered from rickets in childhood, and had always felt constrained in his liberty of motion because of his childhood difficulties in walking. He was an ardent dancer and skater, and was finally killed when he tried to drive his automobile over a dangerous mountain pass at ninety miles an hour. A lady, asked the same question, answered, 'The Italian men! They are divine!' She had always suffered from a feeling that she was sexually unattractive.

'Left-Handedness

A third set of physical disabilities are those that arise from an inferiority, or better, a difference of power in one whole half of the body. The majority of people are right-handed, and the world, from tramcar to newspaper, from corkscrews to traffic regulations, is arranged for their convenience. A left-handed individual is no worse off than a right-handed individual biologically, but socially he is at a great disadvantage. The left- handedness of many is not even apparent, because it is masked by an acquired right-handedness, and while such 'converted' left-handers may become extremely deft, many of them remain clumsy throughout their entire lives. We shall have occasion to demonstrate the splendid compensations open to the left- handed individual in our chapter on compensation. Suffice to say, in this description, that a masked sinistrality, or left- handedness, is one of the commonest causes of relative physical inferiority, and an exaggeration of an individual's total sense of inadequacy.

One special aspect of the difficulty of the congenitally left- handed child deserves especial mention because ignorance of this condition results so often in the diagnosis of feeblemindedness or stupidity. The congenital left-hander finds motion from right to left much simpler and more natural than motion from left to right, which is normal for the right- handed. This tendency also affects the movement of the eyes, and the left-handed child finds reading and writing from right to left much simpler than the usual way, from left to right. When such a child, even though he uses his right hand for most work, attempts to read, he twists his syllables, or reads entirely from the end of the word instead of from the beginning. This condition, which is much commoner than is believed, is best called dyslexia streptosymbolica, which means simply that the child has difficulty in reading because he twists his letters. The condition is often falsely called congenital word-blindness. The following diagram shows how a child of this type tends to read ordinary words.

A. MANHATTAN

Normally read thus, from left to right by right-handed child.

B. Types of pronunciation by child with dyslexia streptosymbolica:

MANHATTAN - NATTAHNAM or NAMTAHNAT or MANNATTAH

C. Normal writing, left to right:

Taxicab

Mirror writing, right to left, normal for left-handed:

Taxicab (mirrored)

We have seen a number of children brought to the Juvenile Court for various school delinquencies because their inability to read was misinterpreted by their teachers as stupidity or wilfulness. When such a child is placed in the ungraded classes, next to morons and feeble-minded children, he quite naturally protests because he knows he is not stupid, even though he cannot read. This type of child is often exceptionally clever at mechanical manipulations. The discouragement that results from this misinterpretation is so profound that the child feels that there is no place for him in school, and he gravitates naturally to the street and to the gang where he can establish his validity by a different kind of courage and wit. We have developed a technique of teaching these children to read as well as normally right-handed children, and once such children master the technique they frequently read better than right-handed children.

Finally, there is a great group of physical disabilities which are not disabilities at all in the medical sense, whose influence on the individual's attitude toward the problems of existence is very profound. It is a psychological truism that severe disabilities, such as the loss of a leg, a complete paralysis of both legs, total blindness, or severe heart disease are not as crippling, psychologically as a tiny disfiguring mole on the end of a girl's nose, variegated colouring of eyelashes, a fat ankle, or a harelip. We once had occasion to see a child who was born with an unfortunate anomaly of the skin of her face. At the age of twelve she had undergone more than thirty skin graft operations, and had spent most of her life in one hospital or another. Her face was horribly disfigured, yet this child was a veritable ray of sunshine in the hospital wards, and was the most thoroughly cheerful and good-natured child we have ever known. On the other hand, we have seen a young girl brought to a psychiatric clinic in the early stages of dementia praecox who dated her depression and discouragement to the use of her brother's cold cream and the consequent appearance of a few innocuous pimples on her otherwise very pretty face.

So it is that exceptional fatness or thinness, birthmarks, red hair, albinism, extreme hairiness or relative hairlessness, an abnormally shaped nose, difference in the colour of the eyes, protruding teeth, cleft chin or receding chin, scrawny necks or abnormally fat necks, sloping shoulders, enlarged breasts or differences in the size of the breasts, large waistlines, wide hips or abnormally narrow hips, long legs and short legs, bow legs and knock knees, large feet or very small feet, baldness or facial hair, acne, freckles, vasomotor instability (as the tendency to blush too easily, or to perspire too freely), feminine bodies in men and masculine bodies in women, and a host of other variations from the physiological norm, may become the basis of an inferiority complex, and thus lead to misanthropy, isolation, and fear because of their social rather than their medical importance.

Beauty and Ugliness

There is no doubt that most people find it easier to get along with a good-looking person than with an ugly person, but on the other hand, nowhere in the world is physical beauty so over-rated as in the English-speaking countries. It has been our custom to console those who are not beautiful with the helpful thought that the world's progress has not been made by chorus girls and showmen. Without exception the men and women who have really contributed most to human happiness have been ugly, misshapen, physically unattractive people. You have only to look at portraits Socrates, with his saddle nose and pot belly, at Beethoven, with his brutal butcher's face, at Daniel Webster, with his rachitic frontal bosses, at Steinmetz, with his crippled body, to prove this point for yourself.

We well remember a charming woman who suffered an inferiority complex because she believed her nose was too long. In order to cure her we made a collection of the portraits of famous, men and women, Alexander the Great, Julius Caesar, Cornelia, the mother of the Gracchi, Tasso, Petrarch, Boccaccio, Cervantes, Rousseau, Voltaire, Mozart, Chopin, Wagner, Elizabeth of England, and Washington, all of whom had abnormally long noses, and finally convinced her with an old Latin inscription, "Non cuique datum est nasum habere, - not everyone can have a nose! - which served to demonstrate the venerable aristocracy of long noses.

While we are on the subject of ugliness and beauty as possible causes of the inferiority feeling, a word about the evil consequences of too much beauty is in order. A very beautiful child is under a severe handicap, and parents should take the utmost precautions lest the old proverb, 'mens Sana in corpore sano' turn out to be 'mens insana in corpore bellissimo'. Every psychiatrist and teacher sees children who have been so spoiled because of their beauty that they are incapable of living in a real world. It is so easy to say to a beautiful child, 'My, what exquisite eyes!' or 'What a lovely face you have!' or 'You are almost too pretty to be a boy!' We fall into these errors because of the undoubted aesthetic appeal of a beautiful body, without thinking what the possible psychological consequences of our words may be for the child.

A beautiful child grows up with the feeling that his or her beauty is the sole contribution that society requires of him. He develops the pattern of a beautiful prince or princess in a drab world, and he assumes the false philosophy that solely because he is beautiful the world owes him a living. And usually he wants a very good living, too. He cultivates his beauty as his sole weapon of offence and defence. While it is true that many a person who has been ugly in childhood acquires the mature beauty that radiates from a wholesome personality, it is just as true that a beautiful child who invests his or her total life's interests in the maintenance of physical beauty, largely spoils that beauty by the shallowness of vanity.

The tragic end is that the hollow shell of mere physical beauty crumbles with time, and the beautiful child, having developed no emergency supports for old age, finds himself mentally bankrupt, commits suicide, or suffers from melancholia as a poor substitute for popular esteem and attention.

The host of women who crowd psychiatrists' waiting-rooms when they reach the 'dangerous age' are usually women who have trusted too much in their beauty to 'get them across'. In a later chapter we shall tell the story of such a woman, and point out the mistakes of her life's pattern, and describe a better technique of growing old gracefully.

2. THE FAMILY CONSTELLATION

Just as no one is born with a perfect body, and all may therefore find physical disabilities a source of an inferiority complex, so no one escapes the dangers of his peculiar position in his family. A good judge of human nature can often tell whether a grown man or woman has been an only child or a youngest child or an eldest child in his family. A young woman once applied to us for a position as secretary. When we asked her what she studied in college she answered, 'You'll laugh when I tell you, but I'm really most interested in archaeology.' We immediately asked her whether she was the eldest child in her family and with a surprised look she admitted that she was the eldest of seven children. This is neither magic nor clairvoyance, but simply an application of the fact that an individual whose focus of interest is in the 'good old days' probably regards his childhood as a lost paradise whose ancient flavour he wishes to recapture, and the family situation in which this most frequently occurs is the situation of the eldest child.

Psychiatric knowledge has sunk so far into everyday practice that almost everyone now regards an only child as an unfortunate child. The reasons for his judgement are very sound. The only child grows up as the central point of a tiny universe, and because of the narrow confines of his little firmament his every act seems inordinately important to his parents. Then, too, the parents of an only child are likely to be less courageous than parents who assume the responsibilities of three or four children, although this is no universal rule. The emotional attitudes of parents and relatives toward an only child are very likely to be over-tense. He is loved harder, cared for more solicitously, guarded more preciously and subjected to a more rigorous scrutiny than a child in a large family. His virtues are usually overpraised, his deficiencies usually made the source of supreme anxiety and worry, while his minor illnesses are allowed to become the object of endless concern.

As we shall indicate in the chapter on the technique of living, self-reliance, independence, courage, and a well-developed social sense, as well as the spice of a sense of humour, are the best tools we know for carving out a successful and happy life. You can easily see how the special situation of the only child is unfavourable for the development of these tools. Dependence, anxiety, doubt, egoism, and the sort of tyranny that is implied in the phrase, "because I love you, you must do what I want' are far more likely to develop in the case of the only child or of any child who for a period of two or more years assumes a position of non-competitive uniqueness in his family.

Now suppose that a child who has been an only child for three years is followed by another child. He has already become accustomed to the advantages of his unique position, and suddenly, with little or no warning, his kingdom is divided, and he usually comes off at a disadvantage because the new-born child requires exceptional attention and temporarily receives excessive affection and regard. The first-born is forgotten, and only a first-born child can understand the bitterness and disillusion of the tragedy of desertion by those in whose confidence and devotion he had invested his sole hope of salvation. The older child frequently develops a neurosis at this point unless the intelligent handling of the situation by his parents opens new avenues of social significance to him. The best course, naturally, is to give the older child the feeling that he has not been deserted at all. This is accomplished by warning him of the advent of the new-born child, and preparing the first-born to find significance and love in the care and custody of the younger child. It is important that the older child should feel that the attention to the younger child is not a detraction of interest from him, but a necessary consequence of the younger child's weakness. It is a very good thing to put the older child in a nursery school at this time, and it is essential that a world of new privileges, new toys, and new activities be opened to him. A practical hint to mothers: if an older child develops night terrors, or bed-wetting, or stuttering, or cruelty, or temper tantrums, or abnormal timidity and shyness after the birth of a younger child, it is a certain sign that he feels himself wrongly dethroned. These are symptoms of a childhood neurosis and should be very carefully treated, by friendly explanation and encouragement. If the child does not react, he should be taken to a competent psychiatrist or teacher schooled in child guidance. These symptoms are not just bad habits - they are critical symptoms of fear, of discouragement, of withdrawal - forerunners of an inferiority complex. Their meaning is always: If you won't pay attention to me and love me as you used to do, I'll compel you to do it by being ill!' The old way of treating such conduct disorders of childhood by liberal applications of the birch and hair-brush is inexcusable. For one thing it seldom cures the habits; for another, the child wins his point and gains the attention of his parents, for he does not discriminate between a kiss and a spanking in these situations.

The limits of this chapter prevent our considering the psychodynamics of all the childhood situations that arise from the family constellation. Suffice it to say that the second child, having a pacemaker ahead of him, is usually aggressive and rebellious. The second child, if not discouraged by the progress of the first-born, is in an unusually good position. The trick is to keep him from becoming a professional iconoclast, who wants to uproot power just for the sake of uprooting it. The aggressiveness of the second-born is a perfect foil to the conservatism of the first-born, who having once tasted the uniqueness of power, knows how to conserve it. The youngest of three, or the youngest of a family, occupies simultaneously the best and the worst position.

Folklore and legends are full of the ambitious exploits of the youngest son - and asylums and gaols are full of youngest sons who, being discouraged by the success of older children, fall by the wayside to become tramps, neurotics, confidence men, bad actors, or long-haired poets. The only boy in a family of girls, the only girl in a family of boys, have exceptionally difficult positions. In a family of girls, the dynamics of the first, second, and third child are usually accentuated because girls are more cruel to one another than boys. The first-born son who is followed by a second-born sister is in an exceptionally dangerous position, while the second-born sister is in an exceptionally good one. Large families usually group themselves into smaller families of two or three children, so that the psychology of the first-born may repeat itself within the family.

You may feel, after reading the facts about the family constellation, that there is no escape from its dangers no matter what your position in the family constellation is. This is not true. While there is no position in the family constellation which in and of itself will guarantee a happy life, there is likewise no position which can doom you to be unhappy if you know something about its dynamics and rationally attempt to counteract its liabilities. The fine art of being happy consists largely in transmuting liabilities into assets, and what holds for the difficulties of the ordinal position in the family constellation holds for all the other factors that so commonly produce fear, discouragement, isolation, and an inferiority complex. No factor, either in your heredity or in your environment, can compel you to be a neurotic or to assume a pattern of inferiority. There is always some good way out in terms of compensation in socially acceptable behaviour. No one is doomed to be a failure; no one is destined inexorably to be unhappy.

3. SEX

It is one of the crazy paradoxes of human life that sex, in and of itself, may be the basis of an inferiority complex. The fault lies not with sex, because other mammals live their sex lives without suffering from their sexuality, but with our history as human beings. It is a sound historical law that the pattern of any given culture is modelled on the organization of its food-getting devices. The two sexes are biologically and psychologically equivalent. Men are no better and no worse than women, and each contributes equally to the chromosomes of the child that is the issue of their sexual collaboration. But economically and historically one sex is usually dominant, and the other sex, of necessity, subordinate. In agricultural communities, such as those of late savagery and early barbarism, the female is the dominant sex, and the male is the subordinate sex. The principle of fertility, the close connection in the mind of primitive man between harvest and childbirth, enables woman to assert her dominance, and such a culture is termed a matriarchy. As soon as a tribe gives up agriculture as its chief source of food supply, and depends mainly on domesticated animals for its sustenance, and as soon as the concept of private property is substituted for the cultural philosophy of communal acres, the male sex becomes dominant.

Engels, in The Growth of the Family, and latterly Dell in Lore in the Machine Age, and Briffault in The Mothers, have traced this change from matriarchy to patriarchy in greater detail than is possible in these paragraphs. For our purpose it is enough to indicate that the history of mankind includes an early epoch in which women were the dominant sex, followed by transition to masculine dominance. The present age, while chiefly characterized by masculine dominance, is again an age of transition. Some writers believe that an era of matriarchy is in the offing, but it is more probable that the next age will be an age of sexual cooperation, not of sexual competition.

After centuries of oppression by exponents of the prevailing patriarchal culture, women are now in a process of emancipation. The two greatest emancipators of women have been the microscope and the machine. The microscope proved conclusively that the role which the female plays in the reproduction of the species is one of biological equivalence with the male. The machine has carried on the work of the scientist by levelling the economic differences between the sexes. The more complicated the machine, the more easily women become the equals of men in its use. The present transition period from the outworn philosophy of the Hebrew fathers, from the horrors of witch-hunting, and from the fallacious belief that women are second-rate men, is characterized by tremendous sexual conflicts.

The embattled males who cling to the alleged superiority of their sex attempt with might and main to maintain the *status quo*. These men (and many women are on their side for lack of courage to participate in the emancipation of their sex) are frantically upholding the old traditions and prejudices. Against them are arrayed the forces of emancipated womanhood who refuse to take the old shibboleths for granted. With every day the battle lines of womankind are extended farther into the terrain which but a few decades ago was considered the sole privilege of men. A great body of laws and traditions still blocks the path to the complete emancipation of women, and not the least of these blockades is the residuum of outworn emotional attitudes in parents and teachers.

The patriarchal system of considering women as the inferiors of men naturally wreaks its worst effects on the growing girl. There are many homes where the birth of girl is still heralded with the damning Tt's only a girl!' The growing girl is not yet allowed to play certain games, go to certain places unattended, nor is she permitted to study certain subjects or choose certain professions. If you are a girl the feeling that you are doomed from the very beginning to an inferior role in life is not calculated to develop a courageous spirit in you. The woman is still rare who refuses to be downed at some time or another in her life by the prejudices against her sex. It is the rarest of women who does not at some time or another find her normal development blocked by the misconceptions of a barbarous patriarchal system. We should not be astonished, therefore, that the majority of women suffer from some form of inferiority feelings just because they are women. It is still a man's world, run by men, and for men.

It might seem at first glance that the prevailing prejudices in favour of men constitute a stimulus to masculine success, and make a man's path toward happiness a paved highway. This is by no means always true. The burden of proving his complete masculinity is not easy for every boy to bear. Where other factors, such as physical weakness, play a subsidiary role, it becomes practically impossible for the boy to sense anything but a feeling of inferiority when he compares himself with Other, better equipped boys. The torturing doubt, I may not be a complete man!' drives many a boy into the by-paths of neurosis, suicide, or homosexuality. Wherever one sex dominates the other, the dominant sex always arrogates the best virtues to itself, relegating subsidiary virtues, which tend to set off the dominant sex's virtues by contrast, to the inferior sex. The "masculine' virtues of to-day, for example, were "feminine' virtues in matriarchal Egypt only a few thousand years ago. The tendency to link superiority and masculinity, inferiority and femininity, is a typical neurotic trick beloved by those hesitant males and over-zealous women who really doubt their own sexual validity. In this fashion the patriarchal code of Conduct stultifies and distorts normal human relations between the sexes, and causes sex to become a source of profound inferiority feelings, whose various ramifications we shall have occasion to examine in more detail in a special section,

4. SOCIAL, ECONOMIC, AND RACIAL DETERMINANTS

In any community which is divided into castes and classes, whether openly, as in India, or tacitly, as in the English-speaking countries, you are likely to become a prey to inferiority feelings if you are unlucky enough to be born into one of the submerged classes. It is an axiom of democracy that all men are born free and equal, but our prevailing social and economic prejudices very quickly change the equality of birth into a decided 'plus' or "minus' in childhood. As in the case of sex, class prejudices have an evil effect both on the "ins' and the "outs'. If your father was a farm labourer your chances of attaining great social significance are very slight, and your opportunities for fulfilling your complete humanity are likely to be very constricted. If your ancestors came to England with the Conqueror, and your father is a cabinet minister, you are just as likely to be constricted by the artificial confines of snobbery and tradition to a very narrow sphere of activity, History is full of the stories of poor men who have risen to fame and of aristocrats who have become splendid leaders of mankind, but the probability is that an unfavourable or unusual social position will exaggerate a normal feeling of inferiority into some form of the inferiority complex,

In America the economic situation is even worse than the social. In a plutocracy, the child of the slums grows up under tremendous disadvantages. Deprivation, lack of proper recreation, early exposure to the evils of economic exploitation, the greater incidence of sickness and the consequent frequency of ugliness, fear of hunger and cold, exposure to crime and vice, are the shameful heritage of the poor child. The immediate evidence of great wealth on every side only serves to exaggerate the helplessness of those who are on the 'outside looking in'. Deprivation leads to the worship of pleasure for pleasure's sake, and pleasure-hunger leads directly to the gang, the brothel, the abuse of narcotics and alcohol, the prison, and the asylum. Nothing is so well designed to produce frustration and inferiority complexes as the lack of proper food, housing, and recreation.

If poverty leads to inferiority, to unfulfilled and inhuman ambition, to a hate of work and a worship of pleasure for pleasure's sake, so also does great wealth. Pity the child of parents who are too rich. Private asylums are filled with the sons and daughters of rich and indulgent parents who have pampered their offspring with lavish bestowals of this world's goods. The rich child meets with difficulty in finding his salvation in work because he is robbed of the opportunity of gaining satisfaction in it. He already has everything that he could gain by work. It requires the utmost emancipation to make a good use of leisure, the curse of the rich, as deprivation is the curse of the poor. There is hardly a sadder spectacle in the whole human comedy than a rich man or woman drugged with leisure, and, as is so often the case, devoid of imagination and the sense of humour which might lead them out of their difficulties. Inferiority complexes grow lushly on the over-fertilized soil of wealth, as the far greater incidence of suicide among the wealthy all too tragically attests. Neither great poverty nor great wealth can compel you to have an inferiority complex - but they make the attainment of human happiness much more difficult.

For much the same reasons an unfavourable social constellation is likely to produce fear and inferiority in your attitude towards life and you are likely to suffer from an exaggeration of the normal sense of inadequacy if you happen to be born into a minority racial or religious group. This tragedy of birth in a minority racial or religious group is the more significant because the child of the under-dog is kicked early in life. The cruelty of children is well known. Any discouraged child is quick to seize upon the false discriminations of society and vent them upon members of the 'under-dog group' to bolster his own sense of security. The child who has fled in shame, anguish, and complete perplexity when the cry "Ikey" has greeted him on the playground, can hardly be blamed for developing inferiority complexes later in life.

5. EMOTIONAL ATTITUDES OF PARENTS AND TEACHERS

Our attitude toward the task of creative self-sculpture is largely determined by the emotional attitudes our parents, guardians, and teachers expressed toward us when we were very young. Whether we go at our task courageously or whether we cringe and hesitate; whether we set impossible conditions for happiness or whether we take our material as we find it, hew merrily at the rock of our heritage, and occasionally take time out to help a fellow-worker, depends very largely upon the form and quality in which we, as children, experienced that quintessential determinant of human happiness men call love. To begin with, when a child is born and begins his life in the environment of adults, he is in the position of an outsider looking in upon a scene in which he will later participate, but which, as yet, withholds its secrets.

He has but the vaguest idea that he will grow up and master the mysteries of speech, of walking, of turning darkness into light, of 'going out', of telephoning, or of driving a car. He sees that his parents are definitely 'in'. They move in ineluctable ways; at their command, food and clothing appear, and at their despotic word one arises from a warm bed, or one withdraws from the bright circle of the fireside and is exiled into the lonesome limbo of the night. The child senses that his parents stand in vague communication with an even more vague 'outer world" of postmen, errand boys, doctors, "uncles", barbers, taxi drivers, or tram conductors. The situation of the young child is that of an alien in a hostile country. Most parents are vaguely aware that the little alien must be domesticated and initiated, and their emotional attitude toward the child determines very largely the nature and quality of his subsequent social adjustment. No child escapes this early process of informal education which is usually far more significant as a determinant of his future patterns than the formal education to which he is exposed in later years. The chief burden of the child's early initiation into the charmed circle of human society usually falls on his mother. *A mother's first duty to her child is to vouchsafe to the child the fundamental human experience of one entirely trustworthy human being.* Without this experience the child remains for ever a stranger in an enemy country. The child need not experience this bond with an entirely trustworthy fellow human being with his blood mother-any human being can play this role, but in the great majority of cases it devolves upon his own blood mother.

When the mother has accomplished her first spiritual function, the initiation of the child into the fellowship of human beings, her second function begins. *A mother's second function consists in training the child to develop his own powers independently that he may transfer the human bond to other members of society - his father, his brothers and sisters, nurses? servants, relatives, playmates? and teachers. She must make him independent and courageous.* The father's role is just as important as the mother's, for it is the father's function to reconcile the child to adults of the other sex, and furthermore to give the child a feeling of confidence in attacking the problem of occupation, because in the prevailing system of civilisation, the father is usually the breadwinner. The roles of father and mother may be interchanged, or they may be assumed by other adults in the child's environment, but unless a child is first reconciled to one trustworthy human being, then trained to find another completely trustworthy human being of the opposite sex, and finally inspired to find a life-work as a source of personal salvation, his social adjustment is destined to be incomplete or distorted.

The problem of initiation into human fellowship and the problem of reconciling the child not only to both sexes but to the vital necessity of work is a problem which is far too difficult for many parents. Some parents have never solved these problems themselves. A mother who has been a very spoiled child will tend to spoil her own child. She is hardly equipped to give the child an objective measure of love. A father who has made a failure of marriage will not encourage his son, and will look askance at his daughter as a potential menace to his sex. Parents who have never agreed about the educational needs of their children will be emotionally incapable of compromise and concession toward them.

Parents who disagree consciously or unconsciously make personal partisans of their children, and herein lies the great fallacy of those who say, 'We would have been divorced a long time ago except for the children. We think they ought to have a home!' It would be safer for such parents to leave their children in the rattlesnake cage at the zoo. Fathers who are failures in business are not capable of inspiring their sons with a sense of joy in work. In fact, every emotional twist, every personality warp of the parents makes itself felt in the development of the personality of the children. Perhaps there is no more discouraging factor in the determination of a child's character than the emotional astigmatism of parents, for while other vicious factors are sometimes escapable by a change of environment, the child cannot escape from the poisonous atmosphere of a neurotic home life.

Parental Mistakes

The commonest emotional warps of parents may be classed under three heads. The first comprises hate, indifference, apathy, antipathy, and resentment. The second comprises pampering, spoiling, over-tenderness, over-solicitude, over- protection, and the murderous misuse of love. The third comprises authoritarianism, patriarchalism, nagging, perfectionism, personal vanity, and ambition. The child who is the victim of any one or more of these false emotional attitudes on the part of his parents and teachers is destined to find difficulties in that most important task of all human life: social adjustment. The hated child, who never experiences the warmth of mother love, remains an enemy of the society which he has never understood. We find him, in later life, a criminal, a pervert, a trouble-maker, and always an isolated outcast. The pampered and spoiled child who has experienced too much mother-love, who has learned to make the social bridge only to his mother, and found complete emotional satisfaction in her, feels no urge to extend the circle of his social interest, and remains attached to his mother by a parasitic relationship. Often when he is faced with the problems of social adjustment, either in the family, in his school, or in his business life, he feels that he has been betrayed by his mother.

A great many of the college suicides are found among dependent, spoiled children who declare their mental bankruptcy, and by giving up the struggle for life neatly lay the blame where it usually belongs, at their parents' door. Or the pampered child may become a pleasure-loving parasite who expects the world to bring him his living on a silver platter. Again he may remain a helplessly timid and incapable adult always looking for something on which to support his languishing soul. Another type of spoiled child becomes a sexual athlete and spends his days attempting to recapture the lost paradise of childhood by being completely spoiled by some member of the other sex.

The child of parents who believe that children should be seen and not heard, of parents who impose a harsh authoritarian education upon him, is likely to be an inconsolable rebel against authority, or in those sad cases where parents succeed completely in imposing their authority on him, one of those helpless robots whose sole use to society lies in his ability to take orders and carry them out without questioning. In the days of kaiserism they made good cannon-fodder, and in these days of economic imperialism they make good drudges for factory and field. Nagging by parents is the very best training school for pedants, compulsion neurotics, religious fanatics, and fussy faddists of one variety or another.

The tragic influence of vanity and great expectations on the part of parents is usually felt very early by the child. Vain mothers and great fathers seldom have adequate children. The weight of the family tradition usually is too much for the child to bear. Often these children protect themselves by appearing stupid, in order to escape the ambitious spurs of their parents' vanity. Or they fly into the enemy's camp, and develop in a direction exactly contrary to their parents' wishes. This is the reason so many doctors' children are hypochondriacs, why the children of clergymen are often immoral, and why the children of lawyers become crooks.

Emotional astigmatism is a contagious disease, and a single, emotionally warped parent is usually quite capable of infecting an entire family with the virus of neurosis. Because there are so few really well-balanced parents, the emotional factors we have outlined in the section play a tremendous role in the discouragement and intimidation of the child. The prototype of human failures is to be found in the childhood situation of the home. The protests, the evasions, the retreats of later life may be demonstrated in the child's crystalline pattern of life. It is for this reason that mental hygienists insist in the necessity of child guidance clinics in every school. While there is no substitute for the emotional environment of a happy home, a good school community is a thousand times preferable to the warped emotionalism prevailing in many homes.

It is our own belief that the common neuroses of western civilization exact a far heavier toll of human happiness than all the contagious diseases that human flesh is heir to, and it is our profound hope that the time is not far distant when the children of parents who are emotionally incapable of educating them will be removed to appropriate children's villages and communities where they may be saved from the poisonous atmosphere of neurotic home life. Certainly there is no sound reason, except that of economic opportunism, for beginning a child's group education at the age of six. Psychologically a child who remains an only child for more than two years is headed in the direction of spiritual dereliction. The psychiatric antitoxins, the nursery school and the pre-kindergarten school, will someday be considered as important as vaccination or diphtheria immunization, although at the present day they are still scoffed at by professional educators, as Jenner was scoffed at by the die-hards of English medicine in 1796.

6. FALLACIES OF FORMAL EDUCATION

Of all the obstacles to the artistic task of self-sculpture which we have catalogued in this chapter, few are so lamentable as the fallacies of formal education because these obstacles are completely unnecessary, whereas physical deformities, the difficulties arising out of the family constellation, social and economic discrimination, sex, and the emotional astigmatism of parents are often beyond social control.

The major sins of our educational systems are derived from the following misconceptions:

1. That the child must adjust himself to the educational system.

2. That some children are inherently more talented than others.

3. That intelligence tests are true tests of ability.

4. That school attainments must be graded, and that school marks are the measure of school success.

5. That the purpose of schooling is the possession of a diploma.

6. That co-education is sometimes undesirable.

7. That the possession of a Training College certificate fits a person for the task of teaching.

To discuss each of these fallacies in detail would lead us too far afield in the philosophy of progressive education, and we must confine ourselves to a brief survey of these unnecessary- complications to the perplexities of the child's life. One of the chief difficulties of our entire educational system is a purely philosophical one originating in the confusion and disorientation of our age. In former times when a people had a single goal in life, the matter of education was simple. In feudal days the goals of education were confined to war and the monastery, and the educational system was effectively designed to •initiate a child into the technical mysteries of these ancient callings. During the guild days a child was educated from his early childhood to take his place in his father's guild. All teachers were specialists in their subjects.

To-day, with thousands of occupations open, and a complete lack of agreement as to the purposes and functions of education, both teacher and child find themselves in the artificial quandary of our age. The growth of technique in all spheres of human life, with the resultant shortening of working hours, brings us again to the problem of the use of spare time for which the first Greek schools - the very word school comes from the Greek word for leisure - were founded.

Our best education is still our business education, for if there is any unit goal inherent in our modern education it is the goal of finding security by amassing riches.

The fallacy of the intelligence test can easily be demonstrated. If three children who have three distinct goals and patterns are given an identical intelligence test, the results will vary widely. A child whose goal is to return to the comfort of his mother's home will pass a very poor intelligence test designed to indicate the degree of progress made by a courageous child who wishes to become an engineer. *The result of the testy moreover does not indicate the nature of the child's failure nor the direction of the failing child's pattern of life.* The tendency of most school teachers is to take the results of the intelligence tests as final evaluations of the child's intellectual ceiling. The child with a very high intelligence quotient demonstrates no more than that he is well prepared at the moment the test is taken to meet just such a test. Some children with exceptionally high intelligence ratings later deteriorate and become victims of dementia praecox. The children with intelligence quotients indicating borderline intelligence can be improved almost without exception by psychological re-education. The chief value of the intelligence tests lies in the field of industry, for they are well adapted to the selection of individuals who can do this or that job on this or that machine. In individual cases they are absolutely valueless unless accompanied by some psychological analysis which indicates the potentiality of the individual for betterment. It has been our constant experience that the I. Q. can be raised in individual cases from ten to sixty points by psychological re-education.

The besetting sin of much school education is the attempt to grade progress by marks, percentages, and the like. The fallacy tempts the child to go to school in order to 'get on' instead of going to school to get an education in the fine art of living. The emotional astigmatism of teachers causes children to develop stealth, craftiness, flattery in order to 'get good marks' by playing on the emotional weaknesses of their teachers, or gives them an occasion to spoil their schooling by open rebellion against the artificiality of the 'system'. In either case the true function of education is lost, and the child pays bitterly for his artificial school successes or failures in later life.

Much of the sexual maladjustment of our times Is due to the abnormal attitude towards co-education still existing in our schools. The theories of the opponents of co-education are direct descendants of the belief that a woman could be intelligent only by virtue of the devil's assistance in the cult of black arts. *Men and women must live together as adults, and they ought to be educated together throughout their entire educational career for this community of living.*

The first task of education is the psychological education of the teacher. Before this task has been accomplished we shall always be in danger of having our children victimized by neurotic, underpaid, emotionally astigmatic, and sexually starved teachers. Anyone who has seen the evil effects of patriarchal authoritarianism on a child, or has suffered from the unreasoning caprices of teachers will understand how inferiority complexes are foisted on children who come to school bright-eyed and eager to learn, only to have all initiative, all imagination, all joy in work crushed by the forbidding formalism of the 'system'

This section on the evil consequences of false educational techniques may well be closed with a few practical hints to parents and teachers:

1. Maintain discipline by interest, never by authority. The interested child needs no policeman.

2. Avoid labels. Every normal child possesses latent talents. The task of education is to evoke these talents, not to impose knowledge which does not fit into the child's pattern of life.

3. When in doubt consult an expert. Most problem children, both in the home and the school, are discouraged. Miraculous improvements supervene when a teacher devotes five minutes of daily, personal encouragement to a child.

4. Mobilise the tremendous social dynamics of your classroom; assign the task of social regeneration of a problem child to volunteers in his own class.

5. Remember that the only true goals of education are independence, courage, social adjustment. Knowledge must always be secondary to these aims.

7. SUBJECTIVE SOURCES OF INFERIORITY FEELING

Our seventh class of inferiority generators comprises a host of subjective experiences which defy logical classification. The sole common denominator of these subjective sources of the feeling of inadequacy is the fact that they are usually based upon ignorance, misinterpretation, or exaggeration of subjective experiences. The case of Edward K. will serve as an example.

Mr K.'s outstanding characteristic is an unpleasant cackling laugh. He is incapable of making a simple statement, such as 'To-day is a fine day' or 'I like to watch race-horses' without completing the statement with his annoying and utterly unwarranted laugh. Analysis demonstrated the purpose of the laugh as a plea for leniency, and traced its origins to his parents' unremitting ridicule of his every attempt at independence during childhood. His first childhood memory is of making a small sailing boat out of a cigar-box, a few bobbins, pencils, and a strip of a discarded petticoat. Edward brought his boat into the sitting-room, proud of his accomplishment,' and expecting his father's approval. The boat was made the source of ridicule and merry-making before a group of visitors, and the child remembers withdrawing in anguish, shame, and resentment from the room, and secretly destroying his boat in a fit of despondency and chagrin. Similar ridicule met his first attempts at drawing, his first poem, his first pair of long trousers, his first attempt to ask a girl to a dance. At the age of twenty-one he timidly announced his engagement only to be greeted by roars of merriment. He broke the engagement and has not been able to approach another girl E. K.'s father is not an innately vicious man. Perhaps he meant his merriment as friendly criticism. Its effect was psychic strangulation. There is hardly a more criminal attitude than ridicule of a child's attempts at creative work. Even monkeys cannot bear to be ridiculed.

Edna B. demonstrates an inferiority complex due to a parental over-religiosity. Her mother is a very saintly woman whose vision is bounded by the Sunday School, the Gospels, a vivid belief in hell, and the hope of a heavenly apotheosis near the throne of God. She has three children, all girls. The eldest escaped the atmosphere of sanctity by becoming a cabaret dancer. The second girl ran away from home at the age of seventeen to meet a dubious fate. Edna is the youngest child. Her saintly mother determined that her youngest daughter should be 'saved for Jesus'. After thirty-eight years of unnatural life in sanctimonious seclusion from every worldly interest, after thirty-eight years of vivid terror of Hell, and an equally vivid belief in the sinfulness of lipstick, rouge, pretty clothes, dancing, Sunday amusements, films, bridge - in fact, everything but prayer and ascetic sanctity, Edna was kissed at a Sunday School picnic by a young minister of her congregation. She believed that she had committed the 'unpardonable sin'. She returned to her home confused and depressed and strangely agitated. At her mother's insistent questioning about the events of the picnic she broke into uncontrollable fits of weeping and laughter. On the following day her expected menstrual period did not appear. She believed that the minister's kiss had made her pregnant. She clumsily attempted suicide and was removed to a private asylum where we saw her first, fondling the only rag doll her mother had ever allowed her to have, mumbling incoherent prayers punctuated by the unforgettable cackling laughter of dementia praecox.

I leave the final evaluation of religious education to theologians and metaphysicians, but as a psychiatrist who has witnessed the untoward effects of intense religious training in countless instances, I advise that religious dogma, doctrines of "original sin', of damnation and hell-fire, of salvation by faith and not by works, and kindred theological fictions be administered in small doses, and very infrequently, by parents who desire their sons and daughters to grow up into healthy-minded adults.

The Role of Sexual Trauma

Ralph M. represents an inferiority complex derived from an unfortunate childhood experience which numerous boys encounter without its resulting in any untoward effects. Ralph was a student in a choir school at which he was a boarder. A proctor, under guise of chastisement for some minor infraction of the rules, assaulted him sexually. Ralph, without knowing the implications of the homosexual attack of this older man, screamed and extricated himself from the situation. The proctor, fearing exposure of his act, persecuted the twelve-year-old boy unmercifully, threatening him with the direst punishment. Ralph dreamed constantly of terrific beatings and persecutions. A fortunate illness occasioned his removal from the choir school. But the seed of guilt and inferiority had already been implanted. He found it difficult to make contacts

with other boys in the new school in which he was placed. His parents were missionaries in a foreign country, and his guardian believed that Ralph's timidity and seclusion were the signs of stupidity. Five years after the attack he failed completely in Ills final examinations, and he was referred for psychiatric care by the intelligent head master who recognized the psychological basis of Ralph's difficulties. It required great patience and constant reiterations of friendship to penetrate the defences which Ralph had erected to keep the world from discovering his 'rottenness'. Even greater eloquence was required to persuade him that the harm that had been done him existed only in his interpretation of his guilt.

Untoward and unfortunate sexual experiences are common in the lives of children. A greater damage is often caused by parents' solicitude than by the actual sexual experience. The Freudian school of psychoanalysis has greatly exaggerated the importance of so-called 'sexual trauma' in childhood. In some cases, the sexual trauma is retroactively utilized as a rationalized cause of neurosis. No sexual trauma can in itself cause an inferiority feeling, but in some cases, such as that of Ralph, the secondary implications, and the child's misinterpretation of the seriousness of the attack, may be elaborated into an inferiority complex.

I am indebted to one of my colleagues for the report of a similar case of a boy who became obsessed with the idea that he was suffering from juvenile paresis after reading Ibsen's Ghosts during the storm and stress of his adolescence. The boy's father had died of a mysterious disease which had defied the diagnosis of several specialists, and the reading of the Ibsen play, together with the surreptitious study of psychiatric textbooks in a medical school library to which he had access, convinced this lad that his father died of paresis and that the germ of syphilis had been transmitted to him. Complete laboratory tests demonstrated normal blood and spinal fluid, but the boy persisted in his belief for months. At my suggestion, my colleague utilized the young man's literary ability to cure him. He was urged to write a play about himself and work out a happy ending, and during the course of literary criticism of his play, he was convinced that it was better to act 'as if' he were not infected, and 'as if' he were as sound as the laboratory tests indicated. New horizons and new triumphs at school served to dispel the black butterflies of a too close identification with Ibsen's Oswald, and a too rigorous and over-imaginative inquest into the probable causes of his father's death.

These few cases serve to show of what thin stuff the inferiority complex may be constructed under unfavourable environmental conditions. We are as miserable as we think ourselves, and most of our fears and doubts and anxieties are based on ignorance, misconception, and narrowed horizons of human activity. There is hardly a human being who has not at some time or another experienced a sense of inferiority whose roots were deeply anchored in one of the seven unhappy sources we have so briefly described. These are the obstacles which stand in the way of every man and woman. They need not be obstacles, as anyone who reads the biographies and autobiographies of really great human beings can easily prove for himself, and any one of these obstacles may become the spring-board to fame as easily as it may be the desperate morass of inferiority.

Before we proceed with our next chapter on the craftsmanship of being happy though human, let us formulate a few maxims for the good life.

If you have an inferiority complex you are in good company. The sense of inadequacy is not confined to you. It is universal.

No matter what the source of your inferiority complex, a careful study of human history will probably show you that some man or woman has used that very source as the basis of his fame or the foundation for his happiness.

Nothing can compel you to keep your inferiority complex if you are not afraid to examine it and if you are not too lazy to do something about it.

If you have retained your inferiority complex you have allowed yourself to be beaten without a struggle. Open your eyes and roll up your sleeves. It is never too late. Ninety-five per cent of the things that you are afraid of never happen. No one has ever built a bridge, written a book, or won a battle by worrying about it. The remaining one per cent is a function of the Inscrutable. To worry about the unpredictable is a crass form of vanity,

An ounce of constructive optimism is worth an entire encyclopaedia of despair. Sackcloth and ashes, remorse and self-reproach, protestations of guilt and lamentations of hopeless inferiority are the sanctimonious excuses of cowards.

Act as if happiness were attainable. The good life is within your reach if you put up a good fight. Give yourself a sporting chance. No one is ever beaten unless he gives up the fight.

CHAPTER FOUR.
Of Craftsmanship: Compensation, and Overcompensation

Four Methods of Compensation - Compensation as a Function of the Total Personality - Social Channels of Compensation - How to Compensate for being Pampered - 'Plus Gestures' mid the Superiority Complex- Valid Uses of 'Plus Gestures' - Fundamental Techniques of Compensation - The Need for Creative Compensations - Hobbies as Old Age Insurance - Neuroses as False Compensations — Two Patterns of Life-The Substitution of Techniques for Goals - Money as a Fiction of Power - Recapitulation

In our first chapters we discussed life as a fine art, the basic principles of creative self-sculpture, the nature of our material and some of the obstacles to the good life interposed by the universal feeling of inadequacy. In our third chapter we surveyed the special situations of human life which sometimes aggravate the vague sense of incompleteness to the proportions of an inferiority complex. Perhaps our description of the various obstacles to the task of successful self-sculpture may have appeared pessimistic at first sight, but the consideration and application of the precepts formulated at the end of each chapter will demonstrate that our problems re not as difficult as they seem. As a matter of fact, it lies quite within your power to transmute the general and specific obstacles and handicaps of your life into very real assets. Knowledge of the stuff of which human beings are made, recognition of the existing dangers together with awareness of the sources of fear and inferiority, constitute the first step toward success as a human being. A general with a good map of a battle-field is far better prepared than his opponent who leads greater forces but is ignorant of the terrain of combat. The craftsmanship of life consists in taking stock of one's defects and liabilities, mobilizing them to the best advantage and converting them into vital assets. It is part of the art of living to realize that no piece of marble is perfect, but that nevertheless its flaws can often be utilized as valuable details in the general design. In the present chapter, therefore, we shall consider the craftsmanship of physical and spiritual compensation in greater detail

Nature provided us with an unbelievably rich arsenal of tools and techniques when she endowed us as individuals and as a race with the ability to compensate for our inferiorities. So elastic are the devices of compensation that it may be stated as an axiom that there is hardly an inferiority that cannot be compensated in some socially useful fashion. The workings of this principle of compensation may be observed throughout the entire world of nature and matter. The story of the human race is the story of the compensation and overcompensation of its human frailties. It began when some pre-human anthropoid was born with a degenerate foot and was compelled to relinquish an arboreal life because he could no longer use his feet, to climb. This great inferiority (from an ape's point of view) compelled him to descend to the plain. The degenerate foot, however, enabled him to stand erect, and thus left his hands free for use. Presently he developed a thumb that was opposable to his other fingers, and finally his brain developed its hidden resources, and man as we know him was born. These first anthropoids who deserve the name of human beings were able to recognize their own weakness and insecurity. They banded together for mutual help and defence. Thus there arose the need for speech, ideas, writing, society. The flower of our present civilization is the final compensation of the sense of insecurity which our weak primitive ancestors felt in the primeval forests.

When we examine this civilization we find that the very accomplishments we pride ourselves on most originate in primitive man's feeling of inferiority. Animals with good eyes do not need microscopes or telescopes. Strong-muscled gorillas do not invent levers, wheels, axes, spades, knives, steam shovels, locomotives, or electric cranes. The keen-eared forest denizens live without a need for telephones, musical instruments, or wireless. Tigers and lions and other pure carnivora have good digestions and need not cook their prey. Fur-bearing animals exist comfortably without clothes. Man, generally, is the weakest and poorest equipped animal in the scale of living things. The period of his relative dependence on his parents is greater than that of any other animal His need of self-protection by means of some communal living is therefore greater, and with the exception of ants and other social insects (whose problem is materially simplified by their limited sphere of adjustment), man's social civilization is the most complicated and effective compensation that is to be found in nature.

What man has accomplished as a race every individual man and woman can do, and must do to survive. Mankind has always lived in groups - and no individual can isolate himself, either physically or mentally, and be happy. There is but one limit to the compensation of the individual, and that is that any individual compensation for defects and inferiorities must fit into the general pattern of human compensation. In other words, happiness is to be achieved solely in terms of socially useful activities. Alexander the Great conquered the world and lost his reason because his boundless ambition led him outside the pale of socially useful striving. All human striving, as we have seen, originates in a sense of inferiority. The goal of all human striving is life, security, and that sense of adequacy which we call self-esteem. Much of the unhappiness of the human race is due to the fact that individuals tortured with an exceptionally severe inferiority complex attempt to break this important law of human living, and seek for individual, anti-social, useless compensation for their sense of inadequacy. Let us examine the mechanism of useful compensations and overcompensations, and then investigate the false compensations we call neurosis, crime, and insanity.

Four Methods of Compensation

Compensation for defects, whether real or imagined, may be effected in the following way:

1. By training of the defective organ or faculty, in which case the function of the inferior organ may frequently become superior to that of a normal organ.

2. By substituting the function of another healthy organ for that of the inferior organ.

3. By the development of a situation in which the defective organ is advantageous.

4. By the construction of a 'psychic superstructure' of compensation in which the whole organism reacts in such a way that the extraordinary sensitivity of the inferior organ or function is translated into socially useful behaviour.

These four methods of compensation, any one of which is usually capable of producing a behaviour pattern that leads to a happy life, deserve a more detailed examination. To the man with poor eyesight the totality of life may be formulated in the phrase 'I want to see everything'. Long before any physician can tell that a defect of the eyes exists, the young child with such a defect senses that he cannot see as well as his playmates, and concentrates his energies upon the task of compensating for his poor eyesight by bettering his technique of seeing. It is notorious that many of the most famous painters and sculptors of all time have suffered from defective vision. The particular form that the compensation for this or any other defect takes, is determined by a host of other factors in the environment. Thus the son of a doctor might become a microscopist, using his technique in the handling of this delicate instrument to see where other eyes were blind, his goal being determined by the medical atmosphere in which he lived. The son of a business man, on the other hand, might more logically find the happiest sphere of his compensation in the designing of advertising posters and the like.

Most of the great philosophers of history, and a great many of the poets and writers of fantastic tales, have been men and women who have been unable to see the world about them, and have compensated by inventing a world of visual images to help them supplement their actual vision. If you suffer from defects of vision it will repay you to read the lives of eminent artists, poets, philosophers, novelists, and astronomers to learn how others, similarly affected, have brought beauty and knowledge and solace into the world. The blind Homer who gave the world the glories of the Odyssey and the Iliad is an example of a splendid line of courageous men and women who have not been daunted by their defects, a line that includes Goethe, Spinoza, Goya, Whistler, Braille, Helen Keller, and others equally notable.

Similarly, that deaf giant Beethoven points the-way to compensation for defects of hearing. Demosthenes, the stutterer, became the greatest orator of ancient times. Moses, also a stutterer, became a great religious leader. The most famous chefs are men who have suffered from dyspepsia, while many of the most famous track athletes and long distance runners suffered from rickets as children; John Hunter, the physician who first described angina pectoris, died of the disease he discovered and first described. Harry Houdini, the Nemesis of handcuffs and locks, utilized an abnormal mobility of his joints until he became a virtuoso in the art of getting out of tight places.

Investigate any genius and you will find that he is compensating for some organic or other defect by intensive training in the compensation of his anomaly in terms of social usefulness. Genius without social usefulness is unthinkable. The infinite capacity for taking pains, said to be the chief characteristic of genius, is part of the job of compensation. Only a man who is spurred to supreme compensation by a torturing sense of deficiency can concentrate so whole-heartedly on his task that he becomes a genius.

The left-handed deserve a special word of encouragement because left-handedness is one of the most common of organ inferiorities. Few other organ inferiorities offer such a wide range of compensation as sinistrality. The left-handed individual is always doing the right thing with the wrong hand.

Therefore, he develops a greater sensitivity to the relation of objects to each other in space. Combined with visual compensation, converted left-handedness is almost a universal characteristic of sculptors. Most of the sculptors whom we have examined have been ambidextrous, that is, born left-handers who have developed a compensatory facility of both hands. Leonardo da Vinci, the most facile genius of the Renaissance, left us a record of his left-handedness in his writings which were all in mirror-writing, the reverse writing so commonly a sign of left-handedness. Left-handed individuals have a great flair for the mechanical. They make the best geographers, mechanics, miniature painters, detail men, pianists, violinists, typists, inventors, fine needle-workers, jugglers, sleight-of-hand artists, or technicians of any sort. Given an anti-social twist by early childhood conditions the converted left-handers become pickpockets, safe-breakers, and forgers. We do not recommend these compensations to our readers.

The second possibility of compensation lies in the substitution of the normal functioning of another organ for that of a damaged or inferior organ or function. Thus, one of my patients who had suffered for years from a defect in her hearing, together with the social isolation and suspiciousness that so often follow in the wake of this condition, was urged to take up sculpture as a life interest. In this art, which requires hours of concentrated work during which the extraneous noises of the great city are only distractions, her loss of hearing was not only not a liability but a valuable asset. The best piano-tuner I have ever found was a blind man who took up piano-tuning early in life at the behest of a physician who wisely recognized the progressive nature of his eye condition. Arturo Toscanini, conductor of the New York Philharmonic Orchestra, has compensated for his great short-sightedness by developing a phenomenal memory, so that he is capable of conducting innumerable symphonies and operas without a score. One of the most daring flying men of to-day suffered a life-long sense of inferiority because of his small size. Not only was aviation a subjective compensation for his smallness (he could look down on the world from the vantage point of his aeroplane), but he capitalized his size by inventing a very small and fast machine which a larger man could never have entered or flown. With this aeroplane he won many races and a great measure of satisfying fame.

The third method of compensation, that of seeking a situation in which the defective organ is advantageous, has already been touched in part in the cases of the deaf woman who became a sculptor, and the small man who invented the speedy aeroplane. Perhaps the best example of this type of compensation is to be found in the case of a man who suffered from ozaena, a degenerative disease of the mucous membranes of the nose which produces a constant stench from the nostrils at the same time that it practically destroys the individual's ability to differentiate odours. Although this disease did not prevent Disraeli from becoming prime minister, it is one of the few diseases which make close social contacts almost impossible. This man was compelled to give up several jobs because his condition made his fellow workmen too uncomfortable. As foreman of a glue factory he found a satisfying occupation which enabled him to hold on to the sheet anchor of work when all else seemed lost.

Compensation as A Function of the Total Personality

The fourth method of compensation is one of the commonest in daily practice, and as a rule offers the most satisfying solutions of inferiority situations. In this form of compensation, the total personality assumes a pattern which is a compensation for the inferiority complex, no matter what its source. Here again the basic rule of all successful compensations, that the compensation must result in socially useful activities, holds as the true criterion of eventual happiness. Perhaps one of the most beautiful examples of socialized compensation in which the entire personality becomes a compensating machine is the example of Braille, himself blind, who gave the blind the famous raised alphabet that brought them light.

The discovery that the individual as a whole seeks a style of life which is in its entirety a compensation for some defective organs or for the sense of inferiority derived from the liabilities of the family constellation, from hate or from cloying love, or from social, economic, or religious disability, is one of the most significant contributions that have ever been made to the science of psychology. We owe this knowledge to Dr Alfred Adler, the Viennese psychiatrist, who announced this epoch-making discovery in a thin volume entitled *Organ Inferiority and its Psychic Compensation* in 1907. Examples of this tendency of the total individual to compensate for single inferiorities fill the history and biography of mankind,

In the matter of organic inferiorities, the story of the numerous physicians, notably Trudeau, who, themselves tuberculous, contributed most largely to the treatment and cure of tuberculosis, is a case in point. A famous French physician who suffered from asthma, bronchitis, and pneumonia as a child was responsible for the introduction of artificial ventilation in French schools; he eventually became minister of health, and developed open-air schools for pre-tuberculous children during his regime. To those who have experienced the tragedy of death in their families, the profession of medicine, indeed, is the most significant compensation.

It Is part of nature's compensatory tendency to make those who have seen death most clearly, the most ardent champions of life. Death and disease are two sources of the inferiority feeling which very few of us escape. In collecting the early childhood memories of physicians we have found an exceedingly large number of recollections of death and sickness in their families. In some instances, these same experiences lead men to become undertakers, and Adler once saw a young boy who wanted to be a grave-digger because he felt this was the best guarantee against being lowered into the grave himself.

Children who suffer from disorders of the digestion frequently devote themselves to the handling of food, the organization of food supplies, or its equivalents, money and securities. This accounts for the fact that so many bankers are either fat and well-fed, or very lean and cadaverous. Nature sometimes not only helps them to overcome their original difficulties by bettering their digestion, but also endows them with what Adler has called a 'psychic superstructure' of compensatory activities which continue to bear the mark of the original inferiority long after the actual need has passed. For example, the elder Rockefeller pursues his pattern, getting security and power through money, long after the original fear of hunger has passed. We see such a man suffering from the various diseases of the gastrointestinal tract as he grows older, and usually any degenerative diseases that affect him are likely to attack the organs of lessened resistance which have determined the direction of his life's pattern.

Social Channels of Compensation

If an individual is faced with seemingly insuperable problems, and develops a neurosis as a defence measure, the neurosis is almost certain to involve the inferior organ or organ system. Recently we had occasion to see a man who had suffered during his childhood from various difficulties of digestion. His life's compensation was a very unhappy one - he became a mean, avaricious miser who squeezed his employees to the limit of their endurance. For years he had suffered from a compulsion neurosis to collect all his old theatre tickets, programmes, newspaper clippings, and the like. His death was like his life, due to a cancer of the stomach which he refused to allow a great surgeon to remove because the surgeon demanded a fee reasonably commensurate with the man's great wealth.

Where organic inferiorities exist, one usually finds functional inferiorities of the sexual organs, and a man's attempt to compensate for these sexual inferiorities often gives us the key to the existence of his inferiority complex. It is probable that the great 'sexual athletes' of history, Don Juan, Messalina, Casanova, and others like them, suffered from a sense of sexual inferiority, and therefore devoted their entire lives to the compensations of this feeling. Certainly this was the case with J. J.

Rousseau whose Autobiography is a textbook of useful and useless compensations of an inferiority complex based on sexual phenomena.

How can social, familial, economic, religious sources of inferiority be compensated? The multiplicity of occupations offered by modern civilization has a place for all these. Dr Norman Haire writes that he was the youngest of eleven children, and was denied the educational advantages of his elder brothers and sisters because his father suddenly became impoverished. He devoted his life to the amelioration of the condition of unwanted children by becoming a champion of the birth control movement. The greatest social reformers have been individuals who have felt the pinch of poverty and have lived the lives of the poorer classes. The best educators of all time were neglected children. Pestalozzi, who put reading and writing within the reach of every schoolchild and did more to remove illiteracy from the world than any other single individual, was a poor, ill-treated, and hungry orphan who translated his own thirst for knowledge, love, and companionship into the basic laws of modern education.

Eldest children often find the best compensation for their familial position in the more conservative professions. They make splendid historians, jurists, archaeologists, classicists, and organizers. Their psychological trends make them the best exponents of the 'old order'. Religion appeals to their sense of authority. To be sure, when the oldest child has not emancipated himself from the feeling of being discriminated against, he is likely to become a bitter rebel, passionately striving for a position of renewed power. This is the reason why so many revolutionaries, so many dictators (Robespierre, Mussolini), and so many paranoiacs, have been eldest children.

The rebellion of the second child is of a different calibre. He is an iconoclast for the pure joy of breaking up the shrines of the established conservatives. The history of the Russian revolution is an interesting example of the activity of some of these chronic rebels. Men who had put their entire lives into the fight against czarism became bitter enemies of the Bolsheviks as soon as these were in power. The French poet, Arthur Rimbaud, is the apostle of all embattled second sons. But the second child has a great future in the world of business and technique. In his desire to catch up with the older child he develops ways and means of establishing short cuts - and not infrequently the world has become the debtor of such a second-born child who developed some new and better way of living, because he refused to play second fiddle in early childhood. The way of social, business, or professional reform is perhaps the best pattern for second-born children whose family situation dominates the picture of their personality.

The hated child, the poor child, the child of the minority group who has suffered his sense of inferiority chiefly because of these factors, will often find happiness in devotion to the task of social service, whether in medicine, in law, in politics, in actual social service, or in the broad field of education. Usually some aspect of their unhappy childhood is distinguished by its especial clarity, and this critical experience usually colours the child's compensatory trends when he becomes an adult. There are, to be sure, many individuals who have been so discouraged that they make no attempts to compensate, but spend their lives blindly enduring and tolerating the evil conditions of their birth, or constructing the wrongs of their childhood into a system of excuses, as if they were saying, I had a hard lot! You must expect nothing of me!' This, as any intelligent reader can see, is pure nonsense. The most brilliant contributions that have been made to human happiness have been made by just such men and women who would not allow themselves to be downed by the untoward circumstances of their childhood.

How to Compensate for Being Pampered

In the case of the spoiled, pampered, and over-indulged child the problem must be solved in a similar manner. The spoiled child sooner or later feels that he is an enemy alien in a 'world which shows not the least inclination to treat him as well as he would like to be treated. Most spoiled children, unfortunately, try the easy way out of their difficulties - they attempt to reconstruct a situation in which someone has the task of spoiling and pampering them. When they succeed at this, they sacrifice their lives and the opportunity of developing most of the worth-while qualities which make men happy. They swell the tremendous army of men and women who remain irresponsible grown-up children,

If you have been a spoiled child you will never find true happiness until you incorporate independence, social feeling, and social courage into the pattern of your life. It may be difficult for you to break the ties that bind you to home and the perennial section of your family, but there is no other way to be a complete human being. The bigger the job you tackle on your own, the more satisfaction you will get from it. To remain spoiled is to surrender yourself to the torture of comparisons with other individuals who do not demand such absolute guarantees of approbation and security. Do not be afraid of people. Most of them are as frightened as you are, and most of them have the same problems that you have. Move to another town, and begin from "scratch" as a contributing fellow-man, make your own decisions, stop depending on the opinions of your relatives and neighbours, and branch out for yourself. Your deficient self-esteem is due to lack of real experience and the avoidance of veritable opportunities for creative activity.

You are probably no better and no worse than the average human being - you are merely unfortunate in having been the victim of too much solicitude. Your ego is hypertrophied. You have never tasted the greatest of human pleasures - that of being useful to someone in your own right. Do not run away from responsibilities - they will make a man of you. Widen your horizons, devote yourself to at least one other human being, surrender yourself to the task of being human; And if you realize your deficiencies, and cannot find a way out of the difficulties, consult a friend, a physician, a teacher, or a psychiatrist who can show you the way.

All good compensations for the inferiority complex have certain attributes in common, (1) They are all useful, (2) They are all expressions of independent thinking and acting. (3) They are all marked by a high degree of social courage. (4) They are all surcharged with social responsibility. (5) They say "Yes!" to life. (6) They result in happiness, self-esteem, social approval, and eventually a normal sense of power which is the logical compensation for the feeling of insignificance.

Good compensations are immediately recognized by your friends and neighbours, and create a sense of "goodness" in your own heart which is often the greatest reward of living.

But not all compensations are good compensations. If your feeling of inferiority is profound, if you are very discouraged, you are likely to demand a goal of power, totality, security, approbation, and esteem quite beyond the reach of human efforts. Under these circumstances when reality interposes insuperable obstacles which prevent you from attaining your goal of power, you are very likely to make a quick about face, and begin seeking the fiction of power instead of its substance.

Plus Gestures, And The Superiority Complex

The fiction of power is much more easily attained than real power and satisfaction, and that is why we have so very many neurotics strutting on the stage of life acting 'as if' they were kings and queens. These strutters are gnawed by a constant fear that their fellow-men will 'call their bluff' or pierce the thin fabric of their disguise. This leads them to isolation, to make-believe, to redoubled, but always useless, efforts to maintain their artificial superiority. To this end they develop a variety of gestures which make them appear bigger and more important than they really are. We have named these character traits 'plus gestures'. The sum total of these 'plus gestures' is usually called a 'superiority complex' by people who do not understand it. Let us examine this superiority complex more closely because its explanation is the key to the understanding of a great many human traits.

The superiority complex is never more than a smoke-screen about an inferiority complex. There is a very good biological basis for an inferiority complex, as we have shown in a previous chapter, but the sole basis for a superiority complex is the desire to prevent others from thinking as badly of you as you think of yourself. The big dog, who is sure of his power, does not bark - it is only the little dog who barks and jumps at the big dog so that he will not pass unnoticed. Similarly, really great men and women do not boast of their greatness because their works speak eloquently enough for themselves. I once asked a patient who denied that he had an inferiority complex why he needed a million pounds to feel secure. Men who are really certain of their value to their fellows do not strive for a million pounds. He had never realized that, in his own mind, his opinion of himself must have been a very unfavourable one if he needed the objective evidence of so much money to feel socially significant.

Much of the mad scramble of modern civilization which is summed up in the phrase 'Keeping up with the Joneses' is a frantic attempt to heap up as many 'plus gestures' as possible in order to impress the world with an outward show of power. The 'will to make-believe' is one of the strongest forces in human nature. The strange thing is that so many really estimable and intelligent people, who contribute greatly to the common weal, spend most of their efforts trying to make an impression in a useless way. They do not realize that a quiet, smooth-running dynamo is immeasurably more powerful than a whole bag of fireworks. The superiority complex is comparable to the whistling of a small boy in a dark alley. It sounds very brave, but it does not destroy fear.

If you have ever observed really superior human beings you will be impressed with their modesty and reticence, their keen appreciation of the responsibilities of their superiority. The inferior individual who wants to 'play big' always betrays himself by the exaggeration of his gestures. The man with the superiority complex is the only one who is deluded by his array of 'plus gestures'. Everyone else sees through the transparent structure of his psychic camouflage. Spurious superiority is betrayed by over-protestations of superiority. Everyone who is burdened with these super-compensations is really afraid that he will be overlooked. Men and women who have more than their share of timidity because of a sense of inferiority are frequently deceived by the impressive barrage of the individual with the superiority complex. In reality nothing is so easily deflated as the uneasy ego of the conceited. If you are annoyed by the boastful arrogance or the unmitigated conceit of someone with a superiority complex you need only demonstrate your knowledge of his underlying weakness to topple the unbalanced superstructure of his 'plus gestures'.

One of my patients, a wise and friendly woman, was driven to defences of a neurotic nature by the constant protestations of her husband's power. These protestations took the form of long and oratorical lectures on the weakness and folly of women, and were usually delivered in the presence of strangers. I advised my patient to procure a little soap-box and wait until her husband was in the course of an especially flowery harangue at a dinner party. Without saying a word, she brought out the soap-box and placed it neatly before him. That was the husband's last lecture.

Valid Uses of 'Plus Gestures'

Unpleasant as the "plus gestures' of the superiority complex are, the principle of 'plus gestures' is a very practical one when applied to an individual with an inferiority complex. Men and women vary a good deal in the range of 'plus gestures' which give them a subjective sense of superiority. 'Plus gestures' never cure an inferiority complex - but they are important aids in establishing that first subjective feeling of power and ability on which further training in social usefulness may be based. There is a story of a hen-pecked labourer who was browbeaten to a pulp by his wife, until one day, while working in a road excavation, the boss gave him a red flag and let him direct traffic. He stopped a shining limousine full of bejewelled ladies for a full ten minutes with his little red flag. He came home a changed man, ordered his wife to cook his favourite dish and generally asserted his newly discovered dignity, much to his wife's delight. The red flag was a 'plus gesture' which gave him a new sense of importance on which he could construct a sense of security and significance.

It is my usual practice to prescribe new hats, facial massages, permanent waves, fashionable lotions, new perfume, expensive gloves, or a new handbag for women in the early stages of depression or melancholia. One of my patients who lived in the depths of depression in a cheap furnished room in a noisy street was constrained, under violent protest, to move into a sunny room in a fashionable hotel. His self-esteem rose like a rocket when he could invite the few remaining friends he had retained to his new quarters. Within a month he had successfully asked his employer for a substantial rise in salary. The employer's reply was significant: 'We would have given you an increase long ago if you had acted as though you were worth it!'

Another patient, an architect, who felt he was a complete failure, was ordered to buy a car he had admired at a distance, as a prop to his self-esteem. He drove his new car to a Country Club which was planning a new addition, showed his plans to the committee in charge of construction, and drove away with an order for the new building. He was an excellent architect, needing solely an external stimulus to his self-esteem, to enable him to realize his own value. A young lawyer who used to sit and worry about his diminishing assets was urged to invest almost his entire fortune in a new wardrobe and a two weeks' holiday in a fashionable seaside hotel. He inspired confidence in an unhappy wife, a guest at the same hotel, took charge of her divorce proceedings, and collected the largest fee he had ever made, and at the same time renewed his zest for the practice of law, and his belief in his own ability.

Silk hats do not make heroes, nor clothes a queen - but they help if you have an inferiority complex. In all the cases we have described, the 'plus gestures' were only accessories - the real compensations were always in terms of social usefulness. The most imposing array of 'plus gestures' is of no value if there, is no underlying willingness to be socially useful. If you have been unduly sensitive to other people's opinions, plan a campaign of convincing yourself, with 'plus gestures' if necessary, of your own validity, remembering always that 'plus gestures' are but temporary devices. If you use 'plus gestures' to help yourself, they are good. If you use them to convince others, they are simply an expression of bad manners.

Fundamental Techniques of Compensation

The art of compensating for the inferiority feeling which every human being inherits as part of the raw material of life, consists of two separate techniques. The first is the art of getting along with other people. The second is the art of getting along with yourself. No compensation is complete without a good development of both these techniques. As part of the first technique we have the affirmation in action of all the bonds that bind human beings together. The sense of personal weakness is best overcome by a close association with humanity. The second method, which we may call internal compensation in contrast to the first which is directed toward the environment, is based upon the fact that a certain quantum of creative energy resides in every individual. Unless this creative energy is harnessed you cannot attain complete happiness. The world is full of stunted musicians, thwarted painters, enchained sculptors, frustrated poets and novelists, frightened actors, hobbled dancers, and intimidated sportsmen. How often have you heard someone say, 'I'd give everything I possess to play that nocturne!' or 'How happy I'd be If I could only write £ Frequently these are men and women who are making a very good outward adjustment, men who hold responsible jobs, women who are good mothers and housekeepers. They are unhappy because they have not tapped the creative depths in their own souls and find themselves with nothing to do when the ordinary tasks of everyday life are completed.

This subject of learning to live with oneself deserves an entire book to itself. Unfortunately, it is but seldom touched by psychological writers. Much muddled thinking about these creative inner compensations, moreover, has been foisted on the world by the Freudians who believe that art and hobbies are 'sublimations' of sex. There is no earthly reason for believing that there is a hidden sexual Energy which, comparable to electricity, can be converted into some form of energy, such as light or heat, when it meets with resistance to its flow. You cannot convert sexuality into poetry or sculpture except by means of metaphysical fictions. If the Freudian concepts were true, they would be equally valid for hunger and thirst or the desire to breathe, secrete bile, or excrete waste products. Each of these physiological functions causes disturbances in the body-mind balance. It is no more reasonable to believe that painting a landscape is a sublimation of a repressed sexuality than it is to believe that a violin concerto is the direct result of constipation. No one ever painted a great painting because he was prevented from drinking the normal amount of water needed by his body for the continuation of life. There is no substitute for, and no sublimation of sex. We do not need this theory to explain man's creative activity, especially when investigation shows that some of the most creative geniuses of all time have lived a thoroughly adequate sexual life.

The Need for Creative Compensations

The necessity of developing some internal compensations is the greater in our machine age because there are so few people whose work and social relations give them a real sense of 'belonging' to their community. If you spend your day turning out financial statements, threading bolts in a motor-car factory, teaching children the mysteries of fractions and decimals, or even selling life insurance, the end of the day may find you a few shillings richer, but you have hardly lived a very thrilling day. The more dramatic professions are not open to everyone, but there is no man or woman who cannot find a hobby in some creative field which can make moments of leisure more interesting. Our civilization, designed to bring people closer together, often accomplishes the very antithesis of its goal, especially in our large cities. As a result of our technical advances you may easily hear on the wireless a running commentary on a boxing contest in New York, but there is an equal or greater chance that you have never seen the man who lives next door. Neither our daily work nor our daily social contacts contain the measure of satisfaction that is open to a Samoan savage who lives, hunts, works, fights, dances, and plays daily with his fellow villagers. The need of creative outlets is all the greater, therefore, for the modern city dweller.

Fortunately, the cities which sin most egregiously against the development of a true social spirit and a deep communal relationship also offer the greatest opportunities for creative outlets, another evidence of the compensatory tendency. The adult education movement is making greater and greater contributions to the increasing number of intelligent men and women who realize that intellectual stagnation is far worse than death. Libraries are so common nowadays that we have blunted our awareness of the enormous sources of personal growth proffered by the world of books. Wireless, at once the curse and the blessing of modern civilization, is rapidly coming to afford more and more extensive cultural opportunities.

There are literally thousands of men and women who suffer from holiday neuroses because they have not developed inner compensations. If you have not learned how to get along with yourself, week-ends become hideous nightmares of boredom and despair. We see case after case of compulsion and anxiety neuroses in men and women who hold important positions and capably fulfil their normal responsibilities toward society, but who find themselves completely unable to solve the problems of a holiday away from their work. Many of these individuals find an asylum from normal social contacts in the turmoil of their daily tasks. Many of them are socially maladjusted.

I have always advised people to begin the task of social adjustment at home. The civilized man must be capable of holding converse with himself without becoming pathologically introspective. The art of getting along with yourself demands an initial investment of self-confidence. Self-esteem is not only derived from the degree of usefulness to your neighbours - the ability to be good company for yourself when the necessity arises immeasurably facilitates the attainment of happiness.

Hobbies as Old Age Insurance

In a sense, the construction of a world of interest in creative activities, hobbies, and avocations is the most certain insurance against the mental depression that so commonly occurs with old age or sickness. Occasionally we hear that someone has been confined to his bed for months by some serious illness, only to discover artistic or literary interests of whose existence he was completely unaware. Willard Huntington Wright, the brilliant writer of the 'S.S. Van Dine' detective stories, developed his technique while suffering from a nervous breakdown. Had he developed his detective-story technique as a counterpoise to his more serious studies, earlier in his life, he might not have been compelled to suffer his breakdown.

One of my patients, a millionaire many times over, came to this country a ragged urchin from Austria, and was compelled to spend his childhood selling papers in order to support his entire family. This man suffered a series of depressions when, at the age of sixty-one, he was compelled to retire from an active business which had been his life's work. He had been a fighter all his life, a good fighter, and a successful one, but in the course of his fighting he had never learned the art of being at peace except in battle harness. When his age compelled him to retire from the active field of battle, he was forced to admit his first defeat. Spare time, the cross of the retired business man who has not developed some avocation, forced this man whom no adversary had ever bested to his knees. In full physical and mental vigour, the passive enjoyments of travel or golf were inadequate stimuli. I prescribed the Boy Scouts as a socially constructive avocation, which represented a psychologically valid compensation for his own poverty-stricken, pleasureless childhood. He became not only an important financial backer of this movement, but spent four evenings a week, and most of his days in active participation in Boy Scout activities. He has suffered no further recurrence of his depression.

If you have ever felt the desire to blow a cornet, to cover canvas with colours, to mould a piece of clay, to collect stamps, to write one-act plays, to do embroidery, to dance, to grow roses or to raise police dogs, to paint lamp shades or to do dry-points, do not procrastinate, do not feel ashamed, but obey that inclination. It may pay rich dividends in self-esteem and security. The prevailing belief that you must be very talented to get satisfaction from an artistic avocation has stopped many from the enjoyment of their own creative urge. Do not let ignorant interferers who are suspicious of any activity which is not strictly money-getting deter you from the practice of these inner compensations.

It may be set down as a psychological axiom that the average adult lives only a partial life. The mad competition for power and money which is the besetting sin of modern life, precludes the graceful utilization of leisure for the acquisition of cultural awareness or the practice of some artistic craft. It is well for those who wish to construct a life of enduring happiness to guard against the temptation to find substitutes for good conversation, creative hobbies, or cultural avocations, in alcoholic excesses. There is no true release from the boredom of an empty life in the continuous repetition of monotonous bridge playing, nor is there any true surrogate for the veritable thrills of any creative or expansive avocation in the artificial exhilaration of stock market manipulations. These are the emergency devices which the human mind, starved for proper intellectual and aesthetic nourishment, is forced to construct as temporary relief measures. Playing bridge or the 'market' are temporary substitutes at best, whose momentary validity soon fades into the arid wastes of lethal boredom. Nor can you escape the problem of the good use of leisure time by hiding behind innumerable cocktails or whiskies and sodas.

Neuroses as False Compensations

When obstacles to compensation, external in social adjustment, and internal in the art of living alone, become too great, it is a common human tendency to seek escape from situations intolerable to our sense of self-esteem in that vague limbo of subjective 'make-believe' compensations which psychiatrists call neurotic behaviour. Probably there is no human being who does not show certain neurotic manifestations in some vital activity. Men who find objective and real compensations in their work often show neurotic patterns in so far as their sexual activity is concerned, and women who meet the problems of sexual union, marriage, or motherhood, are sometimes neurotic in their desire to evade the problems of earning a living. Mental normality i$ not the rule, it is an ideal which he approach as a limit but never completely attain. The purpose of this book is not to demonstrate how to be a perfect human being, but to illumine the major mistakes of unhappy living, and indicate a method of substituting minor, unimportant aberrations from the ideal for grave and tragic errors in the fine art of living. The description of the neuroses which follows, therefore, is intended solely as a map of a large portion of human life which may be avoided by anyone who understands its dangers.

False compensations may be catalogued under several headings. The artificial overcompensations of the superiority complex occupy one. The whining protestation of inferiority with its correlate appeal, I am so unworthy, you must expect nothing of me!' falls into another. The life patterns based on the neurotic 'ifs' and 'huts' fall into still another category. The neuroses which depend on a circumscription of the sphere of activity to some unimportant sector of human activity, and those neuroses which represent such a wide detour about the obstacle that the individual becomes completely perplexed in his way, form another group. One group of neuroses commonly known as neurasthenia consists in shifting the blame for personal failure to pain, sickness, or the inadequate functioning of certain organs.

The profession of sickness, hypochondria, is a very common false compensation in which the responsibility for failure is shifted to the shoulders of society. The hypochondriac says to society, in effect, 'If I were well I would contribute, but I am sick, and you must take care of me.' His secondary goal in life then becomes the maintenance of his illness. In hysteria the obstacle is imagined 2s non-existent, or the hysterical patient converts his unwillingness to meet the obstacle into an actual paralysis which prevents him from approaching it. The general neurotic tendency to shift the responsibility for one's own shortcomings and failures finds its most crass expression in those forms of insanity which we call paranoia, in which the unfortunate patient believes that there are organized plots to deprive him of his rights, money, or the opportunity for happiness, and in dementia praecox, in which the discouraged patient withdraws from the problems of life completely.

The characteristics of all good compensations are these:

1. Social usefulness.
2. Social responsibility.
3. Closer contact with humanity.
4. Acceptance and conquest of difficulties.
5. Social courage.
6. They lead secondarily, to a sense of power, to social esteem, and to security.

Neurotic compensations reverse the emphasis. Their characteristics are these:

1. They lead to an immediate heightening of the ego- feeling.
2. They furnish a make-believe security.
3. They produce an immediate, but subjective, sense of power.
4. They are uniformly futile.
5. They are always socially irresponsible.

6. They lead to isolation.

7. They are cowardly in a social sense.

Two Patterns of Life

Let us consider two typical patterns of compensation. One is the case of a man who was left-handed, rachitic, and hated by his parents as a child. During his early schooling he was a rebel 'against the exceptional brutality of his teachers. His adolescence was marked by isolation, unfriendliness, day-dreaming of extreme power, and the ability to move rapidly. At the age of eighteen he left home to begin work in a motor-car factory. At this point he met a friendly engineer who first initiated him into the amenities of group living. This man enabled him to continue his interrupted studies by proffering financial aid. He became a designer of automobile engines. His friend patented one of his early inventions which brought him freedom from financial worries. Subsequent activities made him a leading designer of engines. He married, assumed the responsibilities of a wife and family. With increasing wealth, he endowed a trade school for boys, and with increasing leisure he began a library devoted to the history of technical research. At the present time he devotes some of his time to teaching engineering at a university, is on the board of numerous charities, a member of the Education Committee, a happy and successful human being.

The other case is that of a typical neurosis. This is the case of a woman who was an only child, and very much spoiled during the first few years of her life. When she entered school for the first time she had violent temper tantrums which quickly effected her return to her home, where she could play the role of a fairy princess without interference. Although she developed very well mentally-a concession to her teachers, in order to be spoiled by them - she was always inclined to be dependent. She was extremely vain of her physical beauty, and disliked the thought that her beauty might some day be marred by pregnancy and childbirth. She married solely as a gesture to her mother's insistence, and remained completely frigid during her marriage.

Her husband was penniless at the time she married him, and she regarded him not as an equal to be loved, but as a child to be mothered and nursed. She pampered him as much as she wanted to be pampered herself. The husband found this state of enforced parasitism very unpleasant, devoted his efforts to work, and after a few years was able to support himself and his wife very well. Although our patient was outwardly well pleased with this situation in reality she felt that she had lost an important prop to her self-esteem. She could no longer maintain her position of uniqueness in her family.

She now developed an anxiety neurosis, showing phobias of every imaginable description. She finally became afraid of her own fears which led to a state of continuous panic. At this point she consulted the psychiatrist. After her analysis the patient lost all her phobias, became sexually adjusted, and developed her musical talent to a high degree,

The Substitution of Techniques for Goals

While we are discussing the patterns of compensation we must consider one other aspect of compensation which occurs constantly both in the world of nature and in the realm of human conduct. It is a well-known fact that every end must be attained by the employment of definite means, or tools. To go back to the analogy of self-sculpture which we proposed in the first chapter, if your purpose is to make a marble monolith, then you must use tools appropriate to the end, and not tools designed for carving ivory. There is a general human tendency to use over and over again a tool that once has proved effective. Sometimes this favourite tool is used so often that it becomes more important than the end itself. The tool thus becomes an end in itself. This confusion of means, and tools, for purposes, ends, or goals, results in the nullification of the original purpose and the elevation of the tool or means into a secondary end.

Examples of this tendency of the means to annihilate and replace the end are common in nature. Consider the dinosaur. His vital goal was to keep alive and propagate his species. The tools he chose from nature's arsenal were protective armour of heavy plates and scales. He added scale after horny scale until he was the best armoured animal that ever walked the earth. He became so heavily armoured that he could hardly walk through the lush swamps of a prehistoric age, much less make love or fight against the obstacles of existence. Finally, his armour became so heavy that he sank helplessly in the marshes, and drowned. When tools are substituted for the goals which they are designed to serve, they annihilate those goals. The armour designed to preserve the dinosaur killed him in the end, when it was substituted for his true purpose to maintain his life.

The same may be said about thought. Thought is a biological tool which nature has given man to help him solve the problems of his existence. When thought breaks loose from man's tool chest, and becomes an independent end in itself, it sets itself impossible problems to solve. We misuse thought when we attempt to solve the insoluble, and eternally futile, problem, the precedence of the hen or the egg, or the equally futile problem of the beginning of time. 'Why are we here?', 'Where are we going?', 'Does immortality exist?', and similar questions are examples of the senseless quandaries that mortals make for themselves when they divorce the tool, thought, from its sole purpose, adjustment to reality.

One of the most potent sources of human unhappiness originates in this misuse of thought and thinking. There are enough immediate problems in the world to occupy all the time of all the thinkers everywhere, without wasting time on metaphysics. When you see a human being deep in the useless problems of metaphysics or theological doctrine you may well suspect that he is neither paying his bills, nor adequately educating his children, nor helping his city clean up its slums.

This does not mean that we should not attempt to search the Unknown and bring it within our reach by scientific and artistic research, or that we should take every mystery for granted. These are the good uses of thought. A practical principle to use if you are in doubt whether you are misusing thought for some futile end, is to ask yourself, 'What difference will it make to my neighbours if this proposition is true or untrue?' 'Does this knowledge make man's communal life on this crust of earth easier?' Only when we are utilizing the faculty of thought either in a creative, artistic activity or in work which helps us to understand the world in which we live and strive, and make it a better place to live in, can we be happy.

The elevation of a technique, a device, a tool of life, to the status of a goal of life is one of the favourite forms of false compensation for the inferiority feeling. A child is faced with the problem of passing an examination in arithmetic. He is afraid he will not pass, and he wishes to avoid the final test of his personality. He develops a headache. He fools his parents and the teachers, but he does not succeed in deluding himself, because he senses the fact that the difficulty of passing the examination is just as great as ever. But he has established a working principle of life: 'If you plead sickness you can avoid unpleasant tests of your self-esteem, and still retain the feeling that you could have passed the test if you had not been ill. Sickness is a good tool. It is worth cultivating.'

This child goes through life fighting all his battles by running to the sick room and pleading for leniency and special privilege. Even though he does meet certain tests in his later life, they are usually preceded or followed by sickness. Finally, he becomes a hypochondriac, a walking encyclopaedia of pains and symptoms. He has succeeded in transmuting what began as a tool into a final goal of life. His technique is often successful, but while he gains the security of the hospital bed he forfeits the happiness of the normal activity of being human. It is well to examine our own mental traits to determine whether we have not fallen into this profound error of false compensation by substituting a neurotic tool of life for living itself.

We shall have occasion to discuss alcoholism and drug addiction in greater detail in a chapter devoted to the side-shows of life, but it is' well to indicate here that alcoholism and drug addiction, gambling, sexual conquest, pedantry, preciosity, piety, snobbery, religiosity, and a host of related techniques of life fall into this type of false compensation. Indeed, it may be stated as an axiom that any man or woman who has one single outstanding character trait or technique such as religious fanaticism, dietetic faddism, crystal gating, or bridge playing which does not contribute to the commonweal - and herein lies the difference between genius and some forms of neurosis - is making the mistake of substituting a tool or a technical device for the real goal of living. Happiness must remain a closed book to such a person.

Money as A Fiction of Power

The most common of all these false compensations for the inferiority complex is the cult of money as a fiction of power. While it is true that many individuals who have achieved great social usefulness enjoy good incomes, and seem to the onlooker to derive their social esteem and power from the money they possess, the quest for money as a source of power, esteem, and happiness is at once one of the most common and perhaps the most deluded techniques of life. We find men and women eating out their hearts and wearing down their muscles in the quest for gold, in the vain hope that its possession will give them security, love, and happiness. The tragedy of this fallacy lies in the fact that this quest not only spoils the lives of the misguided creatures who pursue gold as a goal of life, but it poisons the atmosphere for their neighbours who would be satisfied with other, more reasonable sources of significance. The whole tenor of our civilization has been made neurotic by the insane 'gold rush' of modern life. With the 'gold rush' come hurry, competition, disinterestedness, narrow horizons, disharmony, and the thousand lamentable dissonances of our age. This statement is not a deprecation of the true value of money - the socially useful man needs it as a medium of exchange and acquires it in a greater or lesser measure as the compensation for his usefulness to the group. But it is a footnote of warning to those who seek to compensate their sense of inferiority by the possession of money and the power it represents in modern civilization.

To anyone who examines analytically the security derived from the possession of money, it becomes apparent that wealth is one of the least secure forms of happiness. For one thing, money is very difficult to keep. For another, it cannot buy health, love, or a sense of satisfaction in doing a job well. Above all, money has never been a cure for boredom. The pleasures which it does buy are easily exhausted. Finally, the individual who has concentrated his life on the pursuit of money as the symbol of power, has not had the time to develop other compensatory trends without which money becomes a useless possession in the end. As we indicated in our first chapter, human happiness is not a static thing. It does not result from having something, or from being something - it results solely from doing something which fits into the pattern of human compensation, it derives only from the contribution of something of utility to the social organization of mankind. The fallacy of money as a source of happiness may be easily understood when we interpret the quest of money as an attempt to elevate a means into an end. Whether a rich man can enter into Heaven or not is a matter we leave to the theologians to determine, but we are certain of one thing: he who seeks happiness by getting possession of money has as little chance of attaining his goal as a dinosaur loaded with half a ton of armour plate had of surviving the struggle for existence in the marshes of a long past age.

Recapitulation

This brings us to the end of our discussion of the general laws of craftsmanship. We have sketched the process of compensation and overcompensation, and we have outlined the pit- falls attendant on substituting tools and devices for the veritable goals and ends of life. We have graphically represented two typical patterns of compensation, and discussed the criteria of good and bad compensations. To sum up:

1. The best craftsmanship of life consists in transforming your defects and inferiorities into assets and superiorities. The goal of all successful compensations must lie within the broad field of human usefulness.

2. There is no handicap, either hereditary or environmental, which cannot be compensated if you are not afraid to try.

3. Talent and genius are not hereditary gifts. They represent exceptionally successful compensations, due to exceptionally successful self-training and education. If you wish to develop a talent, get up an hour earlier than your neighbour, and practise.

4. The fine art of living consists in the twofold process of compensating for your inferiorities in terms of social usefulness and in developing your latent creative powers for the purpose of being able to live better with yourself.

5. If you have an inferiority complex, develop a good set of 'plus gestures' for the purpose of encouraging yourself and 'getting yourself across' to your neighbours. Too many 'plus gestures' without an underlying inclination to be useful constitute the superiority complex. The superiority complex betrays the underlying sense of inferiority in its possessor as surely as the brave whistling of a small boy in a dark alley betrays his fear.

6. Neurosis, crime, suicide, perversion, alcoholism, drug addiction, and fanaticism, and some forms of insanity, are false compensations for the inferiority complex. They represent a maximum of subjective power and a minimum of social responsibility. Their common denominators are fear, discouragement, and ignorance. They may be changed into socially useful compensations by enlightenment, encouragement, and social adjustment. They bear the same relation to the fine art of living that doggerel bears to the poetry of Shakespeare, or a shanty to the Cathedral of Chartres. They are bad art.

7. Beware of the temptation to elevate a means into an end. When a tool becomes more important than the process for which it was designed, both tool and process are destroyed. If you would not use a bread-knife to do murder, do not use your thought process to solve the ineluctable problems of the cosmos. Above all, do not be deceived by the madness of some of your neighbours into believing that money will buy happiness.

CHAPTER FIVE.
Of Tools: Character and Personality

The Dynamic Concept of Character - Introversion and Extraversion - 'Good' and 'Bad, Characters - The Ideal Character - The Evolution of a Personality - The Evolution of a Neurotic Character - How to Analyse a Character

What tools are available for the art of self-sculpture? We have learned that living is a fine art, and we have discovered some of the obstacles that stand in the way of our creative efforts to make something of ourselves. Some compensatory technique is available to every human being, and it is our task to know what the techniques and forms of craftsmanship are most appropriate. In the present chapter we shall discuss the choice of tools and instruments most suited to the art of self-sculpture, and at the same time we shall seek an understanding of the perplexity of those unhappy men and women who have, through fear and ignorance, used the wrong instruments.

But before we describe the tools available to each and every one of us, in the quest of happiness, let us determine the purpose and goal of our individual efforts. You will remember that every human child begins life with the handicap of actual inadequacy aggravated by the realization of his handicap. The child compensates by setting himself a goal which promises the consolations of peace, security, a sense of completeness which satisfy his self-esteem. The child's idea of the goal of his striving, vaguely formulated deep in his unconscious, is usually crystallized in some consciously realized, partial attribute of godlikeness (a boy who feels himself small and weak, and whose unconscious goal is to be a complete he-man, crystallizes his unconscious striving in his conscious desire to be a policeman because the policeman seems to have all the qualities of security and bigness that he desires). But whatever the unconscious goal or its conscious crystallization in reality, the goal always represents a substitution of a 'plus' for the 'minus' he has experienced as a child. We have learned that everyone's life is a direct and unit pattern of striving from the 'minus' situation of childhood to the imagined, unformulated, unconscious goal of the 'plus' situation of adulthood, via the half-way goal crystallized in some conscious representation or symbolization of the complete goal of godlike power.

Once the goal of our striving is set in our unconscious, and crystallized, for convenience, in some conscious attribute of totality, we look about us for ways and means of attaining our purpose, and the sum total of these ways and means is called character and personality. It is no more reasonable to believe that Mr Jones is always late for appointments because of deviations in the secretion of his pituitary gland than it is to believe that an epileptic fit is an indication of daemonic domination of the diseased. It is no more reasonable to believe that Mr Johnson always drives his car at the head of a procession because his sexual libido has been repressed, than it is to believe that he wears blue neck-ties because he is habitually constipated. Anyone who really understands human nature must realize that these character traits are not the accidental products of the interaction of blind hereditary or glandular forces. These traits are logical and rational tools which Mr Jones and Mr Johnson have selected from an imposing catalogue of possible habits, traits, reactions, and responses, because they are the most appropriate means of attaining their respective goals in life.

Let us look into the history of Mr Jones. He was the spoiled child of wealthy parents. His childhood was a happy dream, an ideal paradise of parasitic irresponsibility. His parents fell upon evil days, and lost their fortune after Mr Jones had already reconciled himself to a life of leisure and enjoyment. For the first time in his life Mr Jones did not know where he would obtain his next meal, and when his ancestral home was sold to pay for an unsuccessful speculation on the Stock Exchange, he had to content himself with very modest quarters in a boarding house. In short, Mr Jones had to go out and get a job. The world had always furnished Mr Jones with an excellent living, and he had become firmly convinced that the pleasantest possible living conditions, free of all ordinary responsibilities, were his inalienable right. Having spent most of his thirty-two years fostering the cult of his own ego, he had developed only the most rudimentary social feeling. His position as an unimportant underling had been secured for him by a friend of his father who had taken pity on his plight.

Mr Jones very quickly realized that being an employee of a small business house entailed no great honours. Yet his unconscious goal demanded a position of great eminence. His was a chronic craving for the limelight. As he could not attain his goal directly in his work, he attained it indirectly by forcing his customers to wait upon him at appointments. He always appeared pressed for time by the burden of innumerable 'important engagements', and his glib tongue extricated him from numerous scrapes in which his impudence and egoism had involved him. The reader must see how very useful the trait of coming late to appointments was to Mr Jones's unsteady self-esteem. The reader must see, also, how his tardiness, his egoism, his impudence, and his fictional 'business' are all woven of the same cloth. These are not accidental traits - they are the useful tools which

Mr Jones has acquired for the task of maintaining his egocentric self-esteem, subjectively, at the high peak he believes he deserves.

But why should Mr Johnson always wish to drive at the head of any procession of motor cars? Can it not be true that there is an exceptional adrenalin pressure in his blood? Could not his dammed-up sexual libido find its proper expression in this character trait? Mr Johnson is the oldest of three boys. He had a very severe and strict father who constantly belittled his efforts. At an early age he became cruel towards his younger brothers, and attempted in every way to enforce his authority on them as the oldest son, and his father's surrogate. He became pedantic in his exactions of compliance and obedience from his brothers who hated him cordially for his self- assumed powers. He studied hard in school so that he might the more easily retain his place as the head of the three boys. Finally, he developed such a splendid technique of sexual conquest that he was rated the Don Juan of his family, but he took every possible effort to ridicule his younger brothers when they attempted to take out a girl. In this way, and in many other equally fatuous ways, he strove hard to retain his position as the head of the family.

Because his father's campaign of deprecation had materially battered his self-esteem, Mr Johnson was never quite certain that he could retain his position. He left his father's house at an early age because he could not bear to live on the scene of his childhood defeats. He married a timid little woman who offered very little challenge to his self-esteem. His two children were as definitely dominated by his discipline and authority as he had been dominated by his father. He always bought the longest and most powerful car on the market. He passed every other car on the road, scattering curses at every other driver. Whatever circle he found himself in, Mr Johnson either dominated or deprecated. His unconscious goal demanded that he be the first, the chief, the greatest. His profoundest fear was that he might be overlooked, or that someone should get ahead of him and place him again in the intolerable position of his childhood when he was compelled to face his father's ridicule and swallow his humiliation for fear of having a beating added to the insult to his self-esteem.

When we have examined that pattern of Mr Johnson's life we see the usefulness of this strange character trait of driving at the head of every procession. We do not need the fanciful explanation of the endocrinologists or the psychoanalysts. Common sense shows us that driving at the head of the procession is the tangible crystallization of Mr Johnson's secret and unconscious goal in life. Driving at the head of the procession is a useful and necessary tool for a man in Mr Johnson's position.

The Dynamic Concept of Character

Character and personality are the sum total of all the tools, instruments and devices, habits, responses, emotions, and feelings which an individual utilizes for the attainment of his goal in life. This dynamic interpretation of the meaning of character may be tested by the examination of the living laboratory experiments which history and life itself offer to any sceptic. This dynamic point of view requires the assumption of no unseen, unknown forces which are beyond the measurement and understanding of science. It is the modern answer to the outmoded devil-doctrine. Each of us, in striving for his goal, acquires a set of tools and a technique of using them appropriate to his ends.

Much has been written in recent years about introversion and extraversion, and these labels of certain character types have been accepted widely as explaining human conduct. If Mr Adams prefers to spend every evening in his study reading Spinoza, if he is shy in company, if he avoids crowds, if he is inclined to worry about his aches and pains, and prefers studying calculus formulae to attending a football match, he is called an introvert. Mrs Adams, on the other hand, cannot sit still with a book in her hand for more than half an hour, and is happiest on a golf links when there is keen competition. She likes people, cocktail parties, driving a car, selling subscriptions for the little theatre movement in her suburb. Because she dislikes problem plays, philosophy, loneliness, the music of Bach, the novels of Marcel Proust, and cannot sit still at a lecture, Mrs Adams is called an extravert.

The labels introversion and extraversion describe a character but they do not explain it. Let us go back and trace the character patterns of both Mr and Mrs Adams to determine whether we can find why Mr Adams has chosen one set of tools, and why Mrs Adams has chosen tools of an entirely different nature. It will be well to remember that you cannot really judge and evaluate any character trait unless you can fit it into an entire personality pattern. Just as a melody cannot be judged by a single chord, so a personality cannot be understood by the analysis of a single character trait.

Although it is true that we can often make very shrewd deductions about the childhood situation of an individual When we see him sitting quietly beside his fireplace in the company of a volume of philosophy while everyone else in the house is dancing, and we can often reconstruct his probable goal in life, such deductions are usually dangerous unless one is a well-trained psychiatrist. It is better to follow the laws of mathematics and remember that it requires several points to determine the course and formula of a curved line. The amateur student of psychology and of human nature will do well to check his findings and his deductions when he thinks he has discovered the pattern of an individual by adducing further psychological proof that he has correctly evaluated his style of life.

Introversion and Extra-Version

As a matter of fact, when we investigate Mr Adams's early life we find that he was a very weak and sickly child. For years he was practically an invalid because a congenital heart condition compelled him to rest in bed for a considerable part of every day. He felt his weakness keenly in competition with other children. When his playmates where playing football he stood on the lines and watched because his doctor had forbidden any unnecessary running or exertion. He was frequently taunted for not participating, and often children laughed at him, when he explained that his doctor had forbidden him to play, because externally he looked like a very healthy child. Gradually he divorced himself from the playing fields and took to books for companionship. The more his book-world grew, the more he learned to compensate for his physical inferiorities by building up a world of phantasy which soon became quite as satisfying as the real conquests of the playing field. He identified himself with the brave knights of the fairy tales, and he believed definitely in a magic wand which would some day help him to overcome his defects.

Unfortunately for Mr Adams, his preoccupation with the world of dreams and phantasy kept him from making normal contacts. When his heart condition improved with time and he was allowed to go to a public school, he was a shy and timid person, little versed in the art of making friends and playing the game according to the rules which other boys had learned during their early childhood. His greater intellectual development, a product of years of isolation and private tutoring, made him the scholastic superior of his classmates, and this sense of intellectual superiority at once made him deprecate their sports and activities, and devote himself further to his studies. His long years of illness sensitized him to the meanings of life and death and led him almost directly into a study of philosophy. His goal in life became the maintenance of a life of exalted and superior isolation. He avoided any activity which would place him in an inferior role, and yet his years of enforced inactivity had awakened a certain envious appreciation of the free and easy life of those who had not been similarly burdened.

Mr Adams met Mrs Adams at the university. She seemed the embodiment of all the vital qualities which he lacked as a child. She was the captain of the women's tennis team, a leader in the social life of her college. His bookish superiority and his delicate flair for the finesse of living appealed to her as much as her abundant vitality appealed to him. They married, each believing the other to be the fulfilment of their own personality defects. The childhood of Mrs Adams, whom we see now at the age of thirty-five an aggressive, active, worldly woman, was entirely different from her husband's. At the age of six she was thrown into the surf at a seaside resort, and swam out. She could not remember a day of illness during her entire childhood. Both her mother and father were active sportsmen and very courageous social individuals. The family ideal was the ideal of good sportsmanship. The harder the obstacle, the more fun in overcoming it. Thus Mrs Adams was trained to a courageous, socially adjusted 'motor' type of living. Her greatest happiness has always been in finding a worthy opponent and fighting hard to win. Defeats were never to be taken seriously - one must be a good sport, try hard the next time, and never mind if one didn't win. The game was the thing. With this background and this goal, we can understand why Mrs Adams prefers a stiff tennis match to an intellectual bout with Hegel or Nietzsche, and why she prefers dancing to a lecture on the ethics of Aristotle.

'Good, And 'Bad' Characters

We frequently hear our friends saying that Mr X has a 'good' character or that Mr Y is a 'vicious' man. The student of human nature must abjure all moral evaluations of character and personality if he wishes to understand his fellow-men. It is a general human tendency to label people and take those labels seriously, as if they were true interpretations and explanations. If you wish to understand your neighbour (and there is no better practice in understanding your own goal, your own pattern, your own vital formula, and your own character and personality), try to put yourself in the other fellow's place, and by identifying yourself with his actions, really understand them. A good way to do this is to say to yourself, 'Under what conditions, and to what end would I be doing exactly the same thing?' If you can reconstruct the man's goal, you will understand why he has chosen the particular character traits he evinces, in order to attaints end.

As a matter of fact, there are 'good' and 'bad' characters and personalities. We must assume some norm of character, and if we remember that the need of social living is the paramount expression of our desire for self-preservation, it must follow of necessity that all character traits that make communal living easier must be 'good' character traits, and all character traits that tend to disrupt our social life must be called 'bad' character traits. In our evaluation of character and personality we take the commonweal as our measuring rod, but we must never forget that all character traits, dispositions, personalities, and types of human behaviour are 'good', that is effective, from the standpoint of the individual goal.

The importance of this knowledge becomes apparent as soon as we enter the field of self-education or psychological treatment. Most 'bad' character traits sooner or later lead their possessors into conflict with society and with nature. If we wish to rid ourselves of 'bad' character traits, that is, socially undesirable, uncooperative, disruptive, isolating, futile character traits, we can achieve a 'good' character by developing our social horizons and our inner creative interests so that we become more human. Bad and good are questions of degree in human nature. Self-preservation remains the first law of nature, and social life and adjustment is man's best means of preserving himself. It follows, therefore, that all character traits which we term 'bad', that is, all anti-social traits are, in the last analysis, not only socially destructive but also self-destructive. They lead to immediate conflict with the group and with nature, and consequently unhappiness is bound to follow in the wake of a 'bad' character.

Let us analyse some of the good character traits which mark the individual who is living out his humanity to the fullest extent. All good character traits have a common denominator of social courage and social usefulness and common sense. Good traits bind human beings together in a free association. We say a 'free' association purposely because love, one of the greatest and best of all character traits, is frequently misused to effect tyrannical bonds between parent and child, between lovers, between husband and wife. Like the truth which may be misused as the basis of a lie, so love may be misused in psychic enslavement and strangulation. Always observe what happens after the expression of a character trait if you want to understand it. It is sometimes necessary to be harsh, perhaps almost brutal, in order to bring a wandering friend to the path of reason. Under these circumstances harshness and brutality become socially valuable traits. Examples of enslavement and tyranny by the misuse of love are exceedingly common. You have but to observe the murderous love of a vain mother who keeps her 'darling baby' from developing in order to gratify her desire to appear young, or to watch a nagging mother who undermines her child's independence and courage 'because she loves him so' - to understand this prostitution of love.

The 'Ideal' Character

The ideal man or woman, striving for a fair measure of social significance and a reasonable compensation for his own inferiorities in terms of social service, needs as his most trusted tools, courage, common sense, a highly developed social feeling, honesty, sincerity, a sense of humour, the ability to identify himself with his fellow-men. A sense of social responsibility follows as a matter of course. He does not worship luck, and his philosophy is a philosophy of fighting optimism. He regards members of the other sex as equivalent to members of his own sex. He is modest, sincere, honourable, interested in life. He has time for the education of his children, he enjoys the work he has chosen for himself, and he has developed other avocations that help him to widen his horizons and give him a true zest for living.

This ideal 'normal, man is tolerant, and attempts to understand rather than to label his fellow-men. He is generous, patient, good-natured. He is not the victim of his emotions and feelings, but uses them as aids in the pursuit of the major interests of his life. He has time to say a helpful word to a fellow worker, and he is interested in making the world a better place to live in. Wealth as such is not the goal of his life, nor pleasure. He uses his wealth to foster the happiness of others, and his pleasure serves as a necessary relaxation, diversion, and recreation, that eventually contributes to his zest in performing the daily tasks of life. He is devoted to those who are dependent upon him, but interested also in others outside his family.

He is independent in thought, resourceful in work, determined in effort without being aggressive, soft in manner, courteous in bearing, sympathetic in his attitude toward his fellow-men, altruistic without being sentimental, considerate, many-sided, poised with the certainty of one who is at once conscious of his success without losing sight of the insignificant value of that success in the long perspectives of time, place, and civilization. In a word, he is a happy man.

Not all of us pursue an ideal goal, and therefore our characters vary markedly from this ideal picture of an ideal character. Our personality takes form and shape not only from the nature of the goal which we pursue, but also from the manner in which we pursue it. We shall see, therefore, that human beings may be catalogued according to their goal in life, and according to their technique of self-sculpture. We shall find men and women who have set themselves a task too great for human accomplishment because their sense of inferiority is so profound that only a goal of godlikeness can satisfy them. In contrast to these we find others whose fear of the difficulties of life has led them to circumscribe the sphere of their activity to such an extent that they content themselves with being kings in their little side-shows. Furthermore, there are those who, having become panic-stricken because they are so far from their goal, rush at their problems with an aggressive, over-active assault. Other equally unhappy souls who approach their tasks hesitatingly, seek to make a detour about them, or to divert the attention of their fellows by make-believe activity in some useless sideshow. When they are even less courageous, they run away from the problems entirely and attempt to reconstruct the lost paradise of irresponsible childhood. The least courageous of all, perplexed by their own impotence, dazed by the seeming magnitude of the social task, prefer to destroy themselves rather than to make any attempt to solve their problems. The self-annihilation may be actual - as in suicide - or psycho-logical as in the more profound neuroses and insanities which are, in effect, living deaths.

In all these aberrant solutions of the problems of human life we find the common key-notes of fear and discouragement, of personal power, as contrasted with social usefulness, of futility as contrasted with utility, of subjectivity as contrasted with the objectivity of the normal life, of tragedy as contrasted with the sense of humour and perspective of the normal individual, of egoism as contrasted with the optimistic belief in the value of constructive altruism, and, above all, of a private system of logic as opposed to common sense. Personal power is the goal of these individuals, and their goal of personal power may take any conceivable form, whether it be the supposed power of complete enjoyment, the power of irresponsibility, the power of sexual domination, the power of money or of position, or the power derived from the emotional enslavement of others. For want of a better word we call these individuals neurotics.

Every man and woman, in all probability, has some neurotic traits of character. None of us can be entirely brave, none of us can be entirely selfless. No one always follows common sense, and no one has succeeded in compensating for his inferiority complex so completely that he is without vanity and without personal ambition. But it does lie within the power of every individual to modify this striving for personal power so that his ambition is diverted into socially valuable channels. It is not the purpose of this book to instruct you in the art of being an angel. It is enough if we learn to avoid the more egregious mistakes, and substitute minor errors for the tragic aberrations which kill and maim the spirit. The following cases show the processes of character evolution and demonstrate a few of the more typical variations from the ideal norm.

The Evolution of a Personality

John C. was a very small boy. He was teased by his playmates because he was ugly and less capable at games than the average boy of his neighbourhood. He hated his older sisters because they seemed better endowed with the qualities which make people beloved. They succeeded better in their school studies than he did, and he was constantly under the pressure of his parents' criticism for his scholastic shortcomings, and his failure to live up to his sisters' reputation. His mother was indifferent to him, and his father constantly nagged him to 'uphold the family name'. Throughout his childhood he felt himself under pressure.

He sensed his own impotence and satisfied himself as a child by bullying smaller children, torturing animals, and imagining himself a very great man. His father was a chemist, and at an early age he felt that he wanted to master the secrets contained in the rows and rows of mysterious bottles that lined his father's shelves. Surreptitiously he took out the powders and fed the cats of the neighbourhood with them to test his powers, often with tragic results to the cats. As he grew into adolescence a persistent acne made him self-conscious and widened the gulf between him and his classmates. He was a brooding, morose, isolated, uncouth individual. Chemistry was his passion. Ultimately he entered one of the large technical colleges.

At college he made no friends, but he took more honours in chemistry. Explosives were his chief joy. Twice he blew up the college laboratory, and one of the explosions burned his face and the resulting scar left his lips with an almost satanic twist. He enjoyed the disfigurement because it gave him an actual excuse for avoiding the company of his classmates, especially women. During his holidays he worked unstintingly in chemical works in order to repay his father for his education, and thus to sever (as he thought) the last sentimental associations with his home. Women he scorned. At the age of twenty-four he had never attended a dance, never entered a picture gallery except when compelled to do so as part of his school curriculum. He disliked music, art, poetry. He spent any leisure moments in his private laboratory, or hunting and fishing when the opportunity offered.

After graduation, he joined a great chemical combine, and within a year had invented a new explosive which made him financially independent. He continued his experiments, this time attempting to develop a poison gas which would be of great interest in a future war. He is a tireless worker, sleeps only five hours a night, has no real friends, has never contributed a farthing to any charity, has never kissed a girl, has never danced. He wears a suit of clothes until it falls apart or is so badly burned with chemicals that it no longer covers him. His most cherished ambition is to develop an explosive or a poison gas which will immediately wipe out an entire battleship or an army corps.

This unhappy man is considered a success in his profession, but he is a great and unhappy failure as a human being. We can see how the unfortunate circumstances of his youth have given him a warped pattern of life. His goal, a compensation for his own inability to cooperate in the fellowship of human beings, may be formulated thus: I want to be the master of the power of life and death. Since I cannot belong to mankind, I will use my knowledge to destroy it" To this end he excludes every interest and activity which does not lead him immediately to his goal of legal murder. He measures life with an inflexible rule which excludes anything constructive. His passion in life is to destroy life, and his style of life is a direct assault on life itself.

The paradox in this case lies in the fact that John C claims that he is a happy man. If this is true, his life refutes the entire thesis of this book, that a man can be happy only when he is living the good life, when he is contributing to the world's welfare, when he is joining in the world's work. At the age of forty, John C. may still think that he is a happy and successful man, but we know that he has paid a terrific price for his security. Insomnia and vague fits of despondency and 'blues' are the first symptoms of nature's retribution. Mr C. dates his insomnia very definitely to a certain Sunday when his favourite hunting dog was accidentally shot. This dog was the only living thing with which he had anything approximating to a human relation. Perhaps the death of this animal brought his own profound loneliness to his attention. Perhaps it gave him a new perspective of death, brought death close to him for the first time. Perhaps Mr C. has come to the realization for the first time in his life that he, too, might not only die, but die before his grandiose schemes for general destruction were completed.

Because of his isolation John C has never developed a sense of humour, and the prospect of final defeat in his life-plan is not a matter that is conducive to good sleep and jaunty spirits under these circumstances. The spectre of a lonely old age has made even greater men quail. Despondency and insomnia are nature's storm signals: 'Take care! Change your pattern before it is too late!' Perhaps only those readers who have experienced the horror of night after night of sleeplessness can appreciate the fact that John C. is neither as successful nor as happy as he claims.

It is not my purpose at this time to consider the therapeutic approach to this case. I have given this history to illustrate the relation that personality, character, disposition, feeling, and response bear to that dynamic pattern of the individuality which we call the style of life. In the case of John C we see an unbroken dynamic pattern of unsocial traits growing out of his original situation as a hated, oppressed child, isolated from his fellows because of physical inferiorities and the pressure of competition with three older, better prepared sisters. We see the appropriateness of all his activities, from his childhood cruelty to cats and younger children, to his adult interest in wholesale destruction by gas and explosives. His character demonstrates an unbroken unity of conduct leading directly toward his goal: 'If I cannot be admitted to society, I will destroy it.'

A further study of John C. would demonstrate the unity of this dynamic pattern in his dreams, his dress, his choice of sports and recreation, as well as in his favourite characters in fiction and history. As we might have expected, those greatest of antisocial geniuses, Alexander the Great and Napoleon, are his idols, and as we might have expected, he cares little for the amenities of dress or manners which are entirely social in their purpose. A recurrent dream of the last few years beautifully epitomizes his style of life. He finds himself, in the dream, 'alone in a world which has been completely destroyed by a poisonous gas emanating from the tail of a passing comet. I alone, of all the people in the world, have survived because I predicted the advent of the comet and prepared myself secretly by building a gas-proof chamber lined with oxygen tanks and carbon-dioxide absorbing sponges which are capable of sustaining my life for several weeks. In the dream I open my chamber when I am certain that the comet has passed out of the earth's atmosphere. I step out into a desolate world. Dead bodies are strewn all around, many of them bearing the traces of their last agony. I am not in the least concerned about the fact that I am the only man left in the world".

One could hardly desire a more definite proof than the case of John C. of the thesis that character and personality are the sum total of our vital devices for gaining our unconscious goal, nor a more dramatic exposition of the corollary thesis that happiness cannot be attained by an unsocial human being. But for the sake of clarity and for the illumination of the sceptical reader who may. desire further proof we shall illustrate our thesis with a second case, this time of Elsie G., whose neurosis is woven of very different cloth from John C's aggressive assault on humanity. Elsie G., now thirty-five years old, a divorcee, spends most of her time in bed surrounded by rows of medicine bottles, pill boxes, hypodermic syringes, and all the armament of the hospital ward. Unlike John C. she is the only child of kindly and wealthy parents. From her first day in this world she has had every difficulty removed from her path. Her mother, always a very solicitous and anxious woman, still, at the age of sixty-two, lives alone with her daughter and ministers to all her needs and desires.

The 'Evolution of a Neurotic Character

During Elsie's childhood the tender ministrations of her mother kept the 'bad, world from any possible contact with her. When Elsie was six, her father was killed in an accident and all information concerning this important event in her life was withheld from her. At the age of eight, she still believed in Santa Claus, had never crossed a street unattended by a nurse, had never played with a strange child in the street, had never bathed or dressed herself, and had assuredly never been in the position to make any independent decision. She was very beautiful as a child, and was highly praised for her model behaviour. At the age of nine no spark of initiative was left in her little soul. She was timid among strangers, and clung to her imperious, if somewhat anxious mother, whenever they entered a shop or the home of friends together.

At the age of ten, despite the precautions of her mother, Elsie contracted a series of children's diseases which threw her mother into a panic. Half the children's doctors in London were called in consultation to her bedside. A hushed and ominous quiet lay over her sick room, mysterious nurses passed like ghosts through the doors, and the ubiquitous shadow of her frenzied mother pervaded the atmosphere of an entire year of Elsie's life. Precautions were redoubled, contacts with other children were curtailed, interminable visits to doctors began. At this early age Elsie suddenly realized the social value of pain. The least sign of pain was the signal for the convention of doctors and nurses, and a new panic on the part of her mother. A headache was sufficient excuse for avoiding the unpleasant tasks of school for several days.

When Elsie was twenty-one, her mother gave her a fitting 'coming out, party, and in the course of the years her frail beauty had won the hearts of several admirers. During this period of admiration, parties, and dances, Elsie was very happy. They fitted beautifully into her pattern - the life of a misunderstood princess. She married an eminently attractive young man supposedly of good family and estimable character. Her mother, anxious to see her happily married at last, breathed a sigh of relief as the young couple left for a honeymoon in Italy. She felt that she had done her duty, that she had properly prepared her child for life in the world. She had realized her ideal for her child - and as all the elements of this fairy-tale life had been realized almost like clockwork, Elsie's mother did not doubt for one moment that the customary sequel 'and they lived happily ever after' would follow her carefully laid plans.

But as the train left Charing Cross, Elsie's difficulties began. This was her first experience as an independent human being. About sex and the art of love she knew nothing. Her knowledge of the physiology of cohabitation was nil, her ideas about childbirth even more vague than those of the average twelve- year-old child. She knew nothing of men, and when her husband proved to be something of a sexual pervert, and subsequently a professional blackmailer and forger, despite his good family, Elsie was at a loss to cope with the situation. Frantic telegrams to her mother were answered by equally frantic telegrams that bad investments precluded the mother's attempting a trip to Italy. To make matters worse, Elsie became pregnant, and after two months of anguish and hyperemesis her pregnancy was brought to a fortunate end by a miscarriage. She returned to England and instituted divorce proceedings against her husband, and when she had won her case, retired to her bed and did not rise for six months.

Her beauty had not faded and she was urged by her friends to remarry. She fell in love several times, but always with men in the diplomatic service who were never present long enough to be serious contenders for her hand, or with handsome actors whom she loved from afar, or with married men who could not consummate any relation with her because they were tied to the responsibilities of their own families. She did no work, neglecting the music and painting which she had practised in a dilettante fashion as a younger woman. She began narrowing the circle of her acquaintances by insulting all who came to see her until only her mother and an old servant were left in her entourage. Doctors came and went. None was able to diagnose and cure her of her many ailments. Headaches were her constant accompaniment, and at her menstrual periods she retired from the world entirely from ten to fourteen days.

The older she grew, the more slovenly she became, the more introspective, the more concerned with her symptoms, the less interested in the world. She could not hold a civil conversation with man or woman for more than ten minutes. Any caller who dared to remain longer was assaulted by a barrage of symptoms and the catalogue of all the painful sensations in the textbooks of physiology. She hated all her friends who urged her to get out into the sunshine - she lived in a dingy room that looked out on a dingier wall and a group of dingy dustbins - and she hated all her friends who commiserated with her and took her symptoms at her own valuation. She became despondent and thought often of suicide.

She found release from the utter boredom of lying in bed at all times by having a wireless set installed in her bedroom, and by striking up a friendship with John Barleycorn that grew to such proportions that her mother began to interfere. This was the last straw. She had always been an obstinate and self-willed child, but her mother had usually acceded to her whims before any outbursts of anger and temper tantrums supervened. Now when her mother began chiding her for having the wireless going at three in the morning so that all the neighbours complained, and began insisting that she should curtail her drinking, she became a wireless fan of the worst variety, and a persistent and deep drinker. Her drinking went to such lengths that her mother became more than usually anxious about Elsie's health.

The more she drank, the more dilapidated she became, and the more dilapidated she became the more her mother scolded her, and the more her mother scolded Elsie, the more obstinate she became about her drinking, and the more isolated and bed-ridden she was. When friends realized the vicious circle and urged her to move from the house, Elsie produced a sudden access of filial love. She could not leave her aged mother, who was becoming old and weak, and needed her presence. Elsie had read a few books on psychology and realized that her mother was in part responsible for her present state, and she began to hate her mother as violently as she formerly hated the world. Yet Elsie's dependence was so ingrained that she could not leave her.

A psychiatrist was finally called in to consult with her on her symptoms. He insisted on a separation of mother and daughter, and in the face of his seemingly superior knowledge of the case, Elsie acceded for the first time in her life, and took a room in an hotel. She chose a room at the top of the building, moved her medicines, wireless, liquor, and the few French novels that she still read, to her new quarters. On the second day, she walked to the window to look at the view and was suddenly overcome by a terrific compulsion to jump out. With anguished gestures she clung to the curtains in an effort to save herself from this terrific force which beckoned her to destroy herself. After half an hour of struggle she regained her composure, dressed, and went out into the street.

For four days she did not go near the window, did not drink, and did not listen to the wireless. he rather enjoyed her freedom from the nagging of her mother. On the fifth day of independence there was a thunderstorm, but she allowed the rain to pour into her windows until a maid closed them for her. On the sixth day she inadvertently stepped close to the window and again the terrific, compulsion to jump out overcame her. She felt a force like a mighty hand pushing at the back of the neck projecting her to death. The perspiration stood out on her forehead. She put one foot on the window-sill - and fainted.

On the following day she was back in her mother's house. The wireless was going. She was deeply intoxicated. Her mother was scolding her. The family doctor was administering sedatives. She looked out on the dingy wall from her dingy room and watched a dingy cat stalking among the dustbins. She was happy.

How to Analyse a Character

Elsie G. can hardly be considered a successful human being. Most people would consider her lot far from a happy one. Let us analyse her story as we would analyse a Bach fugue, to determine the theme, the counter-themes, and the intricate harmonies on which it is constructed. We see her as a spoiled only child, the centre of all attention in her household, kept out of touch with reality. Her earliest childhood recollection is a dream that echoes her fear of reality and her desire to be protected, and, at the same time, her early childhood suspicion that her mother was her worst enemy. She recalls: 'I was lost in a large forest and wild beasts were peering out at me from behind the trees and making menacing gestures at me. I began to cry and to feel very ill, especially when the trees seemed to make unfriendly sounds. Presently a very large woman who had a hat like my mother's, came toward me and took me under her cloak. I felt very happy, but immediately realized that it was not my mother but an old witch. I became even more frightened, struggled to free myself, and cried out aloud. I awoke and my mother and father were standing over my bed, asking me what the trouble was.'

This dream beautifully epitomizes Elsie's own evaluation of her childhood situation, we know from our acquaintance with psychological mechanisms that her night terrors were the best possible device for attracting and holding the attention of her parents during the night as well as she did during the day by means of all those little obstinacies, tantrums, timidities, and misbehaviours that made up her childhood kit of tools for enslaving her mother. Everything went well. She attained her goal which we could formulate thus: I must be the centre of all attention. My mother and father must always be at my side to help me. I am quite weak alone.' Then her year of sickness provided her with a new and better set of tools. 'Illness is the best weapon. When you are ill, not only your parents, but also the doctors and nurses run to do your bidding and your friends come and bring you toys, sweets, and flowers', she thought.

Her beautiful body, which she cultivated with assiduous vanity up to the time of her marriage, was an accessory weapon. Her fiancé, inadequate human being that he was, had nevertheless acquired an excellent technique for putting people at their ease. It was part of his armament, and he had deluded this innocent child into believing that marriage to him would be a continuation of her childhood paradise, plus the pleasures of love. He was the typical fairy-prince who would always keep her princessdom intact. She had married him at what seemed to be his face value, not inquiring into his motives, his background or his goal in life.

Her marriage was her first contact with reality, and it was a crushing and bruising encounter, both for her body and for her spirit. Her vivid belief in the existence of a very real Santa Claus was cruelly dispelled, and with the disappearance of her illusions came a host of new responsibilities for which she was completely unprepared. Under such circumstances every human being racks his memory for the techniques that have proved effective in the past. Her first impulse was to write to her mother and get help - to re-establish the dependency of her childhood. When her mother failed her she experienced a sense of betrayal for which she never forgave her. At this time, she dreamed a series of dreams which were repetitions and variations of the 'little girl lost in the wood' dream which was her earliest childhood memory. She quickly disentangled herself from her mésalliance, and with this removal of her first human responsibility, the first movement of the symphony of her life ends.

The second movement of her life symphony is opened by the theme: 'The world is a dangerous place. I must avoid all contacts and responsibilities which might get me into trouble.' With this theme she retires to the security of her bed, and circumscribes the sphere of her human activity to her four walls. The counter-theme is stated unconsciously thus: 'It is best to re-establish my security by utilizing all the tried and trusted tools of my childhood - sickness, obstinacy, snobbery, isolation, irresponsibility, egoism, and dependence.' How beautifully appropriate all these devices are to her goal. How could anyone avoid the implications of communal life better than by making a hopeless invalid of himself? What a magnificent sickness it is that defies the efforts of all the specialists. How completely you can make slaves of your family by maintaining such an obstinate disease.

During this period Elsie trained herself for her task in a very naive way. She obtained a set of the Lives of the Saints and read voraciously and assiduously, identifying herself with their sufferings at the hands of a cruel and wicked world. Saint Perpetua, who left husband, a suckling child, and a position of eminence in society for her faith, who suffered a brutal goring by a wild bull rather than recant, was her favourite saint, and she knew every detail of her heroic martyrdom by heart. Even her reading prepared her for her goal of being a misunderstood princess in a cruel and unreasonable world.

For years Elsie avenged herself upon her mother in this fashion for the wrongs she had suffered as a result of her poor training. By her discourtesy she isolated herself completely, surely an exquisite device for alienating the affections of those who came with sympathy and gifts to assuage the boredom of her illness. Her turning on the wireless at all hours was a slap in the face for her neighbours. Alcohol was, at one and the same time, an escape from the boredom of her illness, a thrust at her Puritan mother who was a strict teetotaller, and a trick to concentrate her mother's attention on her night and day.

The rational advice of her friends that she should leave her mother's house was countered by the quickly created filial affection and a hypocritical regard for her ageing mother. Any reader with a primitive knowledge of psychology can see how she really hated and plagued her mother, and how little filial affection there was in Elsie's make-up. But filial affection was an important pillar in the structure of her self-esteem, and effectually silenced all those who advised her to remove herself from the vicious circle of her home life. Finally, the psychiatrist persuaded her to leave and begin life as an independent being.

The strange interlude of her week's life in an hotel room is one of the most instructive episodes in her whole life, because it proves so beautifully the purposive nature of all her character traits. You will remember that while she moved into her hotel room accompanied by all her medicines, her wireless, and her liquor, she did not take any pills, did not turn on the wireless, and drank not a drop of liquor during her absence from her home. The reason: no one in the hotel would be affected by these tricks which worked so beautifully on her mother and neighbours. The hotel had sound-proof walls, and no one could see her headaches, or watch the amount of wine she drank in twenty-four hours.

But the reader must not forget that Elsie had had no training for an independent life. She had developed neither of the two techniques which we have demonstrated as so essential to a happy life - the art of getting along with others, or the art of filling your own life with some meaningful avocation. Therefore she had to look around for some device which would restore her to an atmosphere for which she was prepared. The window of the room on the top floor of the hotel was this ready-made tool. We can imagine that she unconsciously gravitated toward the window and began coquetting with the possibilities of self-destruction. Of real suicide there was no idea. She went through the dramatic fiction of a struggle to resist this 'irresistible force' which seemed to drive her on to the fatal leap. Her vanity and cowardice were far too important to allow her to make such a mistake in reality.

Viewed in terms of its purpose, Elsie's struggle against suicide has but one meaning: 'Now I can leave the hotel and go back to my own room and bed.' Her apartment was on the first floor, a bare ten feet above the ground. A leap from her own bedroom to the drab alley could have resulted at most in a sprained ankle or a few bruises. But the fear of self-destruction led her unerringly to the scene of her life's greatest victories against her mother and her neighbours. She had demonstrated to the psychiatrist the impossibility of living away from home.

CHAPTER SIX.
More About Tools: Conflict and Emotion

Vanity and Egoism - Ambition: Its Use and Misuse - The Meaning of Conflict and Doubt - Some Psychoanalytic Bogeys - The Dynamics of Evasion - Make-believe Superiorities - The Misuse of Mind ~ Fundamental Attitudes of the Good Life - The Profession of Worry - The Purpose of Worry - Analysis of Jealousy- The Relation of Jealousy to Love

From the description of the two cases in the foregoing chapter the reader must realize more clearly that character is not the resultant of the blind interaction of vague forces within our personality. Character and personality traits unveil themselves to the careful student of human nature as tools chosen by the personality from a host of available devices and instruments — consciously sometimes, unconsciously more often — for the attainment of the personality goal, for the execution of the vital formula, or as training for the personality ideal. A character trait can be evaluated only when it has been fitted into the style of life which the individual has chosen as a unit pattern of conduct, as a chord can be understood only when it has been examined in relation to the melody in which it occurs, or as a single figure in a large mural painting can be judged only when its relation to the total design is understood. Once you know the goal towards which a personality is striving, you can very nearly reconstruct the tools which that personality is going to utilize, and if you examine the tools which a personality employs in its life's work, you can deduce the goal of that personality pattern with a fair amount of accuracy.

Does the goal of the personality ever change? Are there individuals who have one kind of a pattern for part of their lives and an entirely different pattern during another part of their lives? These questions must be answered both negatively and affirmatively. The personality goal usually does not change, but the environment frequently does, with the result that an entirely different set of tools is required. The variation of character traits with a change in environment (but the maintenance of the same goal) may be explained by an analogy taken from the business world. A man gambles on the stock market for the purpose of getting rich quickly. When there is a 'bull, market, that is when the prices of securities are rising, he plays 'bull', expecting to capitalize the general tendency of securities to rise in price. Suppose that a crash occurs, and the market changes from a 'bull' market to a 'bear' market. The general tendency of stocks is to depreciate in value. Our friend would lose money if he continued to play 'bull' in the face of a Tailing' market. He changes his tactics, and begins to play 'bear'. In this case he capitalizes the falling value of securities. By changing his tactics, he continues to make money. His goal throughout these operations remains fixed: to make money quickly.

This sudden change of character traits which so often baffles students of human nature who do not understand the purposive nature of all human conduct, is frequently found in its most obvious manifestations in childhood. Edgar I., aged eleven, is a model child at home. He helps in the household, is well beloved, independent, neat, courteous, and friendly. At school he is a problem child. He disturbs the work and the play of other children. He annoys the teacher by making all manner of strange noises during recitations and refuses to study when the other children are studying. He teases his classmates, is mean, vindictive, untidy, unfriendly, and discourteous.

The goal of this child remains the same, although his character seems to change magically the moment he enters his classroom. At home Edgar is the only child, and well beloved. He sacrifices a few pawns in his strategic technique of holding his prestige in his family because he knows that any infraction of the household laws will not only bring down the wrath of his. father, but will also make him forfeit the tender caresses of his mother. At school it is much more difficult to maintain the centre of attention when thirty other children demand a share of the teacher's good graces. We may say in passing that Edgar was very well behaved in class until an unthinking teacher punished him once for a misdeed he had not really committed. From that time, he felt that the teacher was his natural enemy, and used every malicious trick to revenge himself known to an active boy of eleven, and at the same time gain the centre of attention he so badly desired and valued as the fundamental premise of his cooperation. It paid to be good at home — and it paid equally to be bad in school.

Have you not known men who were the most charming of good fellows in their clubs or offices, only to become tyrants the moment they came home? Have you not seen women who praised their husbands lavishly when visiting their friends, but nagged those same husbands bitterly in the privacy of their own bedrooms? These sudden and often quite contrasting character traits which we sometimes see men and women exhibiting do not belie the unity of the conduct pattern, nor do they indicate that our personality goal changes with the four winds. We use different tools, logically, when we cope with different environments. This also accounts for the apparent changes in mood and emotion to which most individuals are subject. When we approach our goal successfully we are elated and happy and good humoured. When we sense an imminent defeat our mood changes to depression, 'blues', tears, anger or rage, according to our pattern. No matter what the variations in conduct, in behaviour, in mood or in emotion, the goal of the personality remains a fixed fiction which we approach now aggressively, now hesitatingly, now with laughter, and now with tears, as the situation demands.

Although we have demonstrated our general thesis of the purposiveness of all character traits, it may serve to clarify the subject further if we discuss in greater detail some of the character traits that most frequently lead to unhappiness. We shall choose for further consideration vanity, ambition, jealousy, indecision, and procrastination, conflict and the sense of guilt, perfectionism, and piety as the most outstanding and most misunderstood character traits.

Vanity and Egoism

Vanity, and with it egoism, conceit, self-centredness are the tools of the individualist who has not gained enough confidence and courage either to contribute to the commonweal, to cooperate with his fellows, or to follow the fundamental laws of common sense that dictate that self-preservation is best attained by alignment with society. All vain individuals are still children, emotionally. Growing up means cooperation; the voluntary assumption of social responsibilities is the only real differential point between a child and an adult. The egoist has centred his total vital energies on his own body and soul. The larger life, the happy life, demands a catholic variety in our experience and action. For this reason, the dividends on the egoist's investment in his ego are very small. Character is nourished only by exposure to the world of men, things, and ideas. The egoist, and all egoists are vain, lives according to a system of 'private logic' in which he tries, with characteristic vanity, to refute the laws of common sense and find values and happiness in life solely in the occupation of his ego with his own ego as object.

All of us are, to some extent, egoists. The boundaries between egoism and self-esteem are sometimes very vague. Because every human being suffers from a sense of inferiority at some time or another in his life, and therefore desires a certain measure of personal pre-eminence and prestige, a quantum of egoism remains in every one of us, and a certain amount of human vanity will always be inseparable from the personality and character of every human being. The completely selfless man has not yet been born, and if he were born we might expect him to have a sense of inferiority because he would be so different from all other human beings. The intelligent human being, therefore, will not try to rid his character of vanity, egoism, self-centredness, and similar character traits, as if they were so many devils. There are some 'saints' and some oriental fakirs who believe that they can attain true humility by torturing the flesh. Theirs is a misguided and frenzied sanctity. The great defect of such saintly labours is their complete futility. Self-torture and the martyrdom of the flesh are not humility but parodies of humility. As often as not the vanity of the saint and fakir peeps out of the holes of his ragged clothes or exudes slimily from his self-inflicted wounds. The objectionable but honest skunk makes a more pleasant household pet than a thoroughly un-egoistic man or woman exuding the odour of sanctimoniousness. Humility is a virtue in the social sense, but it quickly becomes a vice when it is made the chief activity of life. No virtue is sufficiently important to deserve the total investment of our life's energies. The art of life demands a battery of virtues, not one single virtue carried to excess.

What then shall we do with vanity and egoism, if these universal, unsocial traits are ubiquitously present in the personality scheme of every human being? The art of attaining happiness consists in taking egoism and vanity and diverting „ them into socially useful channels. If you are vain because you have a pretty face, a fur coat, an eight-cylinder car, ten thousand pounds in the bank, or a genealogical tree going back to the Norman Conquest, your pride and vanity are childish. One little streptococcus may easily kill you and deprive you of your basis for self-esteem. A playful hurricane may rob you of all your possessions. It is unwise to be vain about any possession, because possessions are notorious for their perverse tendency to vanish. Just as happiness consists in doing something, never in being something or having something, so the cure of vanity and pride, two egregiously disruptive character traits, consists not in putting your possessions aside and courting Our Lady Poverty, but in diverting all your life's efforts to their useful elaboration in the larger cooperation of human life.

If it is childish to be vain about your beauty, it is as futile to be proud of your wealth or intellectual capacity. Intellectual capabilities become interesting only if you can make them pay dividends in social usefulness. If you are proud because you are a better surgeon than your neighbour; if you are vain because you have invented a new electric light which brings illumination to the poorest home; if you feel a personal glow of self-esteem because the bridge you designed brings thousands o£ people nearer to their work or to their homes, then the world will pardon your vanity as reasonably justified. All other forms of vanity anger your neighbours and focus their hostility on your head. In the last analysis, vanity is a waste of time. In a cooperative venture of the titanic proportions of our civilization, vanity, boastfulness, pride, self-centredness are poor tools for acquiring the peace and security necessary to the happiness of each individual. They bring tension and conflict in their wake and preclude the larger awarenesses and the more meaningful experiences of the good life.

Ambition: Its Use and Misuse

A word about ambition which rates as a virtue in the copybooks, but on investigation, betrays itself as a vice in nearly every instance. You have no doubt heard some business acquaintance say: 'When I have made my pile I will devote all my time to charity.' This is one of the most insidious forms of personal ambition. The desire to get ahead at all costs is nothing but a form of vanity. Getting ahead usually involves putting someone else out of the running. The ambitious man has very little time for the communal fellowship that is so necessary for true happiness. Most of the individuals who succeed in 'making their million', promptly keep on making more millions because they become so involved in the toils of their ambition that they can no longer extricate themselves. Frequently they are forced to have a 'nervous breakdown' after they have 'arrived' because they have developed none of the art of living while they are making their 'pile'.

In the psychological laboratory, ambition is laid bare as a partially approved form of egoism and vanity. Beware of ambitious men and women. They are usually more courageous than those who are patently vain and egoistic — but the unsocial nature- of their striving is apparent the moment its goals are examined.

Like vanity and egoism, ambition may become a socially useful force. The ambition to make the world a better place for your fellow-men to live in is the only ambition that is consistent with happiness. When ambition is directed toward socially useful ends it usually brings its possessor the wealth and prestige that are the objectives of the ambitious and aggressive men and women who consciously go out 'to make a name' for themselves because they feel so inferior that life would be intolerable without the prestige of name, of wealth, or of power. Nature does not deal lightly with the aggressively ambitious. More often than not, they ask a prestige which is entirely incommensurate with their actual contribution. In the course of their unfair competition — and it is impossible to be a good sportsman in the battle of life if you have staked too much on the outcome - they make enemies of everyone. Society does not treat them well.

The ambitious are constantly in a state of tension. In their hurry and scurry strategy, the ambitious not only ruin their own health and make enemies of those with whom they should be cooperating, but involve themselves to such an extent in the particular technique they have chosen that they become slaves of their own ambition. As with vanity and egoism, the cult of ambition imposes greater obligations and responsibilities than the normal responsibilities of communal life which the ambitious and the vain seek to avoid.

The special difficulties that lie in the wake of ambition deserve further discussion. Nearly every neurotic is an individual whose ambition has been frustrated. This is almost axiomatic. Just because ambition is so generally egoistic in form and meaning, its goal is one of personal superiority which runs counter to the commonweal and the logical laws of common sense. Sooner or later the ambitious individual is forced to admit that he is beaten and frustrated. To save his face he must divert his ambition to the task of being unique in some useless dugout on the battlefront of life, where he can gain pre-eminence at a cheaper rate. He must either retreat, or shift the blame for his failure to some external circumstance over which he seems to have no control.

If you pride yourself on your ambition, take a mental inventory of its ends, and ask yourself whether you desire to attain those personal ends and forego the opportunities of being happy, or whether you prefer to be happy, and forego some of the prestige that your unfulfilled inferiority complex seems to demand. If your ambition has the momentum of an express train at full speed; if you can no longer stop your mad rush for glory, power, or intellectual supremacy, try to divert your energies into socially useful channels before it is too late.

Ambition. The history of the -world is strewn with the wrecks of egoistic ambitions. Nations have fallen because of their ambitions for aggrandisement. Wars are usually the result of the conflict of two equally vain ambitions. The only normal goal for human ambition is to know more about the world we live in, to understand our neighbours better than we do, to live so that life is richer and fuller because of the quality of our cooperation. All other ambitions end in death, insanity, or the tragic crippling of body and soul.

The Meaning of Conflict and Doubt

No more interesting problem than the problem of conflict and doubt presents itself to the student of human nature. There is hardly a human being who has not at some time or another experienced a sense of conflict in his own soul. The 'to be or not to be?? of Shakespeare touches us all. Our language is full of the evidences of this conflict. We hear much of the struggle between good and evil, between right and wrong, between justice and injustice, between capitalism and labour, between the individual and society. If you have ever experienced conflict in your own mind it will seem to you that there are really two souls in your body, each striving for dominance. The entire psychoanalytic theory of Freud is based on the assumption of a conflict between the libido and the social tendencies. The subjective truth of the existence of conflict is so universal that it seems to refute and deny our thesis of the unity of the personality. How can conflict be part of our striving for a fictional goal of compensation, superiority, security, or power? How can we align this paradoxical character trait 'With all that we have said about the unity of the personality pattern?

The reader will remember that the final test of any character trait or any behaviour pattern is: 'What happens after the expression of this tendency? Who is affected by it? How does it affect the individual's environment?' With this critical yardstick we approach conflict and doubt and find that, like all other character traits, they are exquisitely appropriate for the purpose of the individual personality. Of what possible use are conflict and doubt? Can there be any pragmatic value in the pain and torture of indecision? can there be any utilitarian value in the conflict between good and evil?

The reader must distinguish between an objective choice between several possible actions and the subjective conflict which we mean. If you wish to drive from London to Liverpool and have three possible routes from which to choose, a real conflict, in the psychological sense, does not exist. One route is shorter, one is more picturesque, arid one avoids a great many little towns with crooked and rough streets. You make your decision according to the objective assets or liabilities of each route. If you are in a hurry to see your wife, you take route one; if you wish to avoid traffic, you take route three; and if you are showing a foreigner the beauties of England you choose route two. Such an objective choice of several possible courses is not possible in the case of a psychic conflict.

Let us take a common example from the world of sex. Helen D. is in love with two men. Both have asked her to marry them. Mr A. has all the physical attractiveness of a living Adonis, and comes from a good family, but Helen knows that he is irresistible to other women and gravely doubts his future constancy. Mr B. is not so handsome but he is more 'solid'. He has an excellent position, and he is the soul of honour. Helen doubts whether he has as much zest for life, and knows that he has less of a sense of humour than Mr A. She has never fallen in love before, and her parents are very anxious that she should make a decision and marry. Both men are equally good prospects in her parents' eyes and they have made no attempt to influence her choice. What shall Helen do? Here is a real conflict of emotions and feelings. If we look more closely at her past life we shall see that she has been a very spoiled child, accustomed to allow others to make her decisions for her. She is socially very attractive because of her beautiful body and her grace. She is vain about her looks and ambitious about her future. Her goal is to shine, to be the centre of attention wherever she moves. From the standpoint of future security, Mr B. is the better risk, while Mr A. would appear to better advantage in full dress at the theatre. On the one hand, she cannot bear to have her future husband consider any other woman but herself; on the other, she demands sufficient financial security to enable her to entertain without any thought of the cost. Mr B. could give her the car and the furs that she wants.

These are conflicting considerations, but there is an even deeper cause for this hopeless conflict in choice between the only two men that Helen has ever loved, Helen has always been in keen competition with her younger brother. She has always felt that being a woman was something of a disadvantage. The thought of the pain and possible disfigurement of pregnancy and childbirth makes her shudder. If she could marry and be certain that she would not have any children, the decision would be easy. Helen is still in the toils of an infantile life-pattern. Further investigation shows that she has always shifted every real responsibility from her own pretty shoulders. She has always smiled her way out of difficulties, whether by flirting with the traffic policeman, or by arranging a conflict in the solution of the mature problems of love and marriage. If Helen were a good sport she could make a success of her marriage with either of her two suitors. But her unconscious goal is not marriage, but the avoidance of all responsibilities. The unconsciously arranged conflict of choice, together with her apparent emotional pain (with which her entire family is visibly impressed) is the neurotic device which she utilized in order to avoid a necessary forward movement toward maturity.

Here, then, we have the meaning of conflict, and doubt, the twin sister of conflict. Both conflict and doubt are unconscious neurotic 'arrangements'. Conflict and doubt are the character traits of those who are too timid to move forward.

So few people really understand the meaning of conflict that if you can unconsciously arrange a good psychic conflict, as Helen D. did with her two suitors, you have effectually freed yourself from making a choice or from meeting an obstacle. Conflict, doubt, and indecision are common to almost every neurosis because they are such excellent devices for avoiding responsibilities. The fallacy of attempting an explanation of psychic conflicts in terms of a conflict between two hidden intra-psychic forces or 'drives', the sexual libido and the superego (the social part of the personality according to the Freudians) should be apparent to any intelligent reader.

Some 'Psychoanalytic Bogeys'

One reason for the popularity of such analyses in the past has been the fact that the analysts have fallen into the traps which their patients have set for them. If you are wealthy enough to allow an analyst to search your past for months or years in an attempt to determine whether the fictional 'id' is stronger than the fictional 'super-ego' you not only go through the noble gestures of exposing yourself to a cure, but you very effectually put off the real decisions you must make for the period of the analysis. You may thus indulge yourself in orgies of self-pity or the delicious masochistic tortures of self-examination, without once attempting to look the real problems in the face during the entire procedure.

If you wish to know the meaning of conflict, doubt, and indecision, do not search for causes in the limbo of the unconscious, or in the dead past, but look to the immediate future. Every conflict is a spanner which the individual throws into his own psychic works - to keep them from working. A splendid test is to ask yourself: 'What would I do if I didn't have this conflict?' In the case of Helen the answer was I'd get married in a minute and settle down to married life'. The answer to this question usually betrays the cause of the conflict - it is the obstacle, the obligation, or the responsibility that the conflict is designed to avoid.

The more intense your conflict, the more impossible it seems to find a reasonable solution for it, the more you wish to avoid the solution of your problems. This common-sense explanation of the nature of conflict and doubt coincides with our previous demonstrations of the unity of the personality, the unity of the pattern of conduct, the unity of each individual's style of life. The whole nature of conflict can be graphically described by the dramatic tortures of the man who should be running forward to stop a runaway horse, but stands in one place, jumping from one foot to another because he apparently cannot decide which foot should take the first step. In such a situation no objective bystander could have any doubts about the man's deep intention not to go forward. Conflicts exist largely because of the average man's ignorance of their meaning — and because of the finesse with which they are 'arranged' by those who need such devious tools to excuse their faintheartedness.

The sense of guilt-the most modern of all bogeys - is closely related psychologically to conflict, doubt, and indecision. The sense of guilt is often one of the untoward results of early authoritarian education or of vicious theological training. As most intelligent people grow older and more mature and begin to contribute to the commonweal, thus beginning to earn a sense of self-esteem based on their contributions and cooperation, the sense of guilt, like the fear of spankings, of teachers' censure, of bogey-men, or of imminent hell-fire and brimstone, is largely diluted. Often the sense of guilt is associated with the clandestine practice of masturbation during - childhood. It is distinctly the product of a patriarchal civilization which tends to frown upon any evidences of growing sexual maturity in the child.'

There are, no doubt, a great many adults who grow up in the fear of the consequences of youthful misdeeds, sexual and otherwise, which some strict parent, teacher, or ecclesiastic has impressed upon them. Such a sense of guilt is automatically dispelled as soon as knowledge and maturity sweep away the superstitions and fears of childhood. If the sense of guilt remains, or if it is complicated by tendencies to self-abasement, remorse, self-torture, self-punishment, or penance in what ever form, you may be certain that that individual finds his sense of guilt a very useful tool in the attainment of his goal.

The meaning of the sense of guilt, as well as the meaning of remorse, penance, contrition, self-punishment, and self-abasement can be summed up in the words of one of my patients. 'What can you expect of me, Doctor? I've been a sexual sinner since I was six years old!' in answer to my question 'Why don't you get a job and do an honest day's work?' The unconscious malice of all self-abasement is echoed in this patient's words. The sense of guilt is but one form of this popular character trait whose real purpose and meaning are obvious: the individual who 'wrestles with temptation' avoids all real conflict with the actual problems of existence. The sense of guilt is no excuse for failure, cowardice, or unhappiness, any more than youthful 'sins' excuse an attitude of passive resistance toward life. Despite the fact that long and esoterically complicated monographs have been written about the sense of guilt and the desire for punishment ~ these terms remain no more than scientific synonyms for bad manners and a lack of social cooperation, useful only to those who are too timid to assume the reasonable responsibilities of adult life.

The Dynamics of Evasion

The description of the foregoing character traits and their analysis as tools which the personality appropriates for the efficient pursuit of its unconscious goal will already have suggested to the reader that all so-called 'bad' character traits are to be considered either as good tools designed to effect a false goal, or excellent devices for projecting a courageous solution of life's problems into the indefinite future. This gives us a very good scheme for classifying character traits. We have already sketched the devices which the normal man chooses for the pursuit of the rational goal of fellowship and cooperation in the world's work. All other character traits must, by exclusion, be devices whereby this normal solution of problems is evaded in one way or another.

The normal goal may be evaded by focusing on your own superiority rather than on your contribution to the commonweal. To this end we have such traits as ambition, egoism, vanity, aggressiveness, boastfulness, and the various 'plus- gestures' we described in a previous chapter. The goal of socialized compensation may be evaded, moreover, by the characteristic 'hesitating attitude' of the neurotic who believes that dilatory tactics, if pursued long enough, will buy an eventual escape from the necessity of solving these problems. Under this category we have hesitation, indecision, procrastination, doubt, and conflict, which we have already described in part. Another characteristic evasion of normal adult responsibilities is to be found in what we have called 'side-show' character traits. These are devices which not only evade the issues of reality, but give the deserter a sense of great importance in his useless arena. They also serve to convey to the world the impression that he is very busy. Among these 'sideshow' traits we find all the tricks of pedantry, perfectionism, useless piety, religiosity, ritualism, traditionalism, bigotry, timidity, anxiety, and, above all, worry.

The farther one is from the normal goal, the more frantic the efforts to pursue one's false ends with a great show of activity. That is why those who evade the normal responsibilities of adult life by attempting to re-establish the paradise of their lost childhood, work so much harder at this vain task than those who move forward, taking victory and defeat with a fair sense of humour. Among the traits that betray a retreat from life, we find all forms of human parasitism. In social relations we find a pathological love for some member of the family, together with an insufficient adjustment to men and women outside the family. In the occupational life, the psychologically immature show a tendency to be lazy, to make excuses, to shift from one job to another, to demand a sinecure: in the sexual life we find such infantile forms of expression as the perversions and the parent fixations. The keynotes of this group of character traits are childishness and irresponsibility.

A further interesting method of the evasion of normal responsibilities is found in the trick so often employed by neurotics to make their lot easier. This consists in setting up artificial conditions which must first be satisfied before the individual will contribute. For instance, a man will not work because a woman is- his superior - but he will be unable to find any other job than the one at which he cannot work. Or a woman will say she would marry, but the 'right, man has not appeared on the scene. When questioned as to the qualifications of a possible mate she will describe a paragon of male virtues that has never existed in the flesh. This form of evasion is especially popular with spoiled children, young and old. The spoiled child will not work in school unless the teacher makes a 'pet' of him; and the same spoiled child, grown up, will not take any job or assume any responsibility unless he is certain that the whole world will watch and cheer and praise him for the accomplishment of some minor everyday task.

Another favourite device belonging to this group is the trait of hypersensitivity. People who are for ever having their feelings hurt, others who are for ever being insulted, others again who are for ever walking about with a chip on their shoulder, utilize these traits to avoid the give and take of everyday life, while they arrogate a position of unique importance to themselves. The meaning of hypersensitivity is this: 'Take care! I am a very sensitive creature. You must not disturb my delicate emotional balance!' Viewed in this way the un-social quality of hypersensitivity becomes obvious. The hypersensitive individual not only raises himself artificially to a position of great importance, but also shifts the responsibility for any failure to the unthinking people who do not take his great hypersensitivity into account every moment of the day. Most of the hypersensitive souls demonstrate the validity of this point by being in continual conflict with the majority of human beings with whom they come in contact.

Some people evade the major implications of living the full life by going through their daily activities as if they wore blinkers. They constrict and restrict their activity to a very narrow and unimportant alley of conduct. This gives them a sense of superiority very similar to their fellow-deserters who have made a kingdom for themselves in some little side-show, be the beaten path of human progress. If this is a man's purpose, what better traits than those of snobbery, smugness, traditionalism, self-satisfaction, laissez-faire sanctimoniousness, and bigotry could he choose? By the simple gesture of making yourself blind to the world which is moving beside you, you can attain a smug holiness and satisfaction, and the eminently satisfying belief that you have mastered all the problems of the world. This way of approaching life would be an excellent one were it not for the fact that you get very little out of life if you do not risk anything. To be sure, the risk of living a smug, self-satisfied life is not very great, and those who appreciate security more than the rich satisfactions of great living, will be found in this camp.

Make-Believe Superiorities

We must never forget that human beings are never static. While you are choosing your set of character traits to pursue your goal, your neighbour is choosing his too. Very often your neighbour, having a slightly different goal, chooses a different set of tools and seems to be getting ahead of you. The trick of comparing yourself to other people is a certain index of the inferiority complex. The most painful thing to a man or woman with an inferiority complex is to see someone else getting ahead with a better technique of life. Now there are two ways of getting ahead. One is by training yourself for the objective conquest of difficulties. The other is the neurotic method of putting yourself ahead subjectively by deprecating the efforts of others, or enslaving or fettering them so that they cannot possibly catch up with you.

If your goal in life is not the objective solution of the world's problems, but the attainment of a subjective sense of superiority, then you must choose a very definite set of tools for your purpose. The best of these essentially unsportsmanlike devices for making yourself seem superior, at the expense of the neighbour who is struggling at your side, are deprecation, humiliation of your competitors, trickery, cheating, crime in general, envy, jealousy, ridicule, sarcasm, discouragement, and the insistence of an authoritarian attitude towards those who are in an inferior position by accident of age, birth, or position. Yon have no doubt seen the man who roars at waiters, frightens his office boy, humiliates his servants, browbeats bus conductors, and considers himself greatly superior to the nationals of some foreign country, or to the people sitting in the gallery of a theatre. He is usually the man who is abjectly humble and servile in the face of constitutional authority, a coward who must rescue his unstable sense of self-esteem at the expense of degrading another human being.

The professional patriots, the people who are proud of their class, their good breeding, their social status, their membership of an exclusive club or fashionable church, are to be numbered among these unhappy souls who thus narrow their activity to some unimportant, artificial by-path of human life. They breed revolutions and hate and animosity among their neighbours, and stifling bigotry in their own souls. To those who have followed our thesis it must be quite obvious that no true human happiness is to be found in this way of living. For one thing the individual who narrows his sphere of activity to an artificial and snobbish alley betrays his hidden fear and his unconscious realization of the inefficiency of his technique by making the walls higher and higher, until his defences are so perfect that he chokes all zest and happiness out of his life.

La Fontaine, when he wrote the fable of the fox and the grapes, described another false technique of living in which the evasion of the normal goals of responsibility, contribution, and cooperation is achieved by a categorical denial that these goals are worth while. This raises an important problem of values. If you have been troubled with a doubt about the whence and the whither and the why of human existence - and there is hardly a man or woman who has not at some time faced this problem - it may encourage you to know that these problems are not soluble for the very reason that human thought is one of the tools to help us in our adjustment, and is not suited, and never will be suited, for the examination of the reason or purpose of our existence.

The Misuse of Mind

When you use your thought processes, which were designed to help you build your house, find your mate, choose your vocation, or escape your enemies, to investigate the origin of time and space or the beginning of life, the possibility of immortality or reincarnation, or if you use your brain in an attempt to determine whether the hen preceded the egg, or whether man was created before woman, or to solve any other similarly fatuous and vain riddle, you are prostituting your thought to a false end. The architect does not build his house with the draughting pencil with which he drew up the plans. You cannot pave a street with a darning needle, and you cannot dig a trench with a surgeon's scalpel. Neither can you answer the riddles of the cosmos, using human thought as a tool. To misuse thought to these ends is to divorce it from its one and only true purpose, the adjustment of man to the vicissitudes of life on this planet. As we showed in a previous chapter, the moment you make a goal out of an instrument you not only destroy the tool but also paralyse the original function which the tool might have served.

We live because we are alive, and living is the one and only goal of life. Those who are afraid to live the full and good life often attempt to cloak their own cowardice with an immature cynicism that deprecates life in its entirety. The shabby, we might almost say obscene, spectacle of man, so puny, so impotent, so stupid that he cannot yet remove the annoyances of measles, friction, or rainy holidays from his scheme of things, solemnly announcing that life is a vain mistake, a meaningless, futile, and boring interlude between birth and death, is one of the ridiculous, tragic comedies born of man's enormous egoism and his infinitesimal sense of humour.

Whenever we see men who claim that life is not worth living, men who are bored, disinterested, and predominantly and unproductively pessimistic, we are reminded forcibly of La Fontaine's hungry but impotent fox, looking longingly at the luscious grapes beyond his reach. Show us a woman who is bored and we will show you a woman too timid or too vain to contribute. Show us a man who is surfeited with the futility of living and we will show you a cowardly, uncooperative, and unhappy human being. This technique and these tools, which are becoming more and more common because a high degree of courage and cooperation are increasingly necessary in the complex structure of modern civilization, are the choice of those who, being afraid to risk their contribution, must stand out in the cold and tell us that it is a bad play, badly written, acted by dolts and fools, to no good end.

Of evasion by self-annihilation, martyrdom, suicide, a sense of guilt, or the profession of chronic inferiority we have already made mention; and with this category of spiritual or actual self-destruction, which is the last degree of cowardice and resistance to common sense, we have sketched the various dynamic categories of approaching the tasks of life and the various tools which are appropriate to the various goals we set ourselves. What we call the normal life is no more than a courageous approach to life's problems and the objective solution of its obstacles. All variations from the normal are compassed by the various forms of evasion — aggression, hesitation, detour, circumscription, retreat, and self-destruction. Because no one is free from certain of these evasions, every human being retains some poor or inadequate tools in the form of 'bad' character traits. How shall we discard the useless tools and make the most of those that will lead us to the happy life?

Fundamental Attitudes of The Good Life

Four fundamental tools should be in the kit of every individual who strives for the good life. Of these the first is an awakened awareness of the human comedy in which we all must participate because we are human beings. The second is kindliness, the consideration and appreciation of the efforts of our neighbour, the willingness to identify ourselves with his efforts, the generosity to encourage and to help him on his way. The third is a sense of humour. We do not mean the ability to laugh at a good Joke at the expense of another, less well-off than we, but the ability to laugh at ourselves, to appreciate the infinitesimal

value of our own lives in the cosmic scheme, the willingness to see ourselves as very temporary fixtures in an ancient design whose nobility is beyond our complete comprehension. At the same time a sense of humour demands that we go on, courageously and optimistically, making the best of the realities of existence. Without this sterling quality, life becomes a tragedy full of unnecessary conflict and pain. Men go to war, murder their wives' lovers, suffer from nervous indigestion when the stock market goes down or their golf scores are low, because they lack this quality. Because they lack a sense of humour women slander and libel and gossip. For lack of this quality men kill each other because they disagree about God, religious rituals, or the ownership of a horse, pig, or political doctrine. It is the saving human virtue without which there is little use in living.

The fourth essential quality of the good life is zest. Zest is the correlation of healthy mind and healthy body toward a healthy goal. It implies contribution and cooperation, and the active pursuit and use of the foregoing qualities of awareness, kindliness and a sense of humour. It is the integrating character trait, an essential to life and happiness. It implies the catholic ability to thrill with a sense of belonging, both to the cosmos and to human society, in the meaningful cooperative relationship. It implies the full utilization of all our senses, an openness to the most varied stimuli, and the healthy response to such stimuli in terms of full living. Zest implies an active participation in all the discipline and the arts of human culture, work, play, the dance, music, the theatre, the graphic and plastic arts, as well as the fine arts of social and sexual intercourse. In a word, zest is £he enjoyment of the art of being human.

The Profession of Worry

Let us take a concrete case and examine the dynamics of worry. Elizabeth G. is forty-five years old. She is married to a capable engineer who loves her dearly, and she has three beautiful and well-adjusted children. John, the eldest, is eighteen, Gordon, the second, is fifteen, and Mary the youngest child, Is thirteen years old. Elizabeth herself was the second child of parents whose fortunes declined during her adolescence and young womanhood. The family had enjoyed great social prestige during its flourishing period, only to see it vanish with the general retrenchment and cautiousness that accompanied its decline from former financial and social heights. A great family spirit and family pride remained, however, as a vestige of former splendours. Never, at any time, was the family in actual danger of great poverty, privation, or social ostracism, but Elizabeth, the only daughter, lived for many years as if she were in the shadow of an imminent calamity.

Both her mother and her father, buoyant and energetic during their prime, began to worry about their security in their old age. Both parents were very anxious that their children, by contracting advantageous marriages, should fortify the family fortunes. Their eldest son attained noteworthy financial stability at an early age, and contracted a marriage which gladdened his family's heart. But Elizabeth delayed her marriage until she was twenty-five years old, and finally married a young man who showed promise, but had attained no eminence whatsoever at the time of his marriage. For five years before Elizabeth's marriage her inability to effect a union which would recoup the family's fortune and social status was the subject of continual conversation and the object of a greater amount of whispered criticism. With this background she approached her forthcoming marriage with the fear that she had made a mistake. She hardly loved her fiancé when she did marry him, and looked forward with great misgivings to the dangers of having a family.

Her husband conceded a great many points to her worry in the beginning, and continued to protest his love. Within a very short time he was better off than her brother, and had made a name for himself in the engineering world. Elizabeth's children were born without the slightest danger or injury to her. They developed normally during childhood, and her husband was not only capable of educating them very well, but also of contributing to her parents' welfare in a very handsome way. Elizabeth was envied the calm and quiet and security of her life by most of her neighbours who considered her good fortune remarkable.

Worry would seem to have no place in such a picture of normal family life, and yet there was not a moment of her life that Elizabeth was not worrying about something. She had been brought up in an atmosphere of fear and timidity, and she demanded a degree of security quite beyond the confines of normal human life. Worry had become her profession and as she grew older she practised it with increasing assiduity. The objective triumphs of her husband and the fine development of her children robbed her of any real basis for concern from the very outset, so she confined herself increasingly to vague and unreasoning fears that her children would not find the right professions, or would contract mésalliances, or would become infected with the 'dreadful looseness' of the 'terrible younger generation'. Just what this 'dreadful looseness' might be, Elizabeth was unable to say, and yet it remained a veritable bogey. Nor was her worry confined to her family. She had a great fear that she herself would die of cancer, and visited one physician after another, on any pretext, so that she might be examined for the possible beginning of carcinoma.

Like many another unhappy woman, Elizabeth G. had not learned to enjoy the company of her fellows, or the art of making life worth while to herself by devotion to some avocation. She had, it is true, more or less grudgingly assumed the responsibilities of motherhood, and had not spared herself any effort to educate and develop her children to the best of her ability. But in the course of time her husband had become increasingly involved in his engineering projects, and was frequently away from home for weeks at a time. Her children had developed a fair measure of independence despite her efforts to make them dependent on her, and were well on the way toward adulthood. Even her youngest daughter was more resourceful and more courageous than her mother, and frequently patted her mother on the back, saying, 'Oh, don't worry, Mother. It will turn out all right.'

While the eldest boy resented his mother's worry as unfounded, the second son openly ridiculed her fears, and

often infuriated her by taking unnecessary physical risks which threw her into a pitiful panic. Of all the family, Elizabeth's husband was still the most considerate, and on one occasion he left his work, and came a very long journey by aeroplane in response to a telephone message, to assuage her fears. The second son's comment was very illuminating: 'Mother almost died, thinking of Dad flying over the mountains, but she risked his neck because she was afraid Mary might get pneumonia from her bad cold, and she was afraid to choose a new doctor. I call it poor sportsmanship!'

From her early childhood Elizabeth always feared that she would be deserted in an hour of need. The fear dated from her first day at school when she had lost her way, and was brought home by a policeman after wandering perplexedly past her own house half a dozen times. The tenuousness of her family's fortunes had kept this fear alive throughout the years, and now the spectre of old age and of desertion by her children or her husband drove her to redoubled efforts to maintain her security, in terms of reassuring expressions of concern and attention from everyone about her. Surely no better tool than worry could have been chosen for this end.

She not only worried about possible accidents to her husband during his engineering trips, or injuries to her son who was in his school football team, but she worried about cancer and death, the seduction of her daughter, the possibility of her eldest son's getting syphilis from an infected towel in his boarding school, the danger of crossing streets in the city, the appalling prevalence of infantile paralysis, the danger of communism, and similar vague bogeys. What did she gain by these fears? Why did she choose worry as the best means of attaining her ends?

The Purpose of Worry

If we formulate Elizabeth's unconscious goal with the phrase: I must have greater security than anyone else in the world, and everyone else must help me to attain it,' we can readily understand how important worry is in her armament for gaining both attention and security. Her entire family is tyrannized by her solicitude, because the simplest everyday activity becomes fearful danger in her eyes. Moreover, worry makes her very superior to every other member of her family, because by contrast they appear far less solicitous for the welfare of kith and kin than Elizabeth.

Like the trait of hypersensitivity which we have already analysed, Elizabeth's worry imposes an obligation on every other member of the family. Her worry makes abnormal caution the rule in her family; independence of action, thought, or social contact is out of the question when such a worrying ogress lives in the same house with you. The family, Elizabeth's sole kingdom and interest, is compelled by her worry to remain close beside her - and in this way Elizabeth stills her childish fear that she will be deserted. This fear, moreover, is also a fear that it will be no simple matter to dominate other people as easily as she dominates her family with the tried and trusted device to which its members have responded after years of Elizabeth's dictatorially imposed training.

If any member dares to launch some independent activity which puts him beyond the charmed circle of Elizabeth's over-solicitude, she promptly recalls him by staging a scene of panic. The very vagueness of her fears makes any logical or common-sense reassurance unavailing. There is no logical argument that can convince a woman who spends her days being afraid of cancer or of death that her fears are groundless, because these fears serve only her 'private' logic and her 'private' philosophy of life. Thus worry, commonly believed evidence of a friendly or loving solicitude, unmasks itself, when translated into psychological language, as an effective device to narrow the world to an unimportant side-show, and impose a tyranny of love and a domination of solicitude on those who neither need nor desire such care, while the individual who worries becomes, in her or his own opinion, a saintly and exceptionally considerate fellow-man.

Analysis of Jealousy

Jealousy, which is almost as common as worry, deserves further psychological analysis because there are few traits which have such unpleasant consequences. Jealousy is considered an inborn disposition by the vast majority of human beings, but the most superficial glance at its effects will serve to dispel this fallacy, and show that jealousy is a logical and rational tool, unconsciously acquired for the enslavement of another human being. If there is a single trait which is the unmistakable index of an inferiority complex, jealousy is that trait. It is an artificially prepared emotional feeling-tone which harms both the one who is jealous, and the one who is the object of jealousy. Jealousy has almost as nefarious an effect on the physical economy of the jealous individual as long-continued hate — to which it is closely allied psychologically. And it enslaves the object of jealousy more than if he were bound with gyves and fetters.

Consider the case of Mathilda K., the wife of a physician. She is the youngest of three sisters and has always felt that she has been discriminated against by her sisters and parents. Hers is a suspicious and unfriendly personality. From her earliest childhood she has been continually comparing her lot with those whom she considers more fortunate. Her earliest memory is that on her birthday her elder sister received a doll which could close its eyes. This seemingly innocuous memory may be truly interpreted only when we get her corollary reaction - I got only a rag doll for my birthday.' Mathilda claimed that she loved her husband very deeply; she was very ambitious for his success, and very proud of the progress he made after she married him and began to manage his affairs.

Doctor K. is a very attractive man, and his practice is composed very largely of women who appreciate his gentleness and tact. His patients often call him out during the evening, and occasionally Dr K. must leave a dinner party or a theatre engagement to attend a patient. On such occasions Mathilda would retire to her boudoir with a 'frightful headache'. This 'frightful headache' was no more than a disguised fit of rage which was her usual reaction to Dr K.'s leaving her. Despite the fact that she knew many of her husband's patients socially, and could not impute the faintest trace of infidelity to him, she could not learn to be objective about these night calls. While her husband was out on a call she would construct all kinds of fantastic pictures in her mind, picturing him in the arms of his patients. Dr K. is a jolly, objective, honest physician, deeply devoted to his profession. His own nature is so honest that he was not in the least aware of his wife's jealousy, although all his friends marvelled at his willingness to reassure his wife's unreasonable suspicions by repeated recitals of fidelity which would enrage a less good-natured man.

Once a grateful patient gave Dr K. a beautiful clock. He admired and valued this token very highly. The clock stood near the corner of his desk. To his wife it was the arrogant and impudent symbol of his unfaithfulness. She hated it, and she was annoyed at the idea that he looked at the clock more often than he thought of her. One day she called on her husband in his consulting room, sitting in the chair in which patients usually sat while with her husband. After a brief conversation she arose, and swung her fur stole about her neck in such a way that the clock was caught by the tail, dashed to the floor and irreparably broken. The incident passed as an unfortunate accident, although any psychologist might have been suspicious of Mathilda's unconscious malice, since no one of the doctor's many other women patients had ever touched the dock in rising and putting on her wraps. When Dr K, expressed regrets about the destruction of the clock, Mathilda, who had shown very little concern for her clumsiness, turned on her heel in a high rage, saying, I do believe, J. K, you value that damned clock more highly than you do your wife's feeling!'

Mathilda's sense of inferiority had been stilled to some extent by her marriage to Mr K, and his affection and regard for her had been the first experience of love which she had known in her life. But she could not crush her fear that this treasure might be taken away from her or shared with her. The more popular her husband grew, the more she tortured herself with doubts of his fidelity, and the more she watched and guarded his every gesture. She began to imagine that, when he was called out at night, he was calling on a mistress instead of attending a patient. At first she simply writhed mentally until the doctor returned, but later she insisted on telephoning to him at the address to which he had gone to make sure that he was there, and nowhere else. Her jealousy was a matter of common knowledge in the circle in which the K.s moved. Hostesses were almost afraid to invite the doctor and his wife because some jealous scene was certain to occur if any other woman in the party took the doctor aside for a few moments' conversation.

To test the truth of her jealous beliefs Mathilda made a habit of demanding the sexual embrace from her husband whenever he returned from. a night call. Occasionally the doctor, tired out, after a heavy day's practice and a difficult night case, and needing sleep far more than sexual embraces when he returned to his home, gently denied his wife, kissed her tenderly, and retired to his room to sleep. On these occasions Mathilda became almost apoplectic with rage and jealousy and was certain that her husband was unfaithful to her and had just come from the arms of his mistress. She put detectives on his trail, shadowed him for weeks, upbraiding the detectives when they reported that her husband was a model of good behaviour. Finally, the doctor himself realized that he was being followed, and when he confided his uneasiness to his wife, and asked whether he should apply for police protection, she confessed that she had herself subjected him to these indignities.

This evidence of his wife's lack of confidence aroused the doctor's usually placid nature to profound resentment. When he realized the extent of his wife's pathological possessiveness, he demanded that she should agree to a divorce. Mathilda begged for another chance, and the doctor granted it, although his love for his wife had definitely cooled after the shadowing episode. Within a month his wife had forgotten her good resolutions, and returned to her technique of scenes and 'frightful headaches'. Dr K. realized the neurotic nature of these headaches after the first break, although he had formerly been blind to their meaning, and insisted that his wife should subject herself to psychiatric treatment. This succeeded in giving Mathilda a new and valid self-confidence after the childhood basis of her jealousy had been, discovered, and new paths to social approval and a sense of security indicated to her.

The Relation of Jealousy to Love

To be jealous of someone means to possess him, or to attempt to possess him. Human beings are not chattels, and can never be possessed. One of the most tragic fallacies is the belief that one can buy or command the love or affection of another being. There are fathers who believe that, simply because they are fathers, their children must 'love and respect' them. This is one of the more vicious ideas that we derive from the patriarchal Hebrews, an idea which has caused untold suffering in the world and uncounted conflicts between parents and children. There are husbands who believe that their wives must love them because they are their husbands, and there are wives who believe that, once they have married a man, they have solved all their problems and that love will follow on marriage as the night follows the day, without their lifting a hand to earn it.

Men attempt to buy the love of women by giving them clothes or gifts and are surprised and pained when they find that these women love someone else. Whenever a human being is jealous, he tacitly admits that he feels himself incapable of earning and keeping the love of his beloved, and must have recourse to the artificial restrictions and circumscriptions of jealousy to counteract any competition from outside which might show him in a bad light. Men and women, parents and children, when they feel inferior, try to buy and to own those they love, and to keep that ownership by means of the fetters of jealousy which prevent the beloved that freedom of movement without which love cannot exist.

It is strange that after all these centuries of living, the average human being has not yet discovered the meaning of jealousy. Jealousy is the poison ivy that grows around the tree of love, chokes its branches, and withers its roots. When it thrives, it kills love and the beloved, and enslaves the object of love, thereby making love impossible. When it fails, it brings unhappiness to both. Love cannot exist except between equals; and jealousy degrades and vilifies the person who is being jealously guarded. It does not effect its purpose in holding the beloved against his will, but it does come back and maim the lover, body and soul.

With this description of the major character traits and some of the popular misconceptions of their meaning, we close the chapter on the tools which the personality utilizes in attaining its individual, unconscious goal. The reader who has followed our method will be able to analyse and understand other character traits, personality twists, other patterns of conduct, which the limitations of this study preclude our examining in greater detail. To understand any given character trait, you must fit it into the dynamic unity of a human pattern moving like a planet in its orbit, through a definite pattern between the childhood situation of inferiority and the imagined goal of superiority, totality, security, and peace.

If you would understand the meaning of any particular character trait, observe what happens to the environment after the expression of it. Try to identify yourself with the man or woman who is using that particular tool and try then to reproduce the situation and the end in which, and for which, you would not only use that same tool, but use it in the same way. Analyse the predominant dynamics of your own approach to the problems of life, and if you find yourself running away from the battle, take courage, and look reality in the face. Polish up your sense of humour, realize your neighbour is in the same predicament, and make a fresh start.

CHAPTER SEVEN.
Of Training: Dreams, Humour, and Philosophy

*Psychic Selectivity and Experience - How We 'Make, Our Experiences
Procrustes and the Scheme of Apperception - The Training Formula
The Function of Memory - The Importance of Childhood Memories - About
Dreams - Of Wit and Humour - The Psycho-dynamics of a Joke ~ The Value " of
Sport - Of Basic Philosophies - Mysticism, Fatalism, and Hedonism*

Observing the life and conduct of your fellow-men is like being a Martian spectator at a football match. You see men and women moving, working, striving, and struggling, according to some mysterious plan whose ultimate ends you may appreciate but whose immediate meaning is beyond your comprehension. 'Positions are taken, signals are given. Suddenly both teams clash in a conflict of purposes. You know in a general way that each team wants to get the ball through the other team's goal posts, but you know little or nothing of the immediate strategy of each move in the struggle. You know even less about the practice, preparation, and training that has preceded the contest for weeks.

You see only the dramatic moment - and unless you have been a player yourself, you realize but little of the training that has preceded the successful play. The hours of coaching that preceded and prepare for each single dramatic episode are sensed only by experts who understand that no play is an accident - that every movement has been thought out and prepared by weeks of gruelling practice.

Perhaps you have noticed that, in the great crises of human life, there is always some man who steps into the breach and seems to meet the critical situation as if all his life had been a preparation for that particular emergency. As a matter of fact, we are all in constant training for our goal, and the manner of this training is an interesting chapter in the understanding of human nature. When a dramatic incident occurs and someone rises to the emergency, he has prepared for that emergency either in his imagination or in the actual conduct of his life. The battle of Waterloo was won on the playing fields of Eton. It is for this reason that revolutions whose time has come never lack for leaders, just as the religions required by a certain epoch never want for prophets. Men and woman are constantly training themselves to be leaders, prophets, martyrs, organizers, explorers, experimenters, and the like. It is part of the process of training themselves for their individual goal in life, and when the historical situation appropriate to their goal presents itself, they are ready. This unconscious and conscious training must be understood if we are to be effective human beings, and it must be properly mobilized if we are to lead happy lives.

In the development of a normal personality, the original sense of inferiority is overcome by a process of conscious training and growth until, with maturity, the normal individual is ready to contribute whatever power and technique he has developed during the first period of his life (the period of individuation) to the greater welfare of the race. The conquest of obstacles on the way gives him a sense of security and poise which are the premises of a useful maturity. His early experiences within his family have provided the initiation into the fellowship of mankind that enables him, when he is mature, to turn his efforts to the human cause. In the course of his progress he has trained himself to be courageous, to be objective, to be kindly, to cooperate, and to contribute and to look on his own effort, with a certain sense of humour.

We have shown in previous paragraphs that the individual's goal is always delimited by the particular and specifically individual form of the feeling of inferiority he experienced as a child. We have shown, moreover, that the pattern of any personality is a unified dynamic stream between the original feeling of inferiority and the imagined (and often unconscious) goal of superiority, power, security, totality, which he believes necessary for happiness. But the world is very large, and the possible range of experience is so great that an individual 'muddling through' life will come in contact with a great many experiences which may not only not contribute to his goal, but may actually detract or divert him from his unconscious purpose. We must exercise some selectivity in our experiences. To accomplish this end every one develops a formula with which to test each experience in advance so as to determine whether or not it may be assimilated into his unit pattern. We call this formula the scheme of apperception. The scheme of apperception is the many-branched antenna with which the personality feels its way through life's difficulties.

Psychic Selectivity and Experience

We need not invent a psychological device simply to explain the circumstances of psychic selectivity. As in our other explanations of human conduct we need but apply the sound scientific principles of physiology to our psychological thinking to find the truth. The ingestion and digestion of food is the closest analogy in physiology to the observed facts of psychology. The purpose of eating, comparable to the goal of individual life, is to keep alive. Food is the fuel we utilize to keep alive, just as, in the psychological sphere, we seek experiences to build up our psychic pattern of life. As all the food we eat is not necessarily capable of assimilation in our bodies, so all the experiences we meet in a life-time are not necessarily valuable to our psychic patterns. We must test a morsel before we eat it. To test it we have to use our senses of sight, touch, smell, and feeling, and our experience, plus these valuable feelers, helps us to avoid poisonous food, i.e. material that cannot be assimilated. If a morsel smells as if it were decayed we do not even attempt to put it into our mouths, because experience has taught us that this will lead to pain or disease. In the mental life we have developed an apparatus comparable to the senses of sight, touch, and smell, whose purpose is to pre-view and pre-examine every experience to test its fitness for assimilation in the mosaic pattern of our style of life. This apparatus we call 'the scheme of apperception'. It is the psychic yardstick which we acquire for the purpose of avoiding all experiences that cannot be assimilated into our pattern of conduct.

Suppose a piece of beef-steak is served to you. Your senses and your experiences teach you that this is appropriate food. Your next step is to take this material and reduce it, by the processes of mastication and digestion, to its least common units, which in this case, are the so-called amino-acids. The amino-acids are the units which compose the complex protein molecules called beef. Although human protein contains the very same amino-acids as beef protein, it contains them in slightly different proportions. It is necessary, therefore, in the process of assimilation, to break the complicated beef protein molecule down into its constituent amino-acids and remove only such percentages of each of the constituents as are necessary for the formation of human protein. This process is called assimilation.

An analogous process of psychic assimilation occurs in the mental sphere when you come in contact with a new experience. Your first act is to pre-view and pre-determine whether the experience is fitting to your pattern by measuring it with your psychic scheme of apperception. If the experience seems fairly appropriate, you break it up and remove that part of it that fits into your dynamic pattern, and reject the remainder, exactly as the left-overs of the amino-acids of the beef protein are excreted after digestion in the form of urine and faeces.

How We 'Make' Our Experience

This process of pre-viewing and testing our experiences goes on quietly and unconsciously during our entire lives. When a crisis arises we are prepared for it by virtue of this training. You have no doubt seen men and women who turn every situation to their advantage, while others seem to be constantly in 'hot water' and 'bad luck'. This is not a matter of destiny, fate, or predestination, but of constant training in the choice of our experiences by means of the unconscious application of our scheme of apperception. We do not learn from our experiences; we make them to suit our style of life.

Lest this idea, that we do not learn from experience, should appear too revolutionary, we shall illustrate its dynamics by a few examples. People who are always having good luck are usually happy, and need no instruction in this matter because their scheme of apperception must be based on the normal principles of human cooperation. But the individuals who are for ever having bad luck or 'getting the rough end of the stick' are a problem in human understanding. Let us examine such a case.

John B. is a workman in a furniture factory. He came to my attention because of a claim that he had been injured in an industrial accident that had completely crippled his right arm. The question of the employer's responsibility or the worker's carelessness was raised. The man was given the usual intelligence test, and was shown to have an intelligence quotient well above the average of the workers in the factory. On examination it appeared that this accident was the culmination of a series of accidents, all minor in character, which had prevented John B. from working several weeks. He had, in fact, had twelve accidents in four months. The factory had all the latest safeguarding devices that could be obtained, and John B. was considered an excellent workman when he was not laid up because of injuries.

The psychiatric investigation revealed that he had wanted to be an artist all his life. Because of the pressure of a domineering father and the necessity of assuming a large part of the responsibility for his family's finances, he had been compelled to relinquish his schooling after a half-year during which he had shown fair promise in his artistic work. He had been forced, then, to take up a job in the same factory in which his father was a foreman. John B. had hated his father since his early childhood, and the factory symbolized his father's power to him. The logic of reality compelled him to work for a living, but his scheme of apperception was directed, not to making the best of his situation, but to finding an escape from what he considered humiliating and intolerable work.

The fact that he was a good workman and could have advanced easily did not lessen his dislike of working in the same factory with his father. Unconsciously, he was on the lookout for accidents, and whenever anything went wrong in a factory that had had an almost unbroken record of freedom from industrial accidents, John B. was almost certain to be found bleeding or maimed. We can imagine that this man's goal could be stated in the formula: 'I wish to advance beyond my cruel father by becoming an artist instead of a workman.' Reality prevented him from attaining his goal, and instead he found himself in the most unfavourable situation of working in the very factory where his father's power was a distinct handicap. His secondary surrogate goal became: 'I must get out of this intolerable situation.'

To accomplish this end, he found no better way than to destroy himself by his own inefficiency. He looked for accidents unconsciously, and, when he was injured, he could say to himself and to his father, 'You see, I am in the wrong place. I must get out of this factory.' It seems almost unbelievable that a man would injure himself to the extent of completely destroying the function of an arm, but from the psychological point of view, this is not at all uncommon. In a fashion John R.'s accident is comparable to a 'little' suicide, and has the same psychological meaning. Accidents do not occur so frequently in a well regulated factory, and surely not just to one man, unless that man exercises an unconscious training to get in their way. To be guilty of this form of criminal negligence, directed not against society, but against himself, John B. had only to disregard normal precautions and care.

Procrustes and the Scheme of Apperception

There is a famous old Greek myth of the giant Procrustes whose hut was built at the peak of a narrow mountain pass. This giant would invite all passers-by to sup with him and would force them to spend the night under his roof. Procrustes had an infamous bed for his visitors. If the stranger were shorter than the bed, the giant would stretch him until he fitted the bed exactly, usually at the expense of the stranger's life. If the visitor happened to be too long for the bed, Procrustes would lop off his feet with his sword. We treat our experiences in much the same way as Procrustes treated his visitors. Our 'scheme of apperception' is the bed into which we crowd all our experiences. If an experience does not fit our pattern exactly, we distort it by stretching it or by lopping an essential facet from it. In other words, we fit our experiences into the preconceived pattern of our life, blithely forgetting those experiences which do not help us on our way.

Although it is very human not to learn from your experiences, it is better to make your style of life fit your experiences than to distort your experiences to fit your pattern. Herein lies the difference between subjectivity, which is the application of the Procrustes formula, and objectivity, which implies the broadening of one's style of life to include new experiences. In the subjective life the scheme of apperception is a fixed unit; in the objective life the scheme of apperception is elastic. The happy man expands his pattern to meet reality; the subjective man unhappily tries to distort reality to fit his preconceived ideas of what reality ought to be.

If we return to our analogy of the digestive functions, subjectivity consists in trying to eat glass beads because they look pretty. The subjective man's vanity is so great that he feels he can substitute his private logic - 'if beads look pretty they must be good to eat' - for the common-sense version 'glass beads are indigestible'. The objective man is one who, having been brought up in a Manchester home on roast beef and potatoes exclusively, goes to Paris, tries French cooking, finds that despite its complexity it is just as nourishing as roast beef and potatoes, and thereafter modifies his choice of diet to include the delicacies of the French table. If the objective man has a spark of imagination, moreover, he will extend his discovery that a man can eat more than roast beef and potatoes and survive, to include gastronomic adventures in the cuisines of Italy, Hungary, Austria, or Scandinavia as well as of France.

Needless to say, true happiness lies in extending our scheme of apperception to all the interests and activities which are open to a man. The more elastic the scheme of apperception the more varied and meaningful the experience will be. The cowardly narrow their scheme of apperception to those petty interests which seem to guarantee security by delimiting their activities. The courageous, and they are usually happy, have a catholic interest in the whole world, and are not averse to trying something new if it seems to indicate an extension of their sphere of interest, appreciation, or cooperation. The only way we can learn from our experiences is to allow those experiences to modify our pattern of life by expanding its scope. The truly happy man actually seeks new experiences to broaden his vital horizons. One of the happiest men I ever met could boast at the age of seventy that he had either learned a new language or taken up a new hobby every year since he was thirty. He numbered among his interests and accomplishments such diverse subjects as Japanese poetry, bookbinding, aviation, and the collection of early Persian miniatures.

The Training Formula

Once you have fixed your unconscious goal (the apotheosis of your individual sense of inferiority in the complete compensation of superiority) and have developed a scheme of apperception with which to test the meaning and value of all your experiences, you develop a Training formula' to help you on your way. This training formula is seldom consciously or verbally understood. It is an unconscious motto which you use to guide you through the multiple experiences of life. The happy man, who finds that he can compensate for his original sense of inferiority by cooperating with others, so contributing to society and to the welfare of the world, lives according to a formula that may be stated in its simplest form: 'I must be useful to my fellow-men to be happy and secure.' We could not recommend a better formula to anyone who wishes to attain happiness in this world.

Not everyone has so simple and effective a training formula. The discouraged, the ignorant, and the fearful who make up most of the unhappy people in the world use very different training formulas. The boy who feels that his virility is somewhat under par has a scheme of apperception which divides the world sharply into the neurotic dialectics of superior- inferior, masculine-feminine, strong-weak. This is one of the commonest and most mistaken schemes of apperception, one of the unhappy by-products of our patriarchal civilization. The training formula of an unhappy man who is always trying to prove that being a male and being superior are synonymous is: 'I must be every inch a man!'

If you have met a man who lives according to this formula, you know what unhappiness he suffers in his own life and what discord he spreads among his fellows. In order to carry out this formula the unhappy man who feels that his virility is in question, over-compensates and over-acts the 'masculine' role, until his life becomes a caricature of masculinity. He puts on rough airs, dislikes everything aesthetic, prides himself on his obscene oaths and smutty stories which always show women in an inferior situation. He resents any expression of tenderness, or interest in beauty. He goes to prize-fights, believes that it is necessary to 'hold his liquor well' in order to be a man, considers all women (except his own mother or sweetheart) so many prostitutes, and, if he should happen to encounter a homosexual, believes it his duty to knock the poor fellow down and thus demonstrate his spurious masculinity.

I must be the centre of attraction at all costs V is the training formula of the spoiled child who believes that her right is the brilliant spotlight which she monopolized as a child. The training formula of the dependent spoiled child differs from the arrogant motto stated above. His formula is I must at all costs be supported by someone in power' or related formula: 'I am so weak that you must do everything for me!' The child who has suffered a great deal of sickness and thus tasted the joys and security of invalidism, assumes a vital training formula which might read: It is better to be sick and secure than well and imperilled.' The neurotic who has been intimidated by life assumes the formula: I must avoid all tests of my actual worth!' Another favourite neurotic formula which is very common in these days of almost universal neurosis is 'Keep up appearances. As long as no one knows how weak you are, you are relatively safe.' The woman who has experienced her sex as a source of inferiority, and consequently has the mistaken notion that it is better to be a man than to be a woman, expresses her 'masculine protest' in terms of the vital training formula: 'I must be as nearly like a man as possible.' Her formula is very similar to that of the male who doubts his masculinity, and she uses the same false dialectic in order to exclude any situation which would show her in her true role, a woman.

This particular training formula deserves further elucidation because it is one of the chief sources of unhappiness among modern women. The scheme of apperception of the 'masculine protest' is such that every situation which shows a woman in her normal role is excluded. There is a simultaneous over-valuation of the so-called 'masculine', and an under-valuation of the so-called 'feminine'. It begins in early childhood with the dissatisfied girl's preference for boys' games. Tree-climbing is considered more desirable than dolls, tea-sets, and sewing. It continues with her interest in hunting, athletics, cocktail parties, and smoking (formerly considered male prerogatives) instead of participation in the household and aesthetic arts. In mature life it expresses itself in a disinclination to marry and have children, and a preference for a business or artistic 'career'.

In the sexual relation this type of woman is usually frigid, because, if she were to show evidence of normal passion, she would admit her true femininity. The sexual relation is transformed into an arena in which the "woman with the masculine protest" remains for ever the victor because she seems to express her superiority by the fiction of being incapable of being satisfied or aroused by any man. The physiological differences in the sexual organization of women and men play into the hands of these masculine women. Lesbianism is the final expression of the flight from the feminine role.

The process of training ourselves to conquer our inferiority complex by approaching our unconscious goal of power, security, and self-esteem, requires more than a scheme of apperception to test experiences in advance and to break them up into their unit components, thus rendering them psychologically capable of assimilation. It requires more than a vital training formula which more or less directs the scheme of apperception to those human activities where it is likely to find material for psychic assimilation. The training process encompasses our entire life, and we unconsciously train ourselves to attain our goal not only by looking forward into the future, but also by looking backward into the past to assure ourselves that we are on the right way. The devices which look forward are the conscious processes of reason, planning, will, choice, study, concentration, and attention, together with the more or less unconscious processes of dream, phantasy, imagination, and wishful thinking. Those which look backward are chiefly memory, recollection, and the rationalization of our past actions.

The Function of Memory

To discuss all these tools in detail lies beyond the scope of this study, but it will repay us to know something of memory and its relation to the training formula. The average man believes that memory is a vague hereditary faculty which is valuable to those who happen to possess it and a loss to those who have never developed it. Some scientists believe that memory can be trained in much the same way a muscle can be trained, and to some extent this is true. Yet none of these views helps us to understand the function of memory. Why is it that we remember trivial incidents of our childhood and forget major happenings of our adult lives? Why is it that some people have a vivid and retentive memory of the earliest days of their childhood, and yet are incapable of remembering anything they learned at school? Why is It that we sometimes forget the name of an intimate friend, or the address of an important business acquaintance, and yet recall the colour of a tie we wore on Easter Sunday five years ago?

These are the important facts about memory: the overwhelming majority of the myriad experiences that make up a lifetime are forgotten. What we remember must, therefore, be very important for our training pattern. Psychological investigation indicates that our earliest childhood memories when properly interpreted are found to contain the complete key to our lives. In my psychiatric practice I often ask a patient for his earliest childhood recollection, his most painful experiences of childhood, and his happiest childhood experiences. These three sets of recollections usually give me a picture of what the patient thought of himself and his childhood situation. The earliest childhood recollection epitomizes our first discovery of our own ego, and its relation to the environment at the time when we were first able to understand or feel that relationship. The most unpleasant recollections show how and where our pattern was thwarted, and therefore give a clear picture of the direction we had assumed. The happiest recollection tells how we experienced a single feeling of success or a sense of security.

Many of these earliest recollections are not recollections at all. It is quite possible to "remember' something that never happened. Memory is a creative faculty, and its artistic and creative function is vitally important. You must remember that the adult was a dependent being at the time whence most of his childhood memories are dated. He was being led and guided through the difficulties of life by his parents. If you are being guided through a strange foreign city by a friendly guide, you do not remember any coherent scheme of your wanderings, but certain sites and certain experiences do stand out clearly when you attempt to recall your adventure. These are the experiences that are vital to your style of life. The first or most vivid recollection of your childhood usually epitomizes the first critical situation in which you discovered yourself as partially independent, faced for the first time with the necessity of making some adjustment to life.

For example: the first childhood recollection of a famous night club 'hostess' is that she was given sweets by a genial bald-headed uncle for showing him her knees. A well-known homosexual recalls weeping bitterly on his third birthday because his mother compelled him to put on pants for the first time. A well-known heart specialist remembers the old family doctor coming to the bedside of a younger brother, listening with his stethoscope, and telling the parents that there was no hope for his brother. A patient with dementia praecox recalls a series of memories in which he is being held to his mother's breast, being protected either from a barking dog or from the attacks of an elder brother.

The Importance of Childhood Memories

Childhood memories show how our memory reaches into the past to furnish us with dynamic stimuli to support our efforts to attain our unconscious goal. Many people recall some tragic event in childhood, and say, 'Since the time I had whooping cough I have never been happy!', or 'If I had not been attacked by a big black dog, I should not be so timid now!' No event of your childhood can oblige you to lead an unhappy life, but, if you find yourself unhappy, it is frequently very comforting to be in a position to place the blame for your shortcomings on some so-called 'traumatic' event of childhood. Whole systems of psychology have been built up on this fallacy.

We make our memories just as we make our experiences to fit into the dynamic patterns of our life. This is part of the creative activity of every human being. Very frequently we rationalize our experiences, and act 'as if' these childhood memories were actually reasons or causes for behaviour. As a matter of fact, we invest these childhood recollections with fictional dynamics which they do not inherently possess. Our childhood recollections are often myths which we create in order to rationalize our present behaviour. Memories cannot cause behaviour unless we choose to believe in their motive power.

Why is it, then, that some people remember their childhood more clearly than others? Why can some men remember important current material, names, addresses, and the like, while their neighbours have not this power? Look to the goal of the individual and you can almost predict his memories. The spoiled child who senses his childhood as a lost paradise, and the present as a brutal prison-house full of disappointments and chagrins, will remember the past far better than he will remember matter important for the present conduct of his life. His goal is a goal of retreat. He is more interested in old roads which lead to joys he experienced in the dim distance of childhood than in a map of the roads to the uncertainties of the future. Those who cannot remember the names of their friends demonstrate their essential misanthropy. They are not interested in people because their goal is a goal of selfish isolation.

What we forget is quite as indicative of our personality as what we remember. It is futile, therefore, to attempt to train the memory as if it were an isolated faculty. We have seen no schools of forgetting, yet a course in forgetting would probably be more valuable than a course in memory. But we can train men and women to regard the future with greater optimism, and when they have achieved that optimism, their memory for significant, forward-looking facts will improve of itself. The failure of all memory courses is due to the fact that no tricks of recollection, no exercise of the mnemic 'faculty' can ever replace the courage to face problems and to meet them. Indeed, the futile attempt to train memory and concentration usually ends in the student's further perplexity and discouragement. If you remember the past too well, turn your face toward the future, assured that happiness is more easily acquired in the normal conduct of life in the present than in the vain cult of past glories. If you forget what seems to be essential to the present, remember this: the difficulties and obstacles of the future are no worse than the obstacles you have already conquered in the past!'

Of the instruments we use in our unconscious training for the future, the most interesting, psychologically, are imagination and the dream. Imagination is the process of courageous foresight. It is the extension of the scheme of apperception to the future, the pre-testing and pre-examination of possible events, the trial reconstellation of experiences we have already had, in new terms and new combinations. Imagination is one of the most valuable human faculties when it is applied in the service of the good life, but when it breaks loose from its essential purpose (the process of clearing the mental jungles in advance, like a pioneer breaking a trail to a new frontier) imagination becomes a curse. The daydream is the imagination and phantasy of the discouraged and downhearted. Day- dreamers fear to tackle reality. They prefer to create a phantastic world of wish-fulfilment as a, substitute for the real fulfilment resulting from the conquest of the world as it is. Unfortunately, the daydream leads only to further discouragement.

A child who is discouraged and cannot solve a problem in algebra allows this wish-fulfilling faculty of imagination and phantasy to transport him, by an effortless leap, to the time when he is already an engineer ordering his subordinates to work out the detail problems of bridge construction for him. The inventor who takes the facts of wireless and the facts of the cinema and combines them in his imagination into the new constellation of television, and then proceeds to work out the problem of uniting these disparate techniques to a new end, useful to humanity, is at the other pole. The criterion of social usefulness must be applied before we can interpret the value of imagination. Used constructively, that is, in a socially useful way, imagination is one of the most valuable human faculties; used as a tool of subjective ego-inflation, it becomes daydream and bizarre phantasy, and is only a step removed from delusion and hallucination.

About Dreams

One of the most important discoveries of modern psychology is the discovery made by Alfred Adler that the dream is not an inexplicable, accidental occurrence in the process of life, but a valuable device which we use during the training-process of approaching our individual goal of security and happiness. Although Freud was the first to point out that the dream was determined by our unconscious, it remained for Adler to demonstrate that the dream had a useful function. Like imagination, the dream always represents a bridge between the present and the future. It differs only slightly in its nature and processes from imagination and phantasy, and perhaps its most distinctive quality is the fact that its terms are the terms of archaic thought-processes, similar to the thought world of the young child, of the savage,

The following important facts should be understood in the dream:

1. *The dream is a metaphor written in phantastic terms.* As such it is always a distortion of reality. The distortion is designed to bridge the gap between our private pattern of life and the reality of common sense. It always points to the future, but is rooted in the past or in the present.

2. *The dream is often a trial solution of our problems.* It is as if we built a little marionette theatre, arranged the scenes and sets, and manipulated

an effigy of ourselves along with the other actors. It is an 'as if' solution of a future difficulty.

3. *The dream is a visual process, and the metaphor must therefore be stated in visual terms.* People who are not used to thinking in visual terms do not dream much. The dream is usually built up of the material of everyday life and experience, which is often treated without reference to time, space, gravitation, or historical relativity. Much of the material is symbolized in a variety of 'dream-shorthand' that anyone can learn with a little experience in interpretation.

4. *The important thing about the dream is not its pictorial, but its dynamic content.* To interpret a dream, you must interpret its 'dynamic drift'.

5. *The purpose of a dream is often to establish an emotional mood by an illicit use of the dream metaphor.* If you wake up in terror after a nightmare, you need not look for any causes of the dream. Your unconscious has helped you reinforce your ordinary caution by allowing you to identify yourself with a dangerous situation. Thus the real meaning of a nightmare or other horrible dream is: 'Take care! You are in danger!'

6. *We forget our dreams because we dare not examine the hocus-pocus by means of which we created our illusion.* The purpose of our dreams is to establish an unjustifiable mood by illicit means. We must deceive ourselves before we can deceive others.

7. *No dream can be interpreted unless you know something of the dreamer's dynamic pattern of life.* If his goal is an escape from reality the dream will mirror that escape and foster it. If he is ambitious, the dream will represent him conquering his obstacles, soaring over them without effort. If he is timid and fearful, the dream will encourage him to be cautious, and the like. The correct interpretation of the dream is an artistic process. There may be several approximately correct interpretations of a dream, just as there may be several approximately correct interpretations of a novel or a painting. A 'correct' interpretation of any dream requires the translation of the 'dynamic drift' of the dream and its alignment in relative continuity with the dynamic pattern of the personality.

8. *The interpretation of a dream is never a cure for a mental disease.* The correct interpretation of any dream can only be the corroboration of the style of life which has been established by other facts in the individual's life. So far as the individual is concerned, he is constantly encouraging and reinforcing himself in his already established pattern of life by dreaming of dynamic situations in which his pattern is reinforced. The so-called

prophetic dreams fall into the 'trial solution' type. If you try out several solutions in your dreams and later actually choose one of these solutions in reality, and it turns out just as you had dreamed it, there is nothing prophetic about it. The dreamer alone can supply the magic key of associations which unlocks the hidden meaning of his dream.

A word about the mysterious feeling that you have been in a place before, or have said the same words, or have heard the same reply from an individual. The French authors call this *'déjà vu'*, something that you have seen before. This puzzling phenomenon may best be explained in exactly the same way as the prophetic dream: you have thought of this situation in a dream, pre-figured it, and pre-determined just how it would occur. Occasionally your guesses are correct, and then, when you are carrying out the dreamed-of act, you are struck with the resemblance to the forgotten dream. This is the origin of *'déjà vu'* and related phenomena.

Recurrent dreams are especially interesting because they demonstrate the unity of the dynamic pattern of the personality. All recurrent dreams have a common 'drift'. One of my patients, a steward on a great ocean liner, always dreamed that he appeared at captain's inspection with a dirty uniform, or with a button missing on his coat, or he got to the dock just as the ship was leaving. His inferiority complex was related to his fear of his father, and his constant dread, of being scolded. He trained himself in this recurrent, almost nightly dream of unpreparedness, to redouble his efforts to be perfect. Very ambitious individuals often have recurrent dreams of flying, and fearful neurotics dream of descending from their high estate by falling from high buildings, cliffs, towers, or the like. The one thus trains himself to 'Go ahead!' the other to 'Be careful!'

If you do not dream at all - and most people do dream - you are either not at all visual-minded, which is rare, or you are a completely happy person who solves all his problems objectively during the day. This is also quite rare. It is more probable that you do not remember your dreams because you are satisfied to awake with a definite mood in the morning, and not to question its origins. There are some people who dream a great deal at times, then solve their difficulties objectively, and thereafter do not need to dream. Others, who learn the meaning of dreams, and become more courageous, give up dreaming because they are content to face their difficulties without the artificial props which dreams offer them.

Short dreams indicate greater clarity and courage than long and complicated dreams. If you have long and complicated dreams it is probable that you are an individual who 'muddles through' life rather than one who thinks his way clearly through obstacles. For some, these long, complicated dreams are a substitute for living in a real world. Dreams offer cheap and easy triumphs; their risk is practically nothing, their responsibility is zero, and their subjective gratification seemingly high.

The training of memory, imagination, phantasy, and the dream are examples of the unconscious training which we are constantly undergoing in our efforts to prepare ourselves for the solution of our problems. Other methods of training ourselves fall into the conscious sphere, and include the world of humour, the arts, sports, literature, and history.

The drama is no more than the crystallized dream of the dramatist. There are a great many men and women who have a veritable hunger for the theatre, because, in the observation of a dramatic spectacle, they are enabled not only to identify themselves with the players, and thus often to reassure themselves of their own validity as human beings, but are enabled, moreover, to solve some of their own problems as well, or to get guidance from those who, in the last analysis, are better dreamers than themselves.

The tremendous vogue of the cinema represents a satisfaction of this need for guidance and identification. If you are an insatiable 'film-fan' it is probably because the business of existing in a work-a-day world fails to give normal satisfaction to your ego-feeling. People need some tangible picture of power and security before them as an intermediate goal toward which to strive, and it makes very little difference whether it is a prince or a film star who offers the stimulus to renewed efforts. As with the dream, the cinema may become the symptom of an escape from life into a world of phantasy and cheap triumph for those who are too discouraged to deal with reality.

Of Wit and Humour

At this point we may well consider the role that humour, jokes, puns, comedy, and wit play in the economy of life. The old proverb, 'Laugh and the world laughs with you, weep and you weep alone' indicates that humour is one of the most important devices for securing a deeper solidarity between civilized human beings. The fact that man is the only laughing animal is neither accidental nor irrelevant. We are not only the weakest mammals that inhabit this crust of earth; we have also the greatest difficulties in maintaining body and soul together than any living organism must face. Were it not for the saving grace of our appreciation of the comic and the saving trait of a sense of humour we should ail logically commit suicide. With imagination and the dream, humour is part of our unconscious training toward our individual goal in life.

Like the dream, which may degenerate into the day-dream (useless wish-fulfilment and escape from reality), and like imagination, which may deteriorate into delusion and hallucination (breaking loose from its essential purpose of testing reality in advance), so humour may be diverted from its common-sense purpose of lightening the burdens of existence, and become an instrument of cruelty and social disintegration. The joke is a method of ego-inflation which is effective in giving one an easily attained sense of subjective greatness, without the consequent responsibility of attaining that greatness and power by the application of common-sense training to the problems of life.

The Psycho-Dynamics of a Joke

Examine any joke and you will find that it requires four people. The hero-protagonist, the villain-victim, the teller, and the listener. The teller of the joke always identifies himself in a position of power with the hero-protagonist which elevates him subjectively above the villain-victim. If the listener thinks it is a good joke he must be able to identify himself with the teller and with the hero-protagonist. Otherwise, he feels hurt, because the position of the villain-victim is his own situation. Under these circumstances he feels that it is a bad joke.

An example: A man visits a lunatic asylum and becomes interested in one of the inmates who seems perfectly normal. He tells the inmate, who is the asylum watchmaker, that he would like to get him out of the asylum. 'Could you earn your living outside, my good man?' he asks. 'Of course I could', answers the insane man. 'You see I am a very good watchmaker, and I could always earn my living in a watch-repairing shop. In addition, I am an excellent mechanic and could work in a garage. And if the worst came to the worst', adds the paranoiac by way of emphasis, holding one hand on his hip and stretching his other arm out in a graceful curve, 'I could always be a teapot!'

The obvious incongruity of this man's statement with his belief in his sanity, immediately puts the listener in a superior situation. The transition from a common-sense system of thought to the private autistic logic of the lunatic is imperceptible, but his conclusions are so far-fetched that the listener immediately senses the incongruity, and laughs, because he feels safe in his security and sanity. The joke would not appeal to a paranoid patient in an asylum who was normal in everything but his *idée fixe*.

There are some people who bolster their ego with an extensive repertoire of stories told at the expense and humiliation of someone else. Others - especially in some forms of manic- depressive insanity or in dementia praecox - support their private autistic logic by the belief that the whole world is a joke. This 'senseless laughter' of the isolated schizophrenic patient is one of the earmarks of that form of insanity. Others again cannot laugh at any joke because they take their own lives so tragically. These men and women 'have no sense of humour' because they refuse to build the bridge of encouragement to their fellow-men by participating in the wholesome laughter which, without humiliating anyone, lightens the burden of life by letting it appear as a comic paradox.

The telling of smutty stories exemplifies the attempt of the discouraged to inflate their ego by the defamation of a member of the opposite sex. Whether it is a man or a woman who tells a dirty story makes no difference. They betray their inferiority complex by demonstrating their tendency to achieve an easy triumph at the expense of the other sex. The sophisticated tell stories about the ignorant, whites tell jokes about negroes, Gentiles tell jokes about Jews, adults tell jokes about children, Englishmen tell jokes about Germans, and so on down the line. ' ,

Dostoyevsky once wrote that he could tell more about a man by listening to his laughter than he could learn from a long psychological examination. If you wish to test the dynamic patterns of your neighbour - it is wise to try this out on yourself first - ask for his three favourite stories, interpret the 'dynamic drift' in much the same way that you would interpret a dream, and you will learn his goal and his technique of life very quickly.

Like the dream which establishes a mood or an emotional attitude by the use of an illicit, unconscious metaphor, the joke, the pun, the humorous anecdote, achieves its end, as training of the personality in its path toward its individual goal, by the cheap means of an irresponsible ego-inflation. Like the neurosis, wit and the joke utilize common-sense facts as the premises of the story, but, by a species of psychic legerdemain, substitute a system of private logic which is tangent with the common-sense premise at various points, and thus lead the listener imperceptibly into a situation which vouchsafes him an illicit sense of power derived from the depreciation and humiliation of the villain-antagonist in the inferior situation.

The cultivation of laughter and a sense of humour is excellent training for the good life. There is no better method of establishing a bond between yourself and your fellow-men than to cultivate a genial and humorous personality. Only those who feel reasonably safe and successful can afford to laugh. The forced tragedy of the lives of the unhappy is usually the result of their isolation. No man can laugh when he is isolated from his fellows, because he is in immediate danger of mental strangulation. To those who find the rewards of isolation very meagre we prescribe the following: find a good story and tell it to at least one person during the day. If the first person you tell the story to does not laugh, continue until you have made someone laugh. If you cannot find anyone to laugh at your stories, there is a danger that your sense of humour is perverted. Get someone to tell you a story that he thinks amusing. Tell this story to someone else until you have established the communal bond of good humour. Continue this prescription until you have experienced the reward of citizenship in the republic of laughter.

As we train ourselves by going to the theatre and identifying ourselves with the players, so we train ourselves unconsciously by the books and magazines we read. Some read stories only with happy endings because they cannot bear to look at the realities of life. Men and women with a martyr complex read only tragedies so that they can intensify their hopelessness. Some cannot listen to 'serious' music because such listening requires a surrender of the ego to the dynamic pattern of the composer, others refuse to listen to popular music because a certain musical snobbishness impels them to protect the feeling of uniqueness which they consider essential to happiness. It is as necessary to have a well-balanced mental diet as it is to have a well-balanced menu. Courage and good-humour are the vitamins of the good life.

The Value of Sport

One of the most amazing phenomena of modern life is the growth of popular interest in sports. Football, cricket, and horse-racing attract ever-increasing crowds. When seventy- five thousand people attend a football match a psychological reason greater than interest in the game itself is at work. This psychological reason is the need for empathy with success - that is, close association with the successful conquest of obstacles. Since the days of the Roman circus, mass attendance at athletic contests has been a constant phenomenon of civilization. Modern man, pressed by the drabness of the machine age, needs more frequent opportunities for identifying himself with successful power, both to glory in vicarious compensation for his own weakness, and to encourage himself by identifying himself with the popular hero or heroes of the day.

You will remember that the Roman circus was originally a spectacle for the slaves and the poor of Rome. It was a sop to the hunger- and plague-ridden populace, designed to make their lives more tolerable, a gesture on the part of those who had security to those who were without it. Whenever the conditions of human life become especially burdensome, the human spirit invents a device for strengthening and encouraging its resistance to adversity. The Decameron of Boccaccio was written as an escape from the horrors of the plague. The circus was born of the squalor of decadent Rome. The spectacle of super-football is born of the discouragement of the machine age.

When the human race gets into difficulties that can no longer be faced with equanimity it has developed a saving technique which can be crystallized in the phrase, 'Let's change the subject'. Sometimes the change of subject becomes a real Frankenstein's monster and is elevated into a secondary goal. We have already spoken of the untoward results of shifting our focus from the goal to the means when we discussed the triumph of the means over the end in certain neuroses. History tells of the bestiality and debauchery of the Roman circus.

Both active and passive participation in sport play an important role in the good life. They are closely related to avocations and hobbies; they serve as a means of increasing our knowledge of the world, of extending the sphere of our activities, and of enlarging our opportunities for identification and emphatic training. The chief value of sport lies in the fact that it offers an opportunity of being both a spectator and a participant. The complete human being should interest himself in some athletic sport which will give him not only the opportunity of identification with successful power, but the opportunity of establishing a new arena in which he can gain recreation and diversion. The business of 'Let's change the subject' is one of the emergency devices of the human mind. A great deal of significance and happiness may be attained by participation in a sport, appropriate to your physical constitution and your available time.

There is a very real sense of goodness and happiness to be derived from the playing of golf or tennis, from riding a horse, or sailing a boat. The more decentralized and depersonalized our civilization becomes, the less each individual is granted the opportunities for achieving significance and a sense of goodness in his work or social relations. The importance of having some athletic activity in which one can experience the goodness of one's body in action, and a sense of wholesome fatigue, is all the greater in our machine age when robust physical struggle is almost unknown.

Of Basic Philosophies

There remains one important device by which we train ourselves to the attainment of our goal, and effect the exclusion dreams, humour, and philosophy of unnecessary or interfering experiences. It is perhaps the most difficult of all these devices to discuss in a book devoted to the bare outlines of the art of being human. This device is the elaboration of a psychic map of the world and a mental plan of campaign. We construct and utilize such a plan during the entire course of our lives. For want of a better word this scheme of orientation is called religion by some, a working philosophy of life or Weltanschauung by others. Obviously a man's attitude to the cosmos and his relation to the world in which he lives must bear the stamp of the unit pattern of his personality, and must give us the most profound insight into his own interpretation of his position in the world. While each man's philosophy of life must of necessity be an individual formula, human beings'-tend.to-group themselves in a small number of categories according to their philosophy of life.

Every philosophy of life is a plan of campaign as well as a guiding formula for the progress of the personality toward its individual goal. The relation of this map to the tasks and problems of life is parallel to and coincident with the dynamic drift of the personality. It stands to reason that we can understand something of an individual's goal in life if we can discover his psychic plan of campaign, his vital training- formula, that is, his underlying life-philosophy.

Let us examine the cardinal compass points of human conduct as if we were navigators mapping a new world. The lodestar is the good life; the best course, the course of constructive altruism. The cardinal points are power, crime, social irresponsibility, insanity, neurosis, pleasure, self-complacency, and the good life.

The goals of personal power and egoistic ambition are served by a philosophy of individualistic opportunism. Seize the day. Get what you can out of life while you can. The end justifies the means. The ambitious egoist does not openly war against society, but he exploits it to his own end. Many of our most 'successful' men and women owe their 'success' to their ruthless personal ambitions and the indefatigable cult of their individual ego. Money, prestige, possessions, are the chief symbols of power in our civilization.

Crime, one of the major problems of modern times, is not so much an end result of human conduct as it is the expression of an underlying philosophic attitude toward life. We can understand the criminal better when we remember that he is an individual who has never been adequately initiated into the fellowship of human beings. His philosophy might be formulated as a belligerent misanthropy. The criminal believes that every man within the social scheme is his natural enemy, and he trains himself to continue his depredations against society because he believes that his initiation into human society is impossible. He seeks to inflate his ego at the expense of those who are 'in', and at the cost of those who 'have'.

Beyond crime, but still on the borderland between unsocial optimism and unsocial pessimism, we find the goals of passive resistance to life which lead men and women to choose the professions of tramping, prostitution, racketeering, drug peddling, the employment of child labour and similar forms of human enslavement. The pimp, the profiteer, the gambler, and others of this sort need a philosophy of irresponsible misanthropy to maintain them in their chosen path. Only an individual who doubts the value of human life would exploit his fellow beings. It requires considerable self-justification to continue in the profession of a pimp or a profiteer. Naturally the training formulas of the aberrant forms of human conduct are stricter and less elastic than other philosophic guiding principles, because the irresponsible misanthrope is constantly in conflict with social tendencies in human life, and must fortify himself by rigorous unconscious training.

An increase in the factor of irresponsibility together with an increase in pessimism brings us close to the negation of life itself. In this sector, the goals are self-destruction, either by physical means, as in suicide, or by psychological means, as in insanity. At the criminal end of this quadrant we have paranoia, in which the individual is haunted by delusions of persecution. In paranoia the responsibility is not only renounced but is actually projected on to the persons of imaginary persecutors. The paranoiac is nearly always a potential criminal, and frequently is guilty of homicidal attacks on those he considers responsible for his own shortcomings. By gradual steps we enter the terrain of the maniac-depressive psychoses, in which there are vacillating moods of exuberance and depression, with parallel vacillation in pessimism and irresponsibility, to end in the melancholias and in dementia praecox. In dementia praecox social responsibility is at its lowest ebb, pessimism at its most intense pitch, subjectivity elevated to a *primum mobile* of life. Suicide is frequent in the manic-depressive states, in melancholia, and in dementia praecox. The underlying philosophy is one of irresponsible and subjective pessimism, accompanied by complete and active renunciation and negation of life.

Mysticism, Fatalism, and Hedonism

In the various neuroses the philosophy of pessimism is attenuated to a philosophy of fatalism. Responsibility and objectivity are retained in part. The neurotic unconsciously admits his responsibility by constructing a fictional system of 'ifs' and 'buts' which seems to shift the responsibility to some factor for which he can assume no responsibility. Neurotics are fatalists all: they believe that they are blind pawns in the hands of an irresistible destiny. Pietists and religious fanatics, who shift the responsibility to God instead of blaming their bad physique or the antagonism of their parents, are but a step removed from the frank neurotics who tacitly admit they are afraid to face reality. The neurotic excuses his unsocial conduct on the ground of his neurotic symptoms; he trains himself for his irresponsibility by choosing a philosophy of fatalistic opportunism. The pietist bolsters up his conduct by his affirmation of a particular creed, believing that the affirmation of his credo relieves him of personal responsibility. He puts the whole matter in the hands of God. The goal of all this philosophic training is a maximum of subjective security and a minimum of objective responsibility.

The next great goal of human life is pleasure for pleasure's sake, and the appropriate philosophy is the philosophy of hedonism. Hedonism appeals to adults who have been deprived of the normal joys of childhood. It is a pessimistic philosophy in that the hedonist, like the mystic, despairs of complete satisfaction in this world. His efforts are directed toward the frantic accumulation of as many solacing pleasure- experiences as possible. To this end he makes certain contributions towards the commonweal, but only for the sake of turning his gains into pleasures as quickly and as efficiently as possible. Fie avoids the major responsibilities of life, and remains an egoist throughout. The mystic, by the trick of disparaging life on this planet, prepares for a goal of fictional security in the next world. It is obvious that he usually manages to escape from the obligations and obstacles of the present by focusing his vital energies on an existence in a future and better world where his aristocratic security will be assured by his negation of life on this planet.

By gradations, through sensualism and romanticism, we arrive at the passive cooperation of self-complacency, whose philosophy is that of 'Let well enough alone'. Half-way between pessimism and optimism, half-way between objectivity and subjectivity are the human drifters and the turnips who make up the large majority of mankind. Through ignorance or fear they do not analyse their situations or attempt to improve their human lot, but they do not evade the simple obligations of life. They are the human vegetables, the background of the human comedy, the 'shouts and murmurs' that are heard in the wings of life's stage. Their view is not wide; their mental horizons barely adequate. They pay their grocery bills, take the wonders of science for granted, believe what is printed in the newspaper, own motor cars and wireless sets, obey the laws, and vegetate handsomely on their allotted crust of earth.

We come finally to the consideration of the good life. For those who seek the larger happiness and the greater effectiveness open to human beings there can be but one philosophy of life, the philosophy of constructive altruism. The truly happy man is always a fighting optimist. Optimism includes not only altruism but also social responsibility, social courage, and objectivity. Men and women who are compensating for their feelings of inferiority in terms of social service, men and women who are vigorously affirming life, facing realities like adults, meeting difficulties with stoicism, men and women who combine knowledge with kindliness, who spice their sense of humour with the zest of living - in a word, complete human beings, are to be found only in this category. This is the golden way of life. This is the satisfying life. This is the way to be happy though human.

In this chapter we have attempted to outline the methods of training, conscious and unconscious, which we utilize in the pursuit of our goal in life. In subsequent chapters we shall show in greater detail how the unconscious philosophy of optimistic altruism may be attained by a conscious strategy of approach to the three great human problems - work, society, and sex. Progress toward the good life is a matter of conscious training involving the extension of all human horizons, and the assumption of complete personal responsibility for defeat and success. The quality of happiness must of necessity follow as a consequence of such active participation in the art of being human. And, as we stated in our very first chapter, it is not necessary to attain the finality of the good life to be happy. One must make only the first step, invest only a small initial capital of courage and good will. Once the investment is made, happiness accrues by compound interest.

CHAPTER EIGHT.
Of Goals: The Three Ring Circus

The Importance of Useful Work - The Social and Sexual Tasks - The Battle-front of Life - The Concept of 'Distance'-About 'Nervous Breakdowns' - The Holiday Neurosis - About Idlers - Of Sexual Virtuosity - Emergency Exits of the Soul - Normal Sex Relationships - The Inter-relation of Human Problems - Catalogue of Sideshows - Why 'Normality' Pays

We have spoken a great deal of the goals of the individual personality, and in the last chapter illustrated both the various goals of human striving and the coincident philosophic formulas that help men to attain their ends. In our first chapter we showed that there were certain laws governing all human conduct. Are there also certain goals common to all human beings? Are there certain tasks that every man and woman must solve, no matter what the individual goal? Is there a human goal which is coincident with human happiness?

Our unique situation in the cosmos actually does challenge each of us with three great problems which must be satisfactorily and adequately solved if we would attain the good life and the happiness attendant thereon. These problems are the problems of work, society, and sex. They are peculiarly human problems based on the interaction between our characteristic constitution as human beings and the nature of the world in which we live.

The first of these problems arises out of the fact that, in all except a few favoured places on the Equator, man must either work or starve. Man's brain is not adequate to the solution of the problem of life itself. We do not know why we keep on living, nor do we know the nature of man's place in the economy of the cosmos. But this we do know; being alive, we must work to keep alive. If we do not work, we die of cold and exposure, of hunger and thirst, and, in a civilized state, of boredom and isolation. Without work we should have neither food nor protection, neither tools nor communication. Certainly civilization is unthinkable in its present terms unless every individual contributes and cooperates in the maintenance of society and the social structure. Without work and the recording of man's accomplishments, each of us would be compelled to learn over again all that our ancestors gained by bitter experience. The chances are that most of us would die in the attempt. Work is a fundamental element, therefore, in man's continued existence as a race, and a source of personal salvation to the individual within the social structure.

There are some people who still believe that work is a curse, and that the happiest possible state a human being could exist in would be a paradise of leisure and ease. Whatever the theological attitude toward work may be, it is certain that the civilized man finds work a source of personal salvation. We are endowed with so much energy and activity that we must find some outlet, and the best outlet for our creative energy is in work that helps to maintain the structure of our society. It is the reciprocal formula of human existence, without which society and life would be unthinkable. There are many people who believe it their private concern whether they work or not, and others who are so placed by the peculiar economic conditions of our times that they are practically prevented from working because the immediate goals of work - power, security, prestige, and social esteem ~ are theirs by the right of inheritance from ancestors who worked so hard that they accumulated an excess of worldly goods.

The average, well-adjusted human being is so richly endowed with energy and interest in the world that he not only works to contribute to society's maintenance, but also possesses enough reserve energy to enjoy avocations, hobbies, and artistic interests in addition. When we speak of work as a contribution to society, it does not necessarily imply that every mechanic, hedge cutter, and shoeblack is conscious of any high mission in doing his daily task. Only a few contribute consciously; but it is not necessary to have a conscious insight into the metaphysics of work to be a productive worker. Those who toil know the value and the 'goodness' of their work.

The Importance of Useful Work

In general, it may be said that everyone who is paid for his labour does useful work. This is not necessarily a quantitative index of his social value. The peculiarities of our civilization are such that the greatest and most valuable workers are often badly paid, whereas others, whose value lies chiefly in their usefulness to certain powerful, ambitious, and chiefly egoistic interests, are paid out of all proportion to their labours. Of the first type of workers we may say that the intrinsic rewards of their labours often more than compensate for the lack of material rewards, although in individual cases gross injustices occur.

Suffice it to say, neither life nor society could continue unless every human being made some useful contribution to the commonweal. Certainly the verdict of history favours those who contribute most handsomely to the welfare of their fellows. The inexorable record of time erases the names of all those who have not contributed imposingly to human welfare. Men are not remembered for their looks or for their family connections; not for their money and not for their local prestige: history writes in her golden book only the names of those who have worked well and wisely. This fact should give pause to those who refuse to work, and to those who work only for their personal, egoistic ends. No one knows the names of the richest citizens of Athens during the golden age - but her poets, her thinkers, her artists are as much alive to-day as in their own age. No one remembers the name of the princeling who employed John Sebastian Bach as his organist-but Bach's enormous labours remain as a monument to the entire world.

What if you wish to forego the verdict of history and remain idle simply because it suits you better not to work? This is a very pertinent point. Many say: I can't be a genius. Why shouldn't I just enjoy life?'

The common sense of daily life answers: if you do not contribute and cooperate in the world's work, neither man nor God will punish you. But nature will punish you in her own way for breaking one of her fundamental laws. You eat and drink and sleep. You develop a formidable reserve of vital energy that requires an outlet. If there is no adequate use for this energy, it turns inward and destroys you. The mere pursuit of pleasure quickly becomes a retreat from the hell of boredom. Ennui leads by gradual steps, via the various perversions of human conduct, to suicide or insanity, to the negation of life and the annihilation of the thrill of living. Life without work Is a living death.

Society, moreover, guards jealously against parasites within its body. Those who are not destroyed by nature are isolated by society. The burglar and the thief, whose work is antisocial, the insane and the mentally defective, are removed from the enjoyment of the full fruits of citizenship in their community. Our very word 'idiot' is derived from the Greek word for a non-productive member of society. In earlier days society was more brutal than it is to-day. In savage communities, the aged, the infirm, and the insane are still quickly removed from the community, either actively by being put to death or passively by being allowed to starve. Civilized men are more tolerant of those who are temporarily incapacitated. A greater value is put on past contributions, but any man or woman who remains voluntarily idle for long periods is eventually removed from the usufructs of social life.

We must work, whether we wish to work or whether we prefer to be idle. The question of work is not a matter for us to decide according to our personal whim or fancy. The only choice that remains open to the individual is the manner in which he will make his contribution to the commonweal. Here the chances of individuality are as manifold as the facts of life itself. But work we must - or die. We have already emphasized the fact that the affirmation of the necessity and value of work is part of the good life - it remains only for the individual to choose such work as he is fitted for, preferably work that represents a compensation for his personal feeling of inferiority in terms of social service. The happiest man is he whose personal satisfaction in his work is most useful to his community.

The Social and Sexual Tasks

The second group of problems arises out of the specific human need for communal life. As individuals we are too weak to live alone, and nature has given us the human community as the best weapon against extinction. No other solution is possible for man. The problem of social adjustment, like the problem of occupation, is not a problem for the individual to solve according to his private logic. The manner of his social adjustment admits of a tremendous variety of solutions, but the adjustment itself is fundamental to the good life and to human happiness. So far as any archaeological researches can trace, human beings have always lived in communities, and the history of mankind is the history of the diversification and complexity of social relations. As in the case of work, the individual who does not cooperate in the social life is isolated either by nature or by man, and excluded from the opportunities of living a full and effective life.

The third great problem is the problem of sex. The sexual problem arises out of the fact that there are just two sexes, and that a social and sexual adjustment between the two sexes is desirable and necessary as part of nature's scheme of maintaining the human race. The higher the degree of biological evolution, the more distinct the sexes, and the more complicated the division of labour between them. It is part of the grand strategy of nature to differentiate the human male and the human female for the purpose of facilitating and insuring the evolution of mankind. Not to solve the sexual problem, therefore, is a negation of life, and resistance to the stream of evolution. The conflict of human motives, of private logic, and of individualistic egoism with the profound simplicity and directness of nature is a vain and futile battle. Nature destroys revels and heretics with ruthless celerity.

In contrast to the other two great problems, failure to solve the problem of sex need not result in personal disaster. Failure to solve the social and occupational problems entails death or insanity, but the failure to solve the sexual problem satisfactorily is not dangerous to the life of the individual, however subversive to the life of the race. It would appear, therefore, that the solution of the sexual problem lies within the scope of our individual free will, and it may or may not be solved according to our individual whims in the matter. It is for this very reason that aberrations in the solution of the sexual problem are most numerous. The tyranny of our stomachs compels us to work lest we starve, and the tyranny of loneliness compels us to make certain gestures towards our fellow-men lest we become insane. But men and women can evade the solution of the sexual problems and still live. Those who are vainly seeking to avoid the responsibilities of maturity will be found grudgingly contributing a minimum of work and social cooperation, while the problem of sex is joyously evaded in its entirety.

Just because the solution of the sex problem postulates a previous adequate solution of the other two great groups of problems, it is the problem most frequently left unsolved. In no other problem does the seeker after guidance find so many obstacles in his way. Traditional secrecy and misinformation about sex is still the usual attitude toward the adolescent who asks for guidance, yet in this very problem ignorance leads to the most catastrophic results. Furthermore, many false solutions of the sex problem are tacitly tolerated by society despite their antisocial meaning. Prostitution, homosexuality, sexual asceticism, and sexual perversion are distinctly antisocial solutions of the sex problem. They represent private logic at war with common sense. A man may be a homosexual and retain his place in society, whereas he would be put in a lunatic asylum if he attempted to sell furnaces in the tropics. If a man goes to a prostitute, his conduct is condoned, but if he sells stock that he doesn't own - (an application of the same private logic) - he is sent to prison. The sexual problem is at one and the same time the least understood, the most misrepresented, and the most difficult of all the three problems to solve.

The Battle-front of Life

We sketched the normal attack of an adult when we described the normal character pattern. In adult life this normal attack on the battle-front of life implies a full adjustment to the world in which we live. The institution of a few intimate and meaningful friendships in conjunction with a more extensive acquaintanceship; the affirmation of the bonds of art, science, nature, sports, politics, philosophy, letters, and history; an attitude of optimistic altruism toward one's fellow-men, and a very active cooperation in the business of making the world a better place to live in, are implicit in the ideal conquest of the social sector.

On the occupational front, the adult man finds himself contributing some useful service to his fellows. Usually such services are adequately paid for, although money itself is not the measure of a man's service. Money is so frequently a neurotic end in itself, that we can no longer reckon the mere possession of the world's goods as the sign of an adequate contribution on the occupational front, just as poverty is not in itself the sign of resistance to the necessity of working. The active participation in some hobby or avocation is a necessary concomitant of success on this sector, and no man who has only his business or profession, and nothing beside, can be considered a very objective human being. Either he takes his work too seriously, in which case he lacks the necessary humour to make him happy, or he is running away from other obligations by demonstrating how hard he has to work, in which case his unhappiness is due to the one-sidedness of his life.

On the sexual front, satisfactory solutions allow of greater elasticity of attack. Here, the time element and the element of social and economic success play a role, and while an adult individual should marry, establish a family, and assume the social responsibilities of the education of his children, there are. not only organic, but frequently social and economic, obstacles beyond the individual's control that make this ideal solution nearly impossible. Merely being married and having children is not evidence of success on this front. Any two fools (or any two feeble-minded people) may marry - but the construction of a 'we' relation which represents the merger of two egos, together with the amicable division of labour, the reciprocal sharing of responsibilities, the mutual encouragement and satisfaction of the partners, is an essential attribute of a good marriage.

Without love in the adult sense, and without responsibility, marriage may actually be a neurotic symptom, either of one partner's psychic dependency on the other, or of one partner's attempt to inflate his ego at the expense of the other. The successful marriage is almost never found except in those cases where both the partners have established a well-advanced position on the social and occupational fronts, although occasionally a woman finds her real occupation only in marriage and the education of children. Indeed, the sexual relation may be the only relation which gives meaning and colour to the life of many who are the unwilling slaves of the machine age.

By contrast, many individuals, who are actively preparing for the assumption of the full responsibilities of marriage, but have not yet married, may be said to be farther advanced on this front than their neighbours who have married without adequate preparation. Others again are so constituted organically as to preclude a happy marriage. In these individuals an advanced position on the social and occupational fronts is tantamount to the successful solution of the sexual problem.

The Concept of 'Distance'

With these norms as a guide, we can take a number of individual cases and draw diagrams of their attack on the problems of life and compute their psychic "distance' from the front. We must not lose sight of the fact that time is an element in all cases. Individual development begins with a first attack on the social front. Building up confidence toward one's mother is usually the first problem that faces the individual. Then comes the extension of the social bond to the father, to other members of the family, and finally to playmates and others outside the family group.

Work begins in learning to walk, talk, control the excretions, and coordinate the motor activities. Then come the solutions of the problems of school and education and self-training. The sexual problem begins with the adjustment to one's parents, one's brothers or sisters, and finally to playmates of the opposite sex. With maturity, the occupational problem usually assumes the ascendency.

For the reason that the technical education of the average man is often better than his social and sexual education, a very common mistake in the strategy of life is an over-emphasis on business and work, combined with an inadequate attack on the problems of sex and society. The fallacy of this approach is indicated by the misfortunes that attend it during the attack, and the tragedies that are likely to follow after a complete victory has been gained solely on the occupational front.

The life of the man or woman who approaches life in terms of a 'drive' on work is not very happy. The very intensity of his efforts makes enemies of his associates, and his lack of consideration for the feelings and efforts of his colleagues makes him an inhuman slave-driver toward his employees. No one loves a 'high-pressure go-getter'. Hate and hurry blind him to the beauties of life. At the end of the day he is exhausted by his unobjective work methods, and he seeks relaxation in brutish amusement which he often pursues in the same graceless way. His relations with people are tainted with egoistic ambition. He cannot be interested in anyone who is not immediately useful to him. Members of the opposite sex are similarly exploited for purely selfish ends.

One of the characteristic indicators of this type of individual is the so-called 'holiday neurosis Many men and women are perfectly happy while they are at their job and can sense a certain success in driving themselves and others to the fictitious goal of 'success'. But a holiday is a tragedy to the ambitious 'go-getter'. If possible he remains at work. If he cannot work, he mopes and broods and despairs, is irascible and bad-tempered because he has not prepared for anything in life but an onslaught on his business. These people have no friends with whom to pass the time, and no hobbies to absorb their creative energies. They have developed neither the patience to read books nor the disinterestedness to enjoy nature. Sexual contacts are valued as mere physiological exercises and have no more emotional interest than so many evacuations of bowels and bladder. Consequently, no sexual intimacy can relieve their sense of isolation and depression or help to recreate their fatigued energies.

The holiday neurosis is an epitome of what happens to men and women who 'succeed' as a result of putting over the strategy of massed attack on the work sector. Not infrequently a man of this type develops a veritable genius in his chosen profession or activity, by virtue of one-sidedness, persistence in training, and complete disinterestedness in the rest of the world. Occasionally he reaches the very pinnacle of success and attains the envy and admiration of his friends.

About 'Nervous Breakdowns'

At this point of success, or, let us say, seeming success, tragedy usually overtakes the individual in the form of a 'nervous breakdown'. Having prepared only for conflict, these one-sided warriors do not know how to make the best of their victories. They have never prepared to hold a fort - only to make it capitulate, and this very fact betrays their underlying discouragement. The victory which they really never dreamed of attaining is occasionally won despite their pessimism. This is their weakness. The enemy flanks them on both sides. They have no one to share their victory with, no one whose love gives their victory meaning.

They, who have never surrendered to any obstacle, must capitulate to boredom and loneliness. Suddenly they face the meaning of life, and, in the realization of the futility of their entire past, are seized with the sudden fear of death. The first reaction to their suddenly gained insight is usually depression, which is often followed by a period of frantic searching after gross pleasures. Success, depression, and the quest of enjoyment, however, end in the same blind alley: boredom, satiety, and loneliness. There follows the terror of meaningless, vegetable existence. The mute horror of sleeplessness, anxiety, and restlessness, and the hopeless despair of utter boredom and lack of interest complete the picture.

Unless help comes from the outside, these so-called successful men and women break. Whether the break takes shape as a neurosis, insanity, suicide, as a temporary 'nervous breakdown', or as lasting melancholia and depression, is of little importance at this point. The character of the 'break' depends upon individual physiological and environmental conditions too complicated to describe in a general book. What is of interest to the general reader is, the fact that the prestige, money, power, and security gained by these men and women is completely nullified by their inability to hold their conquests. It seems hardly worth while to slave and sweat at a job from morning to night, all the years of one's life, for the dubious pleasure of being able to afford day and night nurses at an institution for mental diseases.

The whole trend of modern medicine is toward prevention rather than the cure of diseases, and in no medical speciality is the emphasis on prophylaxis more marked than in mental hygiene. The purpose of this book is to help those who have launched a false attack on life's problems to take mental stock of themselves, and to help them to modify their plan of attack before it is too late. While psychiatry offers definite hopes to those who have fought, not wisely, but too successfully, on a single sector of life, only to find the victory not only empty but painful, the number of human failures as a result of this misdirection of energies is out of all proportion to the number of available psychiatrists. Because of this fact, the problem of the care of the neurotic and the insane has become more a problem of housing and administration than of cure and correction.

The intelligent adult will not wait until he has had a mental breakdown or a psychotic episode before taking mental stock of his style of life, any more than he will wait until he is coughing up pieces of lung, or physically unable to walk upstairs, before consulting a physician. The major obstacles to the treatment of high-pressure go-getting, super-business men of this type is their stubbornness and egoism. They are so intensely involved in the mad pursuit of power that they cannot brook correction or the imputation that their goals are false and their success hollow. If you tell a high-powered business manager that his pattern is fast leading him to an asylum, he will laugh at you. "Look at my fine organization!" he will tell you. "Is there anything insane about that?' The intoxication of partial success distorts his perspectives, and the hashish of ambition develops a dangerous sense of well-being in his mind that dulls the danger signals nature has placed along the way.

So much for the successful "go-getter". A more common but equally interesting aspect of this tragic approach to life is the fact that minor defeats tend to assume titanic proportions when one has staked everything on immediate success. Many an individual who begins life with a strategy of assault on work is side-tracked into a neurosis early in the game because of unforeseen difficulties on the way. The solace of excuses is the emergency exit of many whose ambition has been stopped by the actual realities of existence. The deeper security of the nervous breakdown remains for those who fail at the moment of seeming success. Those who fail on the way exhibit a galaxy of neurotic symptoms - chief among which is the "holiday neurosis". The holiday neurosis is the constant accompaniment - the danger signal, so to speak, of this false style of life.

The Holiday Neurosis

The following symptoms characterize the holiday neurosis: it occurs chiefly on holidays, and enforced vacations away from the scene of business activity. Irascibility, irritation, "nervousness", "blues", depression, or Vague anxiety are the most usual emotional symptoms. Frequently the individual with the holiday neurosis is simply more cranky than usual, less considerate of his family or servants, or more critical of his surroundings. Occasionally there is a tendency to drink to excess, to play golf to excess, or to indulge excessively in cards or gambling. One of our patients had a splitting headache every Sunday for twelve years but never suffered a twinge of pain during working hours. Another went to bed as soon as a holiday came. A third got into his motor car and drove at breakneck speed toward some distant point on the map, turned round, and drove back just in time to get to his office.

The reasons for the holiday neurosis are a failure to develop accessory activities and social interests which make necessary or occasional recesses from the active business of earning a living interesting and meaningful. In effect, the holiday neurosis is the prototype of the mental derangement that is likely to follow if the successful 'go-getter' suffers a nervous breakdown later in life. If holidays bore you or drive you to drink take stock of your situation, and begin to broaden the scope of your interests in men and things. This is nature's danger signal of future mental disease.

Then there is the situation which often occurs in the lives of those who are not compelled to work because they have inherited wealth from hard-working ancestors. In this case, the social and sexual fronts are frequently attacked with considerable success, but the work sector is left unguarded. Not every rich man and not every rich woman leads such a life - indeed, like poverty, wealth may be the stimulus to the highest forms of human enterprise, but when wealth is inherited, it frequently distorts perspectives and leads to this form of attack, in itself an index of vital discouragement and a lack of common sense.

Mischief is the work of the man without work, Men and women who approach life in this way are likely to be very charming and gracious individuals, who frequently marry and have families, belong to some of the best clubs, play at this and that sport with mock earnestness. Their essential discouragement lies in the fact that they do not trust themselves to contribute to the world's welfare. They are content to work at the titanic task of defeating their own boredom, Work is the best antidote against boredom - and without this antidote the insidious plague of ennui fastens its lethal tentacles about the soul and body of any man or woman who denies the law that every adult has useful work to do. That is why drug addiction, chronic alcoholism, gambling, sexual perversion, and other aberrations of human conduct are so frequently found in idle men and women. By a queer distortion of vital perspectives, the rich idlers who belong to this group are frequently the ideals of the hard-working masses who do not know how lucky they are to have a job that demands some objective contribution from them, some job that gives discipline and meaning to their life.

About Idlers

As in the case of the 'go-getter' who concentrates on the work sector to the exclusion of everything in life, the rich idler (who is differentiated from the tramp only in the fact that his early environment makes social adjustment and sexual opportunities almost a matter of course) is eventually faced with an insoluble problem. There are men and women who work hard all their lives for the pure purpose of escaping work in the twilight of their existences. These, and others who have never worked at all, gravitate to certain paradisiac spots where human irresponsibility is not too much frowned upon. We find them lolling about on the Riviera; we find them at Cairo and Capri, on the boulevards of Paris, and in the night clubs of London - chasing pleasure and a new thrill in the latest, most bizarre fashion.

Social custom makes it far more difficult for men to follow this technique than for women, and therefore we find that among women who have been brought up to believe that a woman's chief work in life is to be pretty, this is one of the commonest techniques. Women who have followed the strategy of 'no work and all play' cut a sorry figure when they approach the age of fifty. We find them, often bejewelled and beautifully gowned, running around from one gigolo to the other, one watering place to the next, from one charlatan to the next. If it were not for the fact that good human material, degenerated through lack of exercise, both mental and physical, is so tragic a sight, the spectacle of well-educated but non-working women sighing fatuously over the hocus-pocus of some religious or metaphysical cult, would be comic. All too frequently the comedy ends in the tragedy of melancholia and suicide.

The tragedy is all the more appalling because the amount of socially useful work that can be done by women of this type for those who suffer under the heel of economic oppression, physical handicaps, or mal-education, is beyond all comprehension. We have seen women sitting at the gaming tables in Monte Carlo throwing away thousands of pounds in an evening in the hopeless search for a thrill, when thrills entirely unknown and undreamed of could be found at their finger-tips if they were to invest the slightest effort in improving the conditions of the sick and hopeless, or if they were to devote themselves to the task of increasing our knowledge of the world of science or art.

One of my patients who suffered a depression as a result of her inability to experience another thrill was given the task of spending the two thousand pounds she usually gambled away in a season at Monte Carlo in providing recreational facilities for a group of working girls, many of whom were delinquent wards of a certain charitable organization. The initial work opened her eyes to a host of coincident social problems, and, at the present time, this good woman spends eight hours a day, five days a week, administering funds and actively participating in the communal activities of these girls. Her depression has disappeared.

A less common strategy of attack is that in which the focus of life's activities is on the social sector, with various degrees of frustration and non-cooperation on the occupational and sexual fronts.

In this strategy, social contacts and social conventions are elevated into a major interest in life. Form is everything. Snobbery and social prestige are the goals; elegance and manners the chief desiderata. Nothing else matters. One must be graceful and gracious. Let others soil their hands with work. Sex Is possible only when all the social amenities have been complied with. It is more important that the bridesmaids at a wedding should be correctly gowned, the wedding pictures published in the 'correct' papers, than that the bride and groom should be prepared for marriage and capable of making a normal adjustment to one another.

Readers who have followed our philosophic approach to the problems of life will see that a good attitude toward work and toward sex is impossible when there is too much emphasis on the purely social side of life. This type of strategy is usually an admission of failure to solve the other two problems correctly. The problem of social 'form' is one of the easiest to solve. Any fool can master the contents of a book of etiquette with a little effort; it takes a wise man to build a bridge, write a sonata, or raise a family of courageous children.

This type of social self-glorification belongs to the numerous techniques of lying with the truth. Politeness, good manners, social grace, and social ease are among the most valuable devices for social adjustment. To magnify these tools into ends is to annihilate the process of living, and rob the very social graces of their value. Good manners are the lubricating oil that allows the wheels of social intercourse to revolve smoothly. No machine, not even the social machine of our age, will move and work on lubricating oil alone. Adjustment is made of sterner stuff than the precious distillations of etiquette.

Of Sexual Virtuosity

A pattern commonly found in a society which has made sex a special arena of life is that in which the sexual sector bears the brunt of attack, and the social and work sectors are neglected.

The reason for the existence of such a type of attack is deeply rooted in history. Just because the sexual sector is not essential to the continuation of individual life, it is chosen as a side-show of life by many men and women who are afraid to make actual advances on the other two fronts. Our civilization is inclined to overvalue and exaggerate the importance of sexual virtuosity. To many human beings, being human means solely the ability to carry out sexual relations with flair and apparent ease. 'Virility' in sex, that is, a 'plus' of potency in sexual relations, is confused with true virility. Many women see in sexual success the sole path toward significance in life. Many adolescent spirits, no matter what their age, go searching for sexual conquests in their attempt to be 'every inch a man'. Every woman appears a challenge to their virility. Sexual congress, in reality the highest form of social cooperation, becomes an arena in which one sex is subordinated, the other made dominant. If you win, you prove your virility, you are a man. If you lose the battle of sex you are a failure in all else.

The war threw some interesting side-lights on this phase of life. Men who had been subjected to the horrors of barrage and bombardment for weeks, when granted leave rushed to the first woman they could find. Ordinary aesthetic standards were thrown to the winds, and men who were most cautious at home entirely disregarded all precautions. Sexual orgies are a common accompaniment of all wars and all great periods of depression. When the ordinary guarantees of peace and security are abrogated, men and women both tend to find solace in the intoxication of love's embrace.

Emergency Exits of the Soul

The human lot is often a difficult one. Man's brain has fashioned certain emergency exits through which the human spirit can escape into a temporary nirvana of peace or superiority. We have already discussed the value of the Roman circus and modern sports in this connexion. Religion and sex throughout the ages have been the asylums of the fainthearted. Whenever you find a human being who is fanatically religious or fanatically sex-frenzied, you may almost be certain that he is running away from some of the ordinary obligations and responsibilities of being a human being, and seeking a false sense of superiority either by establishing his self-esteem by a fictional intimacy with God, or an equally fictional superiority over his sexual partner. It is for this reason that religion and sex have much in common: frequently in the complicated history of man they have been the two most comfortable avenues of escape from intolerable realities.

The great movements of history are frequently mirrored in the lives of individuals. Discouraged and disheartened men and women are to be found among those who make frantic efforts to establish their virility, just as decadent civilizations are characterized by their tendencies toward sexual orgy and debauchery. Indeed, it may almost be stated as a psychological law that when anyone elects to fight on one of life's fronts to the exclusion of the other two, he is a discouraged and neurotic human being.

Prostitution is the concrete expression of this tendency to make a business of sex. The prostitute, the pimp, the Don Juan, the Messalina, the 'polite adulterers' of Floyd Dell, are all attempting to make sex the be-all and end-all of life. No wonder Freud believed that all neuroses were based on sexual aberrations - the first place in which a neurosis becomes evident is the sexual sphere. Those who seek farther and deeper in the springs of human understanding can see the true relationship, and thus discover the unity of all neuroses as evasions, greater or less, of the complete solution of life's problems.

It is not enough to be a sexual virtuoso - one must follow up the attack on the other fronts as well. The people who consistently follow the attack strategy are frequently the envy of their fellows. One of my patients, who belonged to the strategists of this school, expressed the essential philosophy of this type very well when he said: "What's the use of slaving at a job in an office all day long when the only thing in the world worth having is a beautiful woman's love? That is the true intoxication of life. Nothing else really matters. Show me a beautiful and unattainable woman, and I will lay siege to her as a general would lay siege to a fortress. No matter what the cost, no matter what the effort, success is worth while when it comes. It is the greatest and most thrilling game in the world. Every woman can be had - if you go about it in the right way. It's an art, and one has to be an artist in love. There is no more exalting triumph than the triumph over a beautiful and haughty woman. I'd rather spend one night with such a woman than build the Panama Canal!'

The men and women - and they are about equal in number - who follow this plan of campaign, naturally develop a sexual technique as highly specialized as the technique of a bank director or a surgeon. Are they happy? Yes, but their happiness is very short-lived. The gentleman who expressed this opinion confessed that his pleasure in a woman who had succumbed to his strategy was approximately proportional to the time required to induce her to surrender. If he accomplished his purpose in a week, his pleasure lasted one night, and then he could not bear to see the woman again. If it required a month, a week-end of enjoyment was the upper limit. When the siege lasted for several months, a week or at most a fortnight of bliss was the niggardly booty. He never concentrated on a single campaign - there were always several in various stages of completion. His tastes were as catholic as those of Casanova. A week spent in seducing a hotel maid was as pleasant as a fortnight in humbling a duchess.

His difficulties were comparable to those of the business man who had massed his forces in an attack on the work front to the exclusion of all other human activities. Having become a past master of sexual aggression, a virtuoso in female weakness, he recognized his inability to hold a woman's love. He was getting older, and the spectre of failing virility was beginning to stalk in the ante-chamber. He became pessimistic. Suddenly the whole sexual game began to lose its flavour. He looked with questioning eyes to the neighbouring emergency exit, religion, and began to consider devoting himself to the contemplative peace of yoga philosophy. Business reverses made him falter. Finally, he found himself laying siege to high school girls and older women, and sensed the imminent defeat of his own life's plan in these petty victories. He became blue, irritable, "nervous', and sleepless. He had come to the end of his repertoire of sexual virtuosity, and, for the first time in his life, he had admitted that he was afraid.

Normal Sex Relationships

The correct solution of the sexual problem leads to greater and greater happiness as time goes on, because the sexual relation, as such, is not elevated into a goal, nor made an arena of human significance, but plays its part in the great drama of life. Sex never demands the limelight in the good life. A good actor subordinates his part and his personality to the play, to the players, and to the audience. Similarly, sex and the sex life are satisfying only in the degree to which they are related to all other human activities. Sex is the instrument of the deepest and most vital social communion and the means of the establishment of the family which gives the individual his only true taste of immortality, and often, in the circle of his family, his sole means of finding a social group to which his work and his effort have meaning and value.

Happiness cannot accrue, therefore, in any great measure or in any adequate duration to the men and women who make sex a special arena, and degrade the members of the opposite sex to the role of wild beasts in a gladiatorial combat. The odds are too great against one's sexual partner, the sense of fair play too far outraged when such a campaign is waged. Too many human horizons are excluded, too much human nature is exploited and perverted. It is not necessary to have proof of one's virility every night of one's adult life to be virile. A good job well done, a friend helped in need, a game well played, a child encouraged, a house kept in order - these also are evidences of virility in the best sense of the word. And, as in the world of business, one cannot be happy being a fighter only - one must learn early to make the best use of one's victories. The sexual game, the interchange of aggression and submission which make up the approach to mature sexual relations, are part of life, not the end of life itself. One must live well to love well; one must love well to live wisely.

If you find yourself approaching the problems of life with any of the false strategies we have outlined above, you need not think that the battle is lost. No one solves all his problems perfectly. Every man and woman encounters more or less similar difficulties. If you have a poor strategy, a faulty plan of campaign, it does not in the least impugn your intelligence or spoil your chances of a final victory. As I intimated in a previous chapter, our plan of campaign is really laid down before we are six years old, at a time when we are by no means in full possession of our mature critical faculties. You live your life according to your interpretation of the facts, and your plan of campaign, faulty as it may seem in the perspective of history, is always the best plan of campaign you could have devised.

Our purpose is to provide something of an objective standpoint so that you may measure your relative distance from the ideal 'normal' plan of campaign. Knowledge of the difficulties on the way is half the battle. If you have a mistaken strategy, you need not be involved in any conflict between your old strategy and a new and better approach to life. As soon as you really understand the mistakes of your approach, you will also understand the proper measures to straighten out your lines of attack. This is not a difficult task. It is easier, more practical, and more satisfactory to live a normal life. That is why it is the normal life.

The Inter-relation of Human Problems

If we consider human activities as a three-ring circus, with a number of side-shows, we can understand great numbers of our fellow-men, and a variety of occupations and activities in their true light. The so-called 'normal', courageous, well- adjusted individuals will be found 'doing their act' in the three main arenas, while the neurotic individuals will be found concentrating their attentions on the side-shows. Many of the normal performers will take excursions into the side-shows - and indeed this is a sign of normality. But the neurotics, the incomplete, inadequate men and women will barely touch the main arenas. An interesting confirmation of our thesis that the 'side-show' artists understand that they are evading the realities of the three main rings, is to be found in the fact that neurotics are invariably busier in their side-shows than their normal friends in the chief rings. The over-activity of the sideshow artists is, in effect, a plea for exculpation and exoneration. 'How can you expect me to do my act in the main ring when there are so many fascinating and interesting activities in the side-shows?' asks the neurotic. I am too busy at my job in the side-show to act in the big arena V exclaims the side-show artist. Let us examine the three-ring circus, so that we can better understand the relation of life's side-shows to the realities of the main rings. Some of the side-shows are very closely related to the actual three rings. Family life, for instance, is an important area in the social and sexual rings. When the maintenance of the family becomes the paramount activity of life, it becomes a side-show. Self-esteem and self-confidence are necessary characteristics of any performer in the main rings, but exaggerated to egoism, haughtiness, pride, arrogance, or brutality, these parodies of self-confidence become side-shows. Similarly, games such as bridge, chess, golf, or football are desirable avocations in which one can find recreation. When they become the sole activity - we exclude professional teachers of any sport because these people are necessary and useful members of society - they fall into the category of side-show activities. There are men to whom a low golf score is far more important than the happiness of their wives, the education of their children, or the pursuit of their occupation.

Catalogue of Side-show

The variety of side-shows surrounding the sexual arena are many and diverse, for reasons we have already stated. In no other arena is it so easy to prostitute a normal activity to false ends. The prostitute, the pimp, the gigolo, the 'kept, woman, the procurer, the theatrical and literary exploiters of sex, indicate not only their essential misanthropy, but also their lack of courage to find employment in more useful ways. Homosexuality is the greatest of all the sexual side-shows, and the most characteristic of our times. Romantic infantilism, the cult of the 'perfect lover', the right' man and the 'right' woman, are further sexual side-shows.

So far as work is concerned, side-shows are perhaps less common than in the other fields, because of the inexorable tyranny of hunger. The slacker who denies the validity of work, the criminal who works only at the expense of society, the man who cannot hold a job more than a month, the rich idler, the bridge 'fiend' are to be found in the side-shows round the occupational arena. In a sense, every neurotic, may be said to be in a side-show of the work arena. Every neurosis is a serious profession. It demands a maximum of time and effort, and much explanation and excuse. Neurotics are always the hardest workers in the world - but their work is sterile and pays no dividends in happiness.

All side-show activities are marked by certain common indices. If a man is to be found exclusively in the side-shows of life you may be sure that he has been very discouraged early in life, and is putting up a brave front to keep himself and the rest of the world from guessing how badly he feels about it. Sometimes he succeeds in deceiving himself, but he seldom succeeds in deceiving all his neighbours ~ all the time. Yet if you find yourself in a side-show, you are perfectly justified in a sense. The problems of the main rings appear too difficult. You do not understand how anyone else can possibly muster the courage to go through the ordinary tasks of daily life. If you find yourself in this situation, take heart, and make a fresh start. If you see another in the same boat, and understand his situation, encourage him and instruct him.

We are all responsible for our neurotic neighbours. The normal man is the one who radiates an aura of friendly encouragement and helpful criticism. Scepticism, reserved judgement, and above all divine discontent with things as they are, imagination, and a critical faculty with a constructive turn - these are not to be found in the side-shows but in the main arenas. The man who has mastered a difficulty and surmounted an obstacle recharges his vital courage, and can afford to stop and help a fellow-man over the same obstacles. Only the egoist in the side-show, hypnotized by his own need for excuses, cannot spare the time to listen to the other fellow's story.

Why 'Normality Pays

Every consideration of the problem of living brings us back to the same point: ignorance gives birth to fear; fear is the father of isolation; and isolation spawns further discouragement, irresponsibility, and neuroses of every conceivable variety. Isolation, fear, and ignorance in turn cause a man to constrict the sphere of his activity. They force him out of the main arenas of life, and push him into the side-shows. The risk is less there, and that is why such an imposing percentage of human beings are to be found busily occupied with the useless problems of life's side-shows. It is a truism that the smaller the arena, the less dangerous the encounter, the less imposing the enemy must be. This is the secret of the side-show.

Why is it, then, that anyone should risk the major difficulties of the three chief rings if he can win greater security in the side-shows? Why should any human being strive to earn a living if he can support himself in any other way without too much difficulty? We have already suggested that those who find themselves in the side-shows are entirely justified in their cowardice because they are ignorant of the elements of the fine art of living; they have reacted correctly to life's challenge in terms of their inadequate knowledge. If we are to lure anyone • out of the security of the side-show we must, in the last analysis, show him that it is safer in the main arena, because security is his goal in life. His only mistake is the mistake of strategy and technique.

As a matter of fact, the main arena is not only safer than the side-show, but its dividends in satisfaction, self-esteem, and happiness are incomparably greater than those of the sideshow. If you are in one of life's side-shows you have evaded the main arena and its activities. Something there is in every human being - call it conscience, super-ego, inborn social feeling, race unconscious, or what you will - that pricks him when he evades his responsibilities as a human being. It is the sting of this unconscious realization of the fitness of things that prods the side-show artist to over-act. Look round you and you will find that men and women in the side-shows of life work very much harder than performers in the main arena. A man with a broken leg needs no excuse for not walking, but a man who insists on walking on stilts when the rest of the world is on foot is compelled to spend much of his time explaining and excusing himself. True, he can look down on the rest of mankind, and gain a subjective sense of superiority, but in the last analysis he has assumed a greater responsibility than the ordinary responsibility of walking on the level with his fellow-men, and taking his chances of being noticed and approved because of his smile or his helpfulness.

The side-shows do not pay. That is the chief reason why you should get out of them if you spend your time excusing yourself for not being in the main rings. This is no moral or categorical imperative. We do not arrogate to ourselves any moral superiority when we urge a neurotic to change his ways, to assume his responsibilities, and to take his chances with the rest of mankind. Our advice is the advice of a physician who has just returned from a malaria-infested country, counselling a traveller departing for that swampy country to immunize himself with quinine. It is the imperative of hygiene, not of ethics or morals. Most normal, sane men and women would rather not have malaria, and will take our advice. If they do not do so, they must be ignorant of the discomfort of malarial infection, or insanely confident that a divine providence will toughen their skin against the bites of voracious mosquitoes.

This hygienic imperative is the imperative of common sense, yet it is extremely difficult for many individuals who have become satisfied and reconciled to the narrow life of their favourite side-show to follow it. It is true that a great many people live and die within the confines of this or that side-show, and seem none the worse for it. Some of them become artists of the highest calibre, and actually find their way back to the main rings by virtue of their superlative sideshow accomplishments. This is a rare occurrence. Most of the side-show performers become human derelicts, mental bankrupts, and dilapidated failures. Nature, and not man, visits its punishments on them, sometimes after so many extensions of credit that the side-show performer has been led to believe that he will never really have to pay up. This generosity of nature deceives many into a false sense of security.

Despite nature's apparent kindness, her first principle is that nothing comes to nothing. You cannot make something, or get something, for nothing. Thousands of people have died in the attempt to dispute this cardinal principle of the cosmos; thousands have succumbed in the vain attempt to pit their private beliefs against the inexorable logic of the universe. Boil it down to essentials and the problem of life is as simple as a penny-in-the-slot machine. You put in your penny and you get your piece of chocolate nicely wrapped in silver foil. If you do not risk your penny, you get nothing. And it will not avail you one whit to call the machine bad names, to cast ashes on your head and bewail your past sins, to shake your fist at those who have contributed their pennies and are enjoying their rewards, to believe that you have been discriminated against by a harsh fate, to rail about the uselessness of all penny-in-the-slot machines, or to question the wisdom of this particular type of cosmic arrangement. These are the facts: if you risk your contribution, the chances are very much in favour of your gaining peace, security, happiness, and the esteem of your fellow-men. If you risk nothing, you gain nothing - but heartache and regrets, sorrow, confusion, conflict, pain, and loneliness.

CHAPTER NINE.
Of False Goals: The Side-shows

How the Family Inhibits Mental Maturity - The Necessity of Educating Young Children Outside the Family - The Normal Uses of Individualism-The Evasion of Work-The Sexual Side-shows-The Bogey of Masturbation — The Cure of Masturbation - Homosexuality - Why Homosexuality Can Be Cured - Sexual Athletics and the Double Standard-Prostitution-Minor Conversions of Sex-The Problem of Narcotics - Psychological Aspects of Alcoholism - The Cost of Flight from Reality

A further examination of the side-shows about the main arenas of our lives will illuminate some of the darker corners of human conduct, and help us in our understanding of human nature. The meaning of many traits is often misinterpreted by laymen and psychologists because they treat peculiarities of human conduct as isolated phenomena, and fail to recognize their relationship to the whole scheme of human life. We shall continue to investigate the social side-shows in greater detail.

Perhaps the commonest and most important of these social aberrations is the cult of family relationships to the extent that family loyalty and filial love become the most important ends of life. The family is a product of the same weakness of mankind that gave rise to our social structure and our civilization. If we were not so weak as human beings the family relationship would be a temporary one, as it is among stronger and better-equipped mammals. The older mankind grows, the more dependent human children become. A famous sociologist recently expressed the opinion that forty years would soon be considered the age of maturity in our towns.

In ancient times, and still to-day in savage and barbarian communities, the onset of physical maturity marks the beginning of mental and social maturity, but a fourteen-year-old boy or girl in London or New York is the veriest infant. Social responsibility is hardly ever imputed to him. Although he is allowed to vote at the age of twenty-one, in all probability he is in no position to establish a family and assume his full social responsibilities until he is between the ages of thirty and forty. A not inconsiderable proportion of the population of this country never attains complete social maturity, and our civilization is marked by the irresponsible acts of men and women whose bodies bear the marks of maturity, but whose minds remain at adolescent or pre-adolescent levels.

The permanence of the human family is an outgrowth of the weakness and dependence of the human child. If our children could be thrust out into the world, prepared to take their place in the social structure at the age of ten or eleven years, the family as we know it to-day would never exist. Valuable as the family is as a means of protecting the immature, it carries within itself the dread germs of anti-social disintegration. Physical incest is practically unknown among wild animals, because the young are abandoned to their fate as soon as they can take care of their immediate needs, and the chance of brother mating with sister, or parent mating with child, is reduced to a minimum by nature.

Not so in the human family. Incest (which runs counter to nature's scheme of cross-fertilization and the consequent levelling of individual differences to the advantage of the race) becomes a real problem in civilized communities. Legal bars against incest exist in every civilized community, while some form of taboo is aimed against incest in almost all savage and barbarian communities. But there are no laws, as yet, against the mental component of the over-emphasized family relation which may be called mental incest. This neurotic attitude is far more dangerous both to the individual and to the State, both because of its inestimably more frequent occurrence, and because of its insidious effect on those who come in contact with it. Mental incest may spread its contagion throughout an entire environment, whereas physical incest affects only the contracting parties.

The real purpose of the family is to prepare the young for the assumption of mature social, vocational, and sexual relationships. The family is the testing ground of the social feeling, the proving ground of social cooperation. When the family breaks off from its purpose, and becomes an end in itself, it destroys not only the maturity and mental health of the individuals who compose it, but fails in its ultimate purpose of social preparation and testing. As it exists to-day, the family is a relic of a now discredited patriarchal culture. As such it is in the process of disintegration and reconstellation to meet the needs of a new civilization in which men and women will cooperate as equals. Even the best family life, therefore, with its over-emphasis on the role of the male, and its subordination of women, is not too well fitted for preparing children for a courageous social life. The dangers arising out of the family constellation of the various children have already been discussed in previous paragraphs. The family stands indicted, therefore, in the most favourable circumstances, as not quite adequate to its present-day task.

How the Family Inhibits Mental Maturity

You can well imagine that the dangers of family life are doubly exaggerated when family life, family loyalty, family pride, are held up as the very goals of human existence. You can imagine how objectivity is warped when a brother or a father must be defended simply because he is a brother or a father. You can well conceive how the constriction of the social horizon by the boundaries of family life runs counter to the purpose of nature, and to the laws of mental health that we have already outlined. The family is the breeding ground of envy and jealousy, of personal ambition, of egoism, of hypersensitivity, of suspicion, and sexual perversion.

It is precisely where the family life is most perfect that Its results are most insidious. Bad families cause their children to leave them - bitter medicine, it is true, but often drastically effective if the young rebels are not humiliated and discouraged by their family difficulties to such an extent that they dread to establish families of their own in the future. In many families the mothers still have only one profession - the raising of their families. This leads to mental enslavement. No woman who has invested her total life's capital in her family likes to see her children becoming mature and leaving the family hearth. Despite her best intentions, she tries to keep her children babies, although they have assumed mature and independent sexual and occupational responsibilities.

I have known men, forty years old, who still reported to their mothers every night when they returned to their homes, and accounted for every moment of their time, despite the fact that they were supporting the family. I have known girls who have broken one engagement after another because mother or father did not approve their choice. Independence, social courage, a healthy attitude toward one's fellows, are almost unattainable in the stifling, albeit loving, atmosphere of the professional family.

The over-emphasis of the family is very common among the Jews, who are often cursed with neuroses that hinge on the family situation. During the Middle Ages, when the Jews were compelled to live in ghettoes, their family life saved them from extinction. Without the strong and beautiful family life in which individual Jews found the only available sphere of social significance, the Jews would have perished, and with them their valuable cultural contributions to our civilization. But the translation of this hermetically sealed family life into modern civilization has often worked havoc for the Jewish children of the modern world, brought up 'as if' the dangers and deprivations of ghetto life still existed. The world has outgrown the constricting bonds of patriarchalism. To maintain the family as the end of life and the source of personal salvation, is to be unhappy, because the projection of family influence into adult life runs counter to the purpose of nature.

Every breeder of animals knows that the result of inbreeding is the production of markedly individual, extreme types because inbreeding causes the reduplication of dominant or recessive genes. Mental incest, the result of a too-close family life, leads to mental extremes, to irreconcilable individualities whose uniqueness makes them social incommensurables. We have only to look at dogs to see the result of physical inbreeding. All dogs are descended from a common wolf-like ancestor, domesticated by our forefathers. Generations of inbreeding have resulted in such incongruous differences as those between a Dachshund and a Great Dane, between an Irish Deerhound and a Pekingese. If you continue within the closed walls of your family it is likely that you will become so markedly individualized, so unique, that it will be impossible for you to have any contact, any community of interest with the rest of mankind. In our civilization the results of mental incest are far more serious than those of physical incest: inferior individuals who result from too much inbreeding die out and are eliminated from the economy of the human race, but mental incest evolves unique, unsocial, irreconcilable individualists whose mental attitude is a contagious plague that affects every other human being with whom they come in contact.

The Necessity of Educating Young Children Outside the Family

We hope that the time is not far distant when the communal education of the child will begin at two years, and not at the traditional six or seven when the damage of too close family life has already been done. If, as all psychiatrists and psychologists claim, character is formed in the first five or six years of life, then the character formation of a child must not be left to the haphazard, often well-intentioned, but more often falsely carried out devices of the individual family. The State, usually fifty to a hundred years behind the best scientific opinion, will awaken to the needs of mental hygiene prophylaxis for children, generations from to-day, when the burden of taking care of its criminals, its insane, its psychopathic inferiors has become so great that carefully planned administration and influencing of the young child will appear cheaper in the end.

When the State awakens to the knowledge which is now the property of a few far-sighted individuals, it will no longer subject young children to the pernicious influences of the family environment, as it no longer exposes its children to the dangers of contagious" disease. When the old patriarchal idea that children belong to their parents as if they were so many chattels has been completely exploded, families which are so discouraged that they have but a single child will be legally compelled to give that child a social environment after the age of two years, and continue that group influence until the end of his formal education.

Most of the social side-shows are directly derived from the vicious influence of family life. Thus we have egoistic, antisocial ambition as a result of competition between children and parents, or brothers with older brothers. Pride, and its derivatives, snobbery, bigotry, intolerance, are similarly products of exaggerated and artificial conflicts between the family, or the family group, and the rest of society.

The cult of personal greatness, the elevation of "uniqueness9 and "being different' arises out of the sense of inferiority born of family competitions. From the cult of personal uniqueness to the cult of other cults is but a step. Cultism, whether in social groups or in religious communities, is one of the most popular of all social side-shows.

The Normal Uses of Individualism

Opportunities for individualism abound to-day as much as they ever did, and individualism will never be annihilated. Our purpose is simply to re-direct the channels of individualism from a sterile cult of "uniqueness' to the more valuable cult of uniqueness in service. If you are afraid you may lose your precious ego, look round at the objective problems of housing, transport, hygiene, international cooperation, the conquest of the sources of power, protection against the untamed forces of nature, not to speak of the conquest of the degenerative diseases and the necessity for providing better use for our increasing leisure, and you will find a world of activities open to your individuality. The growing tendency of society to take care of its weaker members gives rise to other social side-show's which depend on the existence of a social consciousness in civilized communities. In prehistoric days a fallen cave-man or a sick cave-man was as good as a dead cave-man. Every individual was so busy with the maintenance of his individual life that he had no time or opportunity to care for a non-contributing member. Today we are kinder to our sick, our old, our crippled - our 'lame ducks'. The professional beggar and the professional martyr who prefer to humiliate themselves rather than take a chance in the open competition of life are exploiters of their neighbour's social feeling. They are social prostitutes who live on the sympathy and kindness of their fellows who have enough to share. Beggars become virtuosos of misery, and social martyrs who go around complaining of the injustice they experience in a harsh society, trick society into taking care of them. Their success, financially and socially, is often great; their happiness in these miserable side-shows very problematic.

Almost everyone has a martyr in his family somewhere near the family skeleton. Almost every family has a 'lame duck' who lives on the industry and responsibility of other, more socially courageous individuals. These human leeches, these social barnacles have usually been prepared for their non-productive lives by the mistakes of childhood training in families so soft-hearted, so over-solicitous, so criminally 'good' to their children that these children, grown up physically, must still be spoon-fed and supported by society. Thus does the cult of the family improve each shining hour, and thus does vanity, the product of the family-cult and dependence, and irresponsibility, and protracted mental infantilism, furnish rich soil and fertile opportunities for the mushroom-like growth of the social side-shows.

The Evasion of Work

An ideal solution of the vocational problem includes a major interest in some socially useful task, complemented by an avocation which gives us a sense of satisfaction for our individually felt inferiorities, or enables us to elaborate some aspect of the creative urge which is the possession of all of us because we are human beings. It includes only work which is of ultimate value to the social group. The happiest mortal is he whose life-work is a combination of Occupation and avocation. Such a profession gives him not only a sense of successful compensation for his own feelings of inferiority, but vouchsafes him the approval of his fellow-men. Variations from this ideal state are many and devious, because the correct solution of the work problem demands a considerable mental maturity, a great degree of social responsibility, independence of thought and action, and an optimistic philosophy of life.

Whatever the immediate causes, and whatever the deeper unconscious causes for a retreat from the task of work in any individual case, the forms of evasion fall into a few simple patterns. If you want to run away from work, substituting your private logic for common sense, you can do it very easily by being very busy at something else, usually something quite useless, which seems to give a subjective sense of importance, occupation, and a ready excuse for not being at work in productive activities. One of the best ways to avoid work is to announce that you have not found the 'right' job. You try one job after another, finding difficulties and disappointments in each, until you are so old, and have tried so many jobs, that you can safely say there is no proper job for you in this world, while you point with reasonable pride to the many and honest attempts you have made to find the proper occupation.

No doubt you have known men and women who are martyrs to the 'wrong' job. We have often heard the complaint 'If only I could have become a doctor' or If only I could have gone into the wholesale grocery business instead of becoming an accountant'. If you really are in the wrong job - and this sometimes happens if your job was chosen for you by well-meaning but misguided parents and friends, or if you chose it yourself at a time when you were mentally immature, and wanted only subjective satisfactions - it is never too late to change to the right job. Usually the men and women who are dissatisfied with their jobs are dissatisfied because they are not doing them well enough.

Granted that, in our mad economic structure, it is not always possible to wait long enough to find a veritably satisfying work to do, because of the necessity of gaining an immediate livelihood, yet it is always possible, by dint of study and effort in your spare time, to acquire a new technique which will fit you for another and better job. Where this is really desirable, the individual usually can find ways and means to attain his ends. But the great majority of dissatisfied workers are dissatisfied with work rather than with their jobs. The spoiled and pampered child considers any job as an insult to his 'face' and his own opinion of his personal value. No job suits him, because he has not grown up to the point where work appears self-explanatory and utterly satisfying as a philosophy of life.

Laziness and procrastination are the commonest side-shows of the work arena. Their popularity is due to their effectiveness. Some men are lazy because they are stubborn, and see in the job they have to do the projected hand of their authoritarian parents. Their protest takes the form of passive resistance to work. Others, and these are in the majority, are lazy because, by being lazy, they attain the fiction: I could accomplish as much as my neighbour if I were not lazy' On occasion they work very hard just to show that they can do their jobs when they feel like it, thus proving the validity of their laziness. If you are a great egoist the inflation of your ego is the only reward work offers you, and if you can inflate your ego by any of the spurious devices of laziness, changing of jobs, procrastination, indecision, stubbornness, dilettantism, criticism, fault-finding, or by setting up impossible conditions under which you will design to work, you accomplish your end much more cheaply and much more effectively than if you had a little more courage and set out to batter down some real obstacles and made a profession of some socially useful work that would help satisfy your personal need for significance.

The Sexual Side-show

The sexual side-shows are the last resorts of the discouraged because in these narrow areas subjective superiority can be bought very cheaply. The tendency of our age is to exaggerate the importance of sexuality, and to many human beings sexual virility and human validity are synonymous. That sexual virility and the normal experience of passion are part of the good life goes without saying, but to the discouraged who are seeking solely subjective, make-believe values in life, the semblance of sexual virility is mistakenly considered an index of human worth-whileness. Because of this common mistake, and also because the sexual arena is the sole arena in which no one is compelled by nature either to do his act or lose his life, deserters from the main fronts of life are chiefly interested in establishing a spurious sense of their sexual importance. Such men and women hope that they can cajole themselves and their neighbours into admitting that their sexual virtuosity carries over into the other fields of human endeavour, and bespeaks a virtuosity in the fine art of being human as well.

The sexual side-shows may be divided into (1) those which are evasions of the problems of love and marriage, *the perversions* (2) those which consist in the misuse of the sexual life to some false social or vocational ends, which might be called the *diversions,* and finally (3) those in which sexual activity is substituted for activity in one of the other spheres of human endeavour. These might be called the *conversions* of sex. They include those forms of sexual neurosis in which men and women find their chief work in consulting one physician after another because of sexual neurasthenia, whose maintenance in the face of all treatment becomes the fundamental premise of their existence.

Of the true perversions of sex, sadism and masochism are the clearest examples. The common denominator of all sexual perversion, as Wexberg[1] has pointed out, is that the sexual partner is degraded into an object of ego-satisfaction. In any perversion we find that one individual misuses another's sexual constitution in order to bolster up artificially his own feeling of self-esteem. This mechanism is beautifully demonstrated in that perversion we call sadism, in which sexual satisfaction is only possible after the sexual partner has been brutally mistreated, physically or mentally.

The sadist wants to feel his personal power, and has no interest whatsoever in his mate. The brutal 'he-man, and the sexual 'gorilla' are common examples of this perverse sexual type. It is not our purpose to describe the horrible crimes that sadists commit in the name of sex. If you

---

[1] Erwin Wexberg: The Psychology of Sex; An Introduction, translated by Dr W. Beran Wolfe.

can experience sexual gratification only after you have beaten or cut or maltreated your mate, you are a very discouraged human being. Only an arrant coward could secure self-esteem at such a price.

The masochists, who seem to be at the opposite pole, because they can be sexually gratified only when they have been maltreated by their sexual partners, are in reality not very different from the sadists. Both sadism and masochism betray a hidden striving for superiority at the expense of the humiliation of the sexual partner. The woman who wishes to be mauled by her man evidences a very spurious submission because, psychologically, she is degrading her mate to the level of a beast. Sadism and masochism are interchangeable. Sadists who are beaten at their game may become masochists, and masochists who have suffered too much may become the cruellest of human beings. If possible, the false martyrdom of the masochist which bespeaks a long neurotic training, is even less human than the downright brutality of the sadist. It is not our purpose to describe the complex manifestations of this linking of sex with cruelty or with abject submission, for such descriptions are suitable only for textbooks of psychopathology. It is sufficient if the reader sees that there is no place for love in these parodies of sex.

Let it be said at the beginning that a great many estimable people look with horror at certain sexual practices which are commonly called 'abnormal' or 'perverted' and are quick to label individuals who practise these variations of normal love as 'perverts'. Nothing could be farther from the truth. When two people really love each other every sexual technique which brings them closer to one another or accentuates their enjoyment of love, must be good and normal. A perversion does not exist until one or the other lover is shocked, hurt, or disgusted by the procedure. Perversions are what we make them. So long as the 'we' relation of the lovers is maintained in its integrity, we should not speak of any sexual technique as a perversion. Perversions of love exist only where the practices destroy love, never where they foster it. A sexual practice becomes a perversion the moment that it is used as an end in itself, when the practise of the perversion, and not the satisfaction of a lover, is its goal.

The Bogey of Masturbation

So much solemn nonsense has been written about masturbation, so much sanctified stupidity has been published by pseudo-scientific writers on the practice of 'self-abuse', and so much fearsome sexual jingoism has been perpetrated on frightened young men and women, that a few common-sense paragraphs on this most widespread of all sexual malpractices are of service. Masturbation is no more than the sexual life of an isolated human being. It begins occasionally as a spontaneous discovery, and is frequently taught in the 'gutter school' of sex to which so many parents send their children when they have forfeited their confidence.

More common in girls than in boys, masturbation is practically a normal phenomenon in both sexes until the age of sexual maturity. Masturbation cannot, in and of itself have the least harmful consequence. Much more harm has been done by those who have preached and thundered against masturbation than by masturbation itself. On occasions of artificial isolation - so common in our society - it may actually be the only available form of sexual expression. Its extent is almost universal.

The psychological implications of masturbation are manifold. It can be spoken of as a perversion only when a mature man or woman practises masturbation to the exclusion of normal sexual relations, and in preference to these. Under such circumstances it is not only self-gratification, but a solacing and consoling practice, well designed to stimulate a subjective sense of power and sexual virility. Among savage peoples, masturbation is practically unknown, because the opportunities for normal sexual congress are present as soon as sexual maturity is reached. But among civilized men and women, who build up walls of fear about themselves, masturbation is a very common phenomenon. It occurs among domesticated animals, but never among wild animals, because, like human beings who have cooped themselves up in mental cages, domesticated animals frequently lack the opportunities for normal sexual gratification.

If you live in a mental vault without doors and windows, if you eat, sleep, and build up a constant reserve of physical energy, you will have the tendency to masturbate, because you have excluded the possibility of normal sexual contacts. Nature by its emergency devices, the nocturnal emission or the automatic orgasm, may help you deplete this store of sexual material. But it is more probable that you will help nature along by fantastic imagination of sexual situations in which you have all the satisfaction of a sexual conquest and none of the risk attendant thereon. The harm of masturbation is never a physical one: it is solely a psychological and a social one. Masturbation is an anti-social sexual device. Its worst possible consequence is that you will become so satisfied with this thoroughly safe method of solving the sexual problem, that you will never afterwards trust yourself to risk a genuine solution in the main arenas of love.

Because manifestations of sex are thoroughly, and sometimes brutally and unthinkingly, suppressed by parents, especially those with a patriarchal cast to their world-philosophy, those who have practised masturbation for a long time sometimes develop a feeling of guilt and remorse. This is based sometimes on their fear of the superior power of their authoritarian parents, but more often on the unconscious realization that masturbation is a kind of sexual cheating, in which all the subjective sense of power and virility is retained, while none of the normal risks of sexual congress are assumed. The necessity of merging one's ego with the ego of the beloved for the purpose of the establishment of a 'we' relation is obviated in masturbation. A sense of guilt or remorse is sometimes built up by unhappy neurotics as a general excuse for their lack of social cooperation. One of my patients, referred to in a previous chapter, when urged to go out and do a day's work, answered in shocked and wounded surprise: 'But, doctor! I've been a masturbator all my life. How can you expect me to work?'

Masturbation is neither a sin, nor a crime, nor an effective excuse for being a lame duck' all one's life. It is a symptom of an isolated and timid style of life. It is always the symptom of some deep-lying discouragement, never in itself the '*cause*' of any psychological abnormality, neurosis, or insanity. It is the sexual asylum of those timid souls who fear that in normal sexual relations they will lose the primacy of their ego. The fact that masturbation in adults is almost always accompanied by phantasies of power and sexual conquest betrays its psychological origin in discouragement. Masturbation in children is an unimportant manifestation of adolescence. Its continued practice, after sexual maturity has been reached, indicates not only a mistaken sexual pattern, but a general withdrawal from reality.

The Cure of Masturbation

If you practise this form of sexual activity, open some windows and doors, and emerge from your self-built sexual vault. Sexual relations have been practised since time immemorial. Men and women have been falling in love, getting married, having sexual congress, establishing families, and finding happiness in these relations for so many thousand years that it is ridiculous for you to pit your private fears against the ancient and imposingly effective devices of nature. Love and marriage cannot possibly be as dangerous as you think they are. If you were not discouraged, and if you did not misinterpret the facts, you would have found someone to love and, eventually, a sexual mate, and would have said good-bye to such childish sexual practices as masturbation. But the more you masturbate, the more you discourage yourself; and the more you discourage yourself, the less worthy you think you are of approaching a member of the opposite sex. This is the vicious circle of masturbation. You cannot stop masturbating by making war on masturbation. You must change the whole vicious circle into a beneficent one.

The 'cure' of this condition does not consist in making war on it, or spending endless hours making good resolutions which last only a few days, and breaking them because you are weak-willed. This technique is the most effective way of preparing a brief against yourself. If you are anxious to prove that you are a thoroughly unworthy soul this is a good way to do it. Yet even if you prove a case against yourself, your self-excuse will not excuse you in the eyes of the world. You are already dimly aware of the truth of this statement, for otherwise you would not protest so often and so loudly that you are unworthy. Even if you are as vile and unworthy as you would like to believe yourself, the world will still demand that you make your contribution, and cooperate to the limit of your capacity. Masturbation is the sign of the lack of sexual and social cooperation.

The first thing to do if you wish to change your sexual pattern is to get some work that interests you. Then go out and make some new social contacts, and widen your mental horizons. Make yourself useful to the community in which you live, and make it your business to bring some happiness or some service to one of your fellows. A job well done, or a favour granted, a new discipline mastered, or a hobby well pursued, will strengthen your courage, and widen your horizons. Your new courage will in turn extend the sphere of your usefulness, and presently you will find yourself in such a good position that not only will you not require the solace and consolation of masturbation, but you will be heartened to begin loving someone. This is nature's way. This is common sense. Once you get into the normal channel of activity, service, interest, and zest in life, you will break down the deadening walls you have built around yourself, and masturbation will vanish from your life. Remember that not masturbation, but isolation, is a sin against nature.

What we have written as advice to those who find in masturbation a sexual hazard applies to other sexual perversions, and indeed to all neuroses which are more or less complicated manifestations of similar constrictions of mental horizons and analogous devices of self-imposed isolation. The fetishist who loves a woman's glove more than a woman, believes himself the victim of some psychopathic tendency, but in reality he is only a coward who chooses to get satisfaction in a cheap way. The woman who can fall in love only with a man with red whiskers, violet eyes, and small ears, hides her unconscious purpose: I do not want to love any man' under the specious conditions which exclude every man while they give her the feeling that she is not cheating nature because she says: I would love a man, if the "right man came along" I' The fact that she knows there is no such man, unconsciously, is carefully hidden from her conscious, rational, responsible self.

Homosexuality

The attempted solution of the love problem between members of the same sex is called homosexuality, and this is one of the most common of all the mistaken solutions of the sexual problem. It is usually difficult to discuss homosexuality with calm and objectivity because the subject is so clouded by misconceptions. Champions of this or the other view become emotionally involved because their 'face' depends too much! on the 'rightness' of their views. Homosexuality is one of the few neuroses whose practice is punishable by imprisonment, but although we consider homosexuality an antisocial solution of the sexual problem, we disagree with those jurists who would attempt to limit it by penal legislation. One cannot legislate sickness out of society. The attitude of most people toward homosexuality is one of misunderstanding and ignorance. There are always some who make a great hue and cry about it, and wish to punish all homosexuals. The homosexuals themselves, unlike other neurotics, are the only neurotics who have any social ties, but, on the other hand, they are also the only neurotics who attempt to proselytize children to their neurotic views. Homosexuality, although a flight from sex, is often an active aggression against society, and so lies on the border between neurosis and crime.

Homosexuals are occasionally impudent about their neurosis, and attempt to set up homosexuality as a higher form of sexual life which has none of the unpleasant features of heterosexual relations. Some homosexuals believe that, because a number of great men in the past have been homosexual, homosexuality is the mark of greatness, rather than the stigma of a neurosis. Even among physicians and sexologists, homosexuality is still considered a congenital anomaly of the sexual function, and literally hundreds of books have been written (chiefly by homosexuals) in support of this view, which, if true, would exonerate all homosexuals from any responsibility for their perverted practices. The prevailing idea that homosexuality is a congenital anomaly, and therefore incurable and unchangeable, has done tremendous harm to those many homosexuals who suffer from their deviation and would gladly become heterosexual if they but knew how the change might be effected.

The truth of the matter is that homosexuality is not a disease and not a congenital anomaly. Homosexuality is a symptom of a sexual neurosis. The truth of this thesis can be tested by the examination of homosexuals with regard to their attitudes toward work and society. If homosexuality were a natural condition, there would be no need of building up a system of justifications and excuses for homosexual conduct.

A blind man need not justify his inability to read. Homosexuals spend ten times as much energy in the pursuit of their sexual affairs as normal heterosexual individuals. They are always attempting to prove that they are victims of fate, but in reality they train themselves to abnormal satisfactions by assiduous avoidance of all normal contacts. All books on homosexuality written by homosexuals are attempts to justify the existence of homosexuality, and to shift the onus for the admittedly unsocial nature of homosexual practices to the inexorable facts of a faulty biological constellation.

Some of the homosexual tracts attempt to beautify the situation by calling attention to the fact that a great many significant artists and musicians have been homosexuals. An equally great number of historical characters have suffered from epilepsy and syphilis, but this is no argument for having epilepsy or syphilis. If homosexuality were only a congenital anomaly, there would presumably be a number of homosexuals who would be normal in every other worldly activity, much as deaf-mutes are normal in every other function. But this is by no means the case. Scratch the surface of a homosexual personality and you will find the anti-social characteristics of that personality in every expression and in every activity.

Why Homosexuality Can Be Cured

Fear of intimate contact with the opposite sex is the fundamental cornerstone in the life of every homosexual. Granted this fear, conditioned in childhood by a variety of factors in the environment, and not infrequently by organic deficiencies which make the assumption of the normal sexual role seem too difficult, then the rest of the homosexual's life and training are thoroughly justified and, indeed, quite logical and rational. The prevailing theory that homosexuality in men and women is due to the persistence of sexual rudiments of the opposite sex is disproved by the fact that in clinical practice a great many homosexuals who are in every way perfectly normal physically, still have the strongest homosexual disposition, whereas other individuals with obvious defects in sexual structure, and obvious stigmata of the opposite sex, are perfectly normal in their sexual attitudes and feelings. Further evidence that homosexuality is a neurosis and not a sexual anomaly is to be found in the fact that male homosexuals are frequently irresponsible, lazy, unreliable, vain, egoistic, and thoroughly subjective, while female homosexuals are commonly of a very effective type, active in their work, thoroughly responsible and reliable in their business relations.

This is accounted for by the fact that homosexuality in a male represents a flight from the responsibilities of the masculine role in life whereas, in woman, homosexuality very often represents an attempt to elevate the personality beyond the limits of the contempt which women still suffer in our civilization. A man becomes a homosexual because he is afraid he will lose his artificial ego-ideal in the sexual contact with a woman. He looks at all women as dangerous threats to his sense of self-esteem. The woman homosexual, on the other hand, mistaken though she is in her belief that sexual congress with a male spells subjugation and submission, spiritual- and physical, frequently contributes to the world's welfare in some other sphere. Though all homosexuals have a tendency to make converts among heterosexuals of a younger age, the legal complications of Lesbianism are few, whereas male homosexuality leads quite generally to conflicts with the police and the law, to blackmail, suicide, and homicide. Unrecognized homosexuality is far more common among women than among men.

It is not our purpose to go into the psychopathology of homosexuality in this chapter: our purpose is to show that homosexuality is a sexual side-show, whose meaning is always a retreat from the responsibilities of normal sexual life. Homosexuality is never a disease in itself, but rather a symptom of a general retreat from the responsibilities of adult life. The male homosexual who attempts to show his femininity betrays the spurious nature of his thesis by over-doing his femininity to such an extent that his behaviour reminds us of a poor actor's impersonation of a woman, not of real femininity. The female homosexual who wishes to protect her masculine qualities is a caricature of a professional he-man. It requires a meticulous and intensive training over a long period of years, for a woman to masculinize herself, or for a man to effeminize himself. The result is always a caricature, valid only in the eyes of the one who believes that these masquerades are impressive and genuine. To normal individuals these cartoonings of sex betray their spurious nature by the very intensity of their protestations. To those homosexuals who are satisfied with their pattern of life - which reminds us of nothing so much as a piece of bad sculpture - and to homosexuals who cannot see that their homosexuality leads to the eventual destruction of their validity as human beings, we have little to offer except the hope that they will study the new psychiatric literature which is rapidly dispelling the idea that homosexuality is a congenital disease. We hope very earnestly that the shreds of remaining decency will cause them to confine their homosexual practices to others of their kind, and not to seek converts among young men and women ignorant of the truth.

For that host of other homosexuals who have unwittingly become homosexuals through the influence of vicious environmental circumstances, who find their lives unsatisfactory, who would like nothing better than to assume normal heterosexual relations, but do not believe that this can be done, we have many words of encouragement. Homosexuality can be cured, and is cured daily, by competent psychiatrists. With the spread of knowledge on this subject, and the establishment of saner legal attitudes toward this form of neurosis, homosexuality will tend to vanish from the world, just as the major forms of hysteria, so common in the days of Charcot, are practically not to be found in our clinics nowadays, or, to take an even more obvious example, as the small-pox scarred faces of the eighteenth century are but rarely met in a civilization which has learned the value of vaccination. Fifty years from to-day homosexuality will not be looked on as a congenital anomaly, but as a form of bad manners.

Sexual Athletics and the Double Standard

The progress of knowledge of human nature makes some of the more crass examples of sexual aberration impossible in our day. During the Middle Ages, when knowledge of human nature was at its lowest ebb, and the misconceptions of a patriarchal system were most obvious, chivalry and witch- hunting were the chief forms of sexual aberration. The knight who divided all women into Madonnas and whores, and considered as a witch any woman who desired to raise herself out of the slough of man-imposed parasitism by developing her mind, still has his counterpart in the "sexual athletes' of our day, whose technique may be more refined, but whose essential psychological attitudes are still those of the Middle Ages.

There are still men to-day who divide all women into those who are "bad' and those who are "good' - usually reserving the latter epithet for their mothers, sisters, and wives, and the former for all other women. Such an attitude is inconsistent with a normal sexual life. These are the men who are potent with prostitutes and impotent with their wives because they believe that sex is a bestial, degrading form of animalism. The so-called double standard is a relic of the Middle Ages and a decrepit patriarchalism. Anyone who makes these dialectic divisions of woman finds himself inextricably involved in one of the most common of all the sexual sideshows. That happiness is not to be found in this degrading practice goes without saying.

A word should be said about the increasingly common type of sexual "athlete' who attempts by the demonstration of sexual virtuosity to indicate his universal human validity. There are men who sleep with a different woman every night in the year, so eager are they to prove that they are men, and so deep and profound is their doubt that they are not. These men become masters in the strategy of approaching and besieging the female, but they are the veriest tyros at the finer art of holding the love of one woman for any length of time. The same may be said of women who see in every man a challenge to their sexual power. They develop a belligerent sex appeal, an aggressive and predatory "it' that enmeshes every stray male who comes within their reach. One contact, one conquest, and they have proved that the man can be made to fall, that he can be had. To all these men and women sex is a form of legitimate warfare in which the prize is one's sexual validity, to be measured by the scalps of the victims who have succumbed to one's sexual blandishments. The extension of these sexual athletics into the realm of psychopathology gives us satyriasis and nymphomania.

One might believe that asceticism and a life of celibacy and sexual continence were the very opposites of sexual athletics, but these apparent contradictions of sexual athletics represent psychological over-valuations of the sexual act in the economy of human life. The sexual athlete and the sexual ascetic have the same goal in life - the avoidance of complete, mature, sexual responsibilities. They vary only in the means they choose to attain their ends. In the Middle Ages, when venereal diseases were more common than they are to-day and religious ideas of the devil-possession of women were more commonly accepted, asceticism was the preferred way. To-day, sexual athletics fit the modern neurotic better, and we have more Don Juans and Messalinas than we have St Anthonys or scrawny anchorites.

Let us reiterate that fear of the opposite sex is the keynote of every perversion and aberration from the normal sexual life. Fear of adult responsibilities runs parallel to the fear of the opposite sex. This is true of the sexual side-shows as it is true of the social and vocational side-shows. In the sexual life, however, aberrations are frequently more dramatic, and more likely to lead to immediate complications; moreover, because of general ignorance of the mental hygiene of sexual relations they are surrounded with a greater air of mystery. Sexual sideshows are as simple in their origin, in their explanation, and in their cure, as the other side-shows which originate from fear and ignorance and discouragement in other spheres of human activity.

Prostitution

We have discussed the perversions and the diversions of sex. Prostitution is the best example of the conversion of sexual activity. The man who patronizes a prostitute attains the semblance of a sexual triumph, a sexual union, whereas, as a matter of fact, the only result has been a business relationship. The prostitute is the product of patriarchal civilizations which deny sexual maturity to adolescents, and place insuperable obstacles in the way of normal sexual expression and contacts to young adults. Therefore, we have the seeming paradox of a civilization that hunts down the prostitute, and simultaneously builds her brothel for her. Everyone knows that prostitution is anti-social, but prostitution must be winked at unless young adults are given the opportunities for the early choice of a mate, and the free choice of a love-object (which runs against the patriarchal grain, because patriarchal men still consider women chattels, and value an intact hymen more highly than a normal mental attitude).

From the prostitute's point of view, the sale of her sexual constitution amounts to the arrogation of masculine privileges. Often prostitution represents no more than a poor girl's desire for the finery which was denied her in childhood. She is usually frigid with her client, but allows herself the luxury of passion with her pimp. In our great cities, where morals are regulated by the police, the prostitute pays dearly for her freedom from the constraint of bourgeois morality, unless she can make her way into the 'kept woman' class. The risk of venereal infection is a constant liability in her profession, the possibility of victimization by unscrupulous police agents, the danger of blackmail, together with the tendency to drift into the shadowy by-ways of alcoholism and drug addiction (which are no more than side-shows within side-shows), make her masculine prerogatives of choosing her own mate when and where she wills, rather dear.

The only solution of the problem of prostitution lies in the education of our children to a more normal attitude toward sex, the gradual abrogation of patriarchal ideas, the support of young married couples by their parents, or even their subsidizing by the State. Such a course would be far cheaper and healthier than building institutions for prostitutes and their hangers-on. Prostitution would be impossible in a civilization where women were considered the equals of men.

Minor Conversions of Sex

The cheap dance halls, which are no more than legalized opportunities for mutual masturbation (again without risk), the publication of pornographic literature and pictures, and their patronage, are lesser sideshows about the tremendous arena of sex. Smutty stories, so dearly beloved by the hesitant male, are a further evidence of an attempt to solve the sexual problem by the substitution of an artificially prepared superiority for the responsibility of mature sexual relations.

Impotence and frigidity (commonly believed to be physiological aberrations like homosexuality) are forms of 'organ jargon', in the realm of sex. Impotence, like frigidity, answers a loud 'No!' to sexual responsibility, while the fiction of good intentions is maintained. They fall naturally into the category of the sexual neuroses.

Romanticism is the most hallowed of all the sexual sideshows. The search for the 'true' mate, the cult of the 'right' man or woman (who usually does not come along) is another way of negating the fundamental premise of sexual cooperation.

Romanticism is the sexual life of the adolescent. When practised by mature men and women it represents a narrow horizon, a high degree of subjectivity, a desire to be pampered, to be treated as a prince or a princess. It is a sign of the inferiority complex in the sexual field. There are men and women who are always unlucky in love. They are usually the men and women who do not want to love at all, and unconsciously stack the cards against themselves, by falling in love with the wrong mate. Mature men and women make mistakes in love, and tragedies sometimes grow out of these mistakes; but the large number of men and women who cultivate sexual unhappiness by imitating the tragedies that occur as a result of the real difficulties that beset human beings in the conquest of life, believe that their pseudo-tragedies excuse their unconscious lack of cooperation. One mistake in love is allowable. Two mistakes are suspicious. Three mistakes, and constant mistakes thereafter indicate unconscious bad intentions, self-sabotage, sexual defeatism.

No chapter on the side-shows of life would be complete without some consideration of drug addiction and alcoholism, piety and mysticism, gambling and the cult of luck', the search for pleasure and power as ends in themselves, the belief in superstition, and cults of the various pseudo-sciences of astrology, numerology, and spiritualism based on superstitious premises. These are vague side-shows, never referable to a single arena of life's activities, but affecting all vital conduct.

It is important, therefore, that the intelligent adult who is devoting himself seriously to the task of creative self-sculpture should understand the meaning of these side-shows the better to orientate his own life and the better to encourage those of his friends whom he finds hopelessly entangled in them.

The Problem of Narcotics

It is an admitted fact that life is not easy for man on this planet. There are problems and obstacles to our task of living happily which at times seem completely insuperable. Nature has presented man with a number of solacing devices which act as buffers between him and the stark realities of nature. Chief among these are human love and the gift of laughter, tears, forgetfulness and the soothing nirvana of sleep, dreams, and imagination; secondarily: music, poetry, and the ecstasy of the other arts. In the physical realm, fainting and coma bring relief from intolerable pain and anguish.

But man, not content with these devices, or ignorant of their uses, has gone questing through the ages for accessory agents which shall bring him quick relief from the oppressive burdens of reality. To many men the emergency relief measures which nature has provided are too slow, to others too long deferred. The more civilized man becomes, the more he becomes aware of his miseries, the more discouraged he becomes if he does not live according to the rules which have been laid down by the inscrutable forces of life, the more frequently, therefore, he seems to require immediate relief from the pain and anguish of intolerable situations. Modern medicine has secured relatively certain relief from physical pain, but mental anguish, because of its intangible quality, often defies the ordinary consolations.

In every age and in every climate, therefore, men have cultivated drugs which have hastened the solace of nature. Placed in the service of humanity these drugs are the basis of valuable anaesthetics without which modern surgery could not exist, placed in the service of deserters from the front of life, they have given rise to the curses of drug addiction and alcoholism. And there have always been panic-stricken men and women, too sensitive or too timid for this world, who have sought and abused the precious peace of the poppy, or the transient stimulus of alcoholic intoxication.

No matter how the use of narcotics and intoxicants begins in the life of the individual, their continued use is an escape from the oppressing realities of his vital situation. The morphine addict frequently begins the use of his drug to relieve pain, and continues its use until the consequent state of peace becomes a psychological necessity. In turn, the further use of morphine depresses the general functioning of the body, and leaves him less capable of meeting the realities which he has essayed to escape. The addict gradually increases the dose of the drug, as his body becomes accustomed to the initial dose and no longer responds with the same physiological euphoria.

The more of the drug he takes, the less capable of meeting his problem the addict becomes. At periods of extreme depression, he may whip himself to a false sense of superiority and ability by the additional use of cocaine, which counteracts the effects of morphine or heroin. The vicious circle is begun. Because these drugs cannot be obtained legally, the drug addict soon becomes the victim of unscrupulous pedlars who exact enormous payments for their contraband. The step to crime or to the disgrace following the discovery of the unfortunate habit is a short one. Painful periods of withdrawal of the drug are followed by succeeding depression, and again the temptation to use morphine recurs with overpowering force.

The cure of the morphine habit must be two-fold - a physiological removal of the drug, followed by a psychological treatment which removes the temptation to avoid reality and mental pain by the development of a better attitude toward life, and by training the addict in a better technique of living. The psychological cure is the more important part of the treatment.

Psychological Aspects of Alcoholism

The use of alcohol as an intoxicant and narcotizing agent is well-nigh universal. Used in moderation, by normal people, alcohol in the form of wine and beer probably has a legitimate use as a beverage, and in certain countries the use of alcohol has always been an adjunct of civilized living. In America, under Prohibition, drinking became a political football, a holocaust of crime, racketeering, and adult infantilism. Temperance can never be achieved by law - it can be achieved only by education to normal living. To run counter to this fundamental psychological law is to court the very disaster that has followed on all attempts to limit human nature by legal compulsions.

If we look aside from the national aspects of the problem of alcohol to its place in the economy of the individual, we find that the urge to abuse alcohol is comparable to that of abusing morphine and its derivatives. The unnatural puritan tradition under which all Anglo-Saxon peoples still labour prevents a normal expression of life forces in daily life. Authoritarian education develops pathological inhibitions and excesses. The 'censor' artificially developed by a stultifying tradition must be abolished if an individual is to have any sense of freedom. For repressed individuals, no matter what the source of their repression, alcohol is the Open Sesame toward personal expression. Psychologically, this expression is usually an attempt to attain an irresponsible freedom to break traditional taboos which run counter to the normal stream of human behaviour.

It is well known that an intoxicated man is not responsible for his actions. Many men and women drink solely in order to attain a state of irresponsibility and a semblance of happiness, through freedom from the chains of a constricting tradition. Excesses committed in alcoholic intoxication are often sexual because our tradition is most cruel to normal sexual expression, but often the irresponsibility is expressed in words or foolish actions. 'Oh, you mustn't mind what I said last night. I was drunk' is the excuse we often hear after an alcoholic orgy; frequently the individual conveniently forgets any irresponsible acts, inconsistent with his sober personality, committed during intoxication.

Need we explain that this irresponsibility is not real? Need we explain that drinking whisky in order to be irresponsible bespeaks a timid approach to life? Need we say that real happiness, which must originate from the conscious, calm utilization of life forces to a useful end, can never be gained by the artificial use of stimulants and intoxicants? While it is true that a man is not responsible for his actions while he is drunk, be is responsible for getting drunk. It is a cheap, and yet very ephemeral happiness, that is bought at the expense of simply checking the critical faculties at the gate, and letting go, in the semi-delirium of alcoholic intoxication.

The exaltation of the inhibited man in his cups is short-lived. When the intoxication has worn off, his sense of guilt, inferiority, and remorse is far worse than before. His first tendency is to drown this artificially heightened sense of guilt in further alcoholic excesses, and thus the vicious circle of the alcoholic neurosis is begun. Some men and women, again, drink not so much to cast off the oppressive burden of parental authority, as to escape reality. They suffer an exaggerated sense of their own inferiority, and attempt to bolster up their self-esteem by the use of alcohol. During alcoholic intoxication they feel 'as if' they were very important, very clever, very sophisticated, or very powerful. Their conversation seems to sparkle, they feel good", their sense of power is temporarily increased, and the grim problems that hover on the outskirts of their lives fade into nebulous mists.

When alcoholic intoxication wears off it is followed by a definite physiological depression. In this consequent depression the problems of reality appear in even sharper focus. The sense of inferiority is increased and the feeling of insignificance intensified. The drinker makes a half-hearted attempt to shoulder his responsibilities and to face the tasks before him. Weakened by alcoholic excesses, he fails miserably in his first steps. The whisky bottle beckons alluringly with a promise of another subjective victory, another cheap intoxication with power. The drinker forgets his resolutions, and succumbs again.

The Cost of Flight from Reality

The process is endless, and progresses to a gradual deterioration of mental faculties and physiological powers. Unlike morphine, alcohol causes definite pathological changes in the body which are irreversible. From a purely medical point of view, therefore, the alcoholic neurosis is more dangerous than morphine addiction, although the social and legal consequences of morphine addiction are usually more serious than those of alcohol.

If you find yourself in the vicious circle of alcohol or morphine, we should counsel immediate consultation with a reputable psychiatrist who understands both the medical and the psychological treatment of these conditions. Like all other devices for the evasion of reality, morphine and alcohol diminish in effectiveness the more they are used, while their toxicity increases with time. It is not the province of this book to outline the treatment of these conditions, but the writer hopes that the analysis of the psychological mechanisms at the basis of both morphine addiction and alcoholic excess will encourage those who find themselves the victims of these abuses of nature's devices to examine their life patterns and face their problems with greater courage.

Neither the chronic alcoholic nor the drug addict understands the uselessness of desertion, the inevitability of final accountings, nor his eventual responsibility for his acts. Both these habits may be permanently broken if the individual will apply himself to the task of facing reality with the same assiduity with which he has run away from it. A constructive scheme of living is within the reach of everyone. Once the constructive pattern has been initiated, the further use of both alcohol and morphine becomes unnecessary.

The basis of the use of both alcohol and morphine is an over-valuation of pleasure as an end in itself. Hedonism, as we pointed out in a previous chapter, is in itself the philosophy of the discouraged. Pleasure is not the end of life: it is an 'attribute', like happiness, of the good life. It cannot be gained by running away from life. The cult of the greatest possible pleasure with the least amount of pain, so common in our neurotic civilization, is an essentially infantile quest, as out of place in the machine age as the quest for the fountain of youth or the gold of *El dorado*.

Men and women who believe that pleasure can be gained in the pursuit of pleasure and the flight from pain are chronic believers in Santa Claus. Pleasure, gained in sport, in games, in recreation, is a necessary and important means of attaining the relaxation and renewal of energy demanded by the difficult tasks of living. Recreation, no matter in what form, is a desirable adjunct to the business of living, but it is never life itself. If you spend your life seeking pleasures, you quickly exhaust the available means of recreation. Boredom pursues you. The field of normal recreation soon becomes uninteresting, and the field of the pathological beckons alluringly. But even the pathological palls, and the only adventure left is the great adventure of Death. Suicide is the shadow of boredom born of pleasure-hunting and the satiation of pleasure-hunger. The meaning of life, significance in living, peace and happiness, are not to be found in the hedonistic side-shows.

As in the case of the drug addict and the chronic alcoholic, the pleasure-intoxicated build their lives on the mistaken notion that life is unsatisfactory and vain. This is in itself the height of human vanity. Life declares no dividends until you - have made an investment in the fine art of living. If you look at life as if it were a business, and consider it in terms of 'What can I get out of it?' you will sooner or later find yourself madly hunting either pleasure or power. The pleasure and the power neuroses are the commonest aberrations of human conduct in our present-day civilization. When pleasure and power as goals of life elude you, as they must because they are not things but qualities of the good life, you are likely to find yourself denying the validity of life itself. The gate then opens into the realms of pietism and mysticism.

St Augustine and St Francis of Assisi, failing to attain their goals of significance by profligacy and the riotous pursuit of earthly pleasures, sought the same superlative significance in saintliness and the cult of poverty and piety. These techniques cannot he recommended to modern men and women. The founder of a well-known religious cult, unsuccessful in her quest for health, took refuge in the belief that disease does not exist, and died in her paranoid belief that she was the victim of malicious animal magnetism. Her tragedy lay in her disinclination to reconcile herself with life as it is, her folly in her obstinate refusal to admit that life was other than she would have liked to have imagined it.

The attempt to escape from the inevitable responsibility for what we have made of ourselves by our own creative self-sculpture leads directly to mysticism and the allied hocus- pocus of numerology, astrology, spiritualism, and other pious forms of voodooism. No one likes to assume the responsibility for his own failures when it is so much easier to believe in luck than to put one's shoulder to the wheel and push for one's own salvation. Gambling and the cult of good luck are but other aspects of the tendency to shift the responsibility for one's shortcomings to fate and destiny.

Superstition and the belief in magic, as well as the search for a second chance in another world (while contributing little or nothing to life on this planet), together with the various theories and beliefs in reincarnation, are woven of the stuff of escape. The frantic, and tragically vain, attempts of spiritualists, clairvoyants, telepathists and others of their kind to pierce the veils of the supernatural originate simultaneously from their sense of frustration in this world and their obstinate denial of scientific data.

The cult of the side-show is evidence of a sense of defeat, as is the denial of the validity of life itself. The meaning of life is not to be found in the denial of life. Medals have never been struck for those who ran - no matter how well - from the battle-front; nor has anyone found the elusive quality of happiness in life's side-shows. The side-shows are the false goals of life, and those who pursue these false goals require special techniques to attain them. We call such false patterns the neuroses.

CHAPTER TEN:
Patterns of Failure: About Neuroses

The Neurotic Decalogue - Types of Neuroses -'Fallacies of Freudian Psychoanalysis - Adler and the Hormic Point of View - Fundamental Dynamics of Neurotic Behaviour - Techniques of Evasion - The Flight from Reality – 'Split Personality': A Neurotic Fiction - Suicide - The High Cost of Neurosis - Psychological 'Rackets', and the Cure of Neuroses - How a Neurosis is Cured - Who Shall Treat the Neurotic?

Every age and every people has its characteristic plagues. Locusts troubled the ancient Egyptians, the Black Death ravaged mediaeval Europe, syphilis spread like wild-fire during the fifteenth and sixteenth centuries, measles has decimated the South Sea Islanders, and yellow fever, until recently, has made the tropics uninhabitable for white men. The neurosis is the characteristic plague of the machine age. This insidious and almost universal condition affects every walk of modern life, nations as well as individuals, parents as well as children, capitalists as well as proletarians, intellectuals as well as morons, and you.

Although the neurosis has never been so prevalent as it is to-day, its origins are veiled in prehistoric antiquity. The first written description of a neurosis is in the Book of Genesis. When Cain answered God "Am I my brother's keeper?' he voiced a typically neurotic rejoinder and betrayed a full- fledged neurosis (as did his parents when they blamed the serpent for their disobedience). The modern neurotic who says, 'I would marry but I am afraid I shall be impotent' or his equally neurotic neighbour who believes 'I could be happy if people did not treat me so badly'; the modern woman who excuses her idleness with the statement, 'I should like to work, but you cannot expect a woman to compete in this man's world!' and her sister who believes she 'would marry if the right man came along', are all repeating Cain's words in a different form. Modern problems are more complicated, perhaps, than the problems of the Biblical ancients, but the forms of escaping the responsibilities and obligations of mature life in a grown-up world are much the same to-day as they were in Eden six thousand years ago.

The interesting thing about this modern plague, the neurosis, is that it is not, strictly speaking, a disease at all. The neurosis is an attitude towards life, and a technique of living, characterized by the fact that it is directed, always, at an escape from life and an evasion of life's problems. The neurosis is always a bad technique of living, as we shall show, because its effectiveness is limited by the harsh reality of the cosmic logic that governs men and matter. The neurosis is based, like other false techniques of life, upon ignorance of the common-sense laws of human behaviour, and upon the fear born of this ignorance. But for the general ignorance of the meaning of the neurosis, it would long ago have ceased to exist. The neurosis is one of the tragic fallacies of human life; eventually it will disappear from the earth together with the belief in magic and Santa Claus, alchemy, the geocentric universe, witchcraft, and wizardry, perpetual motion, and human infallibility, the attempt to get something for nothing, the search for the fountain of youth and the philosopher's stone.

As it is, the neurosis is the profession of uncounted thousands who seek to substitute their private logic for the inexorable logic of immemorial aeons of life and living. Its tragedy and its problem lie largely in the fact that it is a contagious disease and affects young children before they realize their danger. It is passed on from mother to children, from rulers to people, from one age to another by the written word of neurotics who wish to justify themselves not only in the present but for all time. One neurotic will infect an entire family or group with the insidious virus. One neurotic teacher can contaminate the minds of class after class of children, one neurotic book can contaminate thousands of readers, as history proves only too well. It is obvious that a civilized man should be capable of recognizing a neurotic style of life when he sees it, as he should be prepared to guard against its evil effects. Because of the widespread distribution of neurotic ideas in politics, religion, business, and education, it becomes the duty of every intelligent man to spread the knowledge which alone can remove this curse from modern life. In this sphere of life every adult can make himself useful.

How shall we define the neurosis, and what are the characteristics by which we can recognize it? A neurosis may best be defined as a style of life, aimed at the evasion of mature social responsibilities, in which an 'I cannot' is substituted for an 'I will not' by the construction of a system of plausible, often exceedingly painful excuses. The neurotic individual builds up the fiction of his irresponsibility with the help of any material that lies at hand. Every neurosis is a relative matter. Its form and content depend not only on the physical and mental constitution of the neurotic, but upon his tradition, the prejudices and ignorances of his environment, the nature of the problems he seeks to avoid, his age, and the tenor of the society against which the neurosis is aimed. Often the neurosis is an exceedingly clever and elaborate structure, comparable to the over-decoration of shoddy art. Every neurosis is a creative work. It is art, but bad art, useless art, irresponsible art.

The Neurotic Decalogue

Every neurotic trait and all neuroses have ten cardinal characteristics all of which must be present if the neurosis is valid. While it may be difficult occasionally to make a differential diagnosis between a neurosis and an organic disease, the presence of several of the ten cardinal cornerstones is presumptive evidence that the others can be found on further investigation. These ten cardinal characteristics are: (1) ignorance of the meaning of life and the value of social cooperation; (2) the primacy of the individual ego and the cult of individual uniqueness ; (3) an emotional undercurrent of fear; (4) the establishment of a subjective sense of power and security; (5) purposiveness in the attainment of the neurotic goal; (6) the substitution of 'I cannot' for 'I will not'; (7) the creation of a scapegoat; (8) the cult of personal irresponsibility for failure; (9) futility; and, finally, (10) isolation and the constriction of the sphere of activity to the bare minimum consonant with life. When we examine these ten cardinal points of the neurosis more closely we can understand the psychodynamics of neurotic behaviour and establish the unity of all neuroses.

(1) The first point, ignorance of the meaning of life and the value of social cooperation, is perhaps the clearest index of all neurotic behaviour. All neurotics are individualists, par excel- knee, and are interested in the cult of their own personality as a goal in life. The neurotic ego is the most precious jewel in the cosmos, to the neurotic. The ego must be kept intact and unbruised by the evil forces of a bad world and selfish, ignorant people. This attitude bespeaks a certain infantilism which is normal in the case of a child who has not learned to find satisfaction in the use of his powers for social good.

Egoism is natural in a child, but egoism projected beyond maturity is a neurosis. The egoistic neurotic finds little comfort in a world in which service and cooperation are the criteria of appreciation, and deduces that the world is bad, its problems not worth solving, and its opinion false and unjustified. Herein lies the basic ignorance of the neurotic. The meaning of life is to be found only when you have cooperated in the world's work, and contributed to the best of your ability to the commonweal; but the neurotic has been so busily occupied in the cult of his ego that he has not discovered this basic law of human life. If we grant the neurotic his fundamental fallacy, we must agree that the rest of his life's pattern is logical and rational. We may now frame the first commandment of the neurotic decalogue: *Thou shalt cultivate the primacy of thy ego above all the things in the cosmos. Let thy ego be the sole measure of the value of all things.*

(2) The second basic characteristic of all the neuroses follows directly on the fundamental fallacy of the primacy of the individual ego and the belief in the egocentric scheme of the cosmos. If the intactness of the ego be maintained at all costs, it follows inevitably that the problems, tasks, and activities of the objective world must be abjured and avoided. Were the neurotic to attempt the solution of the three great problems of social adjustment, vocation, and sexual fulfilment, the primacy of his ego could not be maintained. Reality and common sense would intervene and teach him that cooperation, not egoism, is essential to a happy existence.

The primary goal of each neurotic style of life is the avoidance of the objective problems and tests of ordinary life. To this end each neurosis is a purposive pattern of behaviour, logical in conception (according to the private logic of the neurosis), and rational in technique (according to the goal of the neurosis). Single neurotic traits and activities can be understood only when you understand the neurotic's objective, and once you have understood that the neurotic is attempting to maintain the uniqueness of his ego you know that he must retreat from reality and all its implications, and must substitute a system of egocentric values, private logic, special privileges, and unique behaviour for the universal values, simple logic, ordinary behaviour-in a word, the common sense of normal behaviour. The second commandment of the neurotic decalogue follows: *Thou shalt abjure and avoid all tests and problems which might detract from thy belief in the magical primacy of thy ego; Thou shalt maintain a special code of individual ethics and of private logic. In the neurotic cosmos, common sense, cooperation, and reality shall be taboo,*

(3) The third distinguishing characteristic of the neurosis is the underlying emotional undercurrent of fear pervading all neurotic conduct. Ignorance of the meaning of life causes the neurotic to exaggerate the difficulty of the problems he must solve, and isolation from the normal contacts of life robs him of a true perspective of his own value and ability. The neurotic acts as if every problem were insuperable. He compares himself constantly with other fellow human beings whom he cannot understand because he has never taken the time to identify himself with their problems. Their seeming poise and security deceive him into believing that every other man and woman is a superman, and that he, by comparison, Is an impotent and Insignificant derelict.

The average neurotic believes he is a misunderstood god, and acts as if he were a discouraged worm. This attitude reinforces his sense of worthlessness and makes him afraid to test his real powers in any objective problem. The specific problem that a neurotic fears may be determined by asking him what he would do if he were immediately cured of his neurosis. If I did not have these terrific headaches when I go into a social gathering, I would get married immediately' the neurotic will answer, thus betraying his unconscious fear of sexual responsibilities. If I could rid myself of this gnawing doubt and indecision I would open a bookshop' answers another who thereby betrays his fear of independent work. The third commandment in the neurotic decalogue is: *Safety first; Never risk an open test of your ability when you can be secure behind the smokescreen of a neurosis.*

(4) The fourth cardinal criterion of the neuroses is the establishment of a subjective sense of power and security, or the elaboration of a make-believe superiority. The neurotic's code insists that he shall maintain his precious ego on its pedestal, but the same code forbids any attempt toward the actual conquest of life's problems (which would normally produce a sense of poise and superiority). The neurotic solves this woeful dilemma neatly and effectively by the unconscious utilization of the side-show technique described in a previous chapter.

By constricting the arena of his activity the neurotic achieves the desired subjective sense of superiority or security. Instead of applying himself to the business of earning a living he takes refuge behind an unswerving belief in his constitutional laziness, If I were not lazy I could do just as well as anyone else' says the neurotic, and thereby saves his face. Instead of taking her chances in a social gathering, a neurotic young woman, suffering from agoraphobia (the fear of open places), remains secure in her well-established despotism over the small domain of the home in which she can easily tyrannize every member of her family by means of her neurosis. She avoids all tests of her value by remaining at home, and, in restricting her horizon to the four walls of her bedroom, she achieves the subjective experience of queenliness. The compulsion neurotic who washes his hands eighty times a day similarly achieves a subjective sense of power and goodness, for by comparison with him, the other human beings who wash their hands only five or six times a day are filthy swine. The fourth neurotic commandment reads: Seeming is more important than being or doing. Thou shalt make believe.

(5) A fifth, and most important aspect of every neurosis, is its purposiveness. Every neurosis has a hormic drift. It is a useful, rational, logical structure designed to bring the neurotic most speedily to the realization of his unconscious goal of super-superiority, super-security, and super-irresponsibility. *No neurosis is an accident.* No neurosis is the result of any blind interaction of instincts or 'drives'. The *purpose* of the neurosis

can best be interpreted by the observation of its *effect* on the environment. Thus the meaning and purpose of doubt, fear, vacillation, conflict, procrastination, and indecision is to avoid a test of personal validity. The purpose of homosexuality is the avoidance of mature sexual relations. The purpose of the fear of blushing is the avoidance of social responsibilities.

Every neurosis, being purposive, demands a constant unconscious training and cultivation. To this end reality is distorted and denied, and experiences, feelings, emotions, reactions are unconsciously created to order. The anxiety neurotic, whose goal is super-security, trains himself by dreaming of dangerous situations from which he awakens, shaking with fear, wet with perspiration, and reinforced with a conscious motto 'Take care! The world is dangerous!' to take care and precaution during his waking life. The homosexual man trains himself to prefer men by looking only at handsome youths, and confining his experiences with women to frowzy prostitutes or unattractive old women. Every neurosis is a profession which requires a long and arduous preparatory training. This training is transparent to the experienced psychiatrist. The fifth neurotic commandment reads: *Day and night shalt thou train thyself by thought and by dream, by creed and by the creation of moods, affects, emotions, feelings, likes and dislikes, to approach directly thy goal of subjective super-security and subjective superiority.*

(6) The substitution of 'I cannot' for 'I will not' by the construction of an apparently logical scapegoat whose existence is accepted as an excuse for failure, is the sixth fundamental characteristic of the neurosis. Every intelligent human being is dimly aware of his obligation to cooperate in the world's work. When early conditioning factors lead him to believe that he is incapable of joining with his fellows in the cooperation of social life, he must establish a set of extenuating circumstances which tend to exonerate him for his personal failure. Society knows that the sick and the lame cannot contribute as well as the hale and the healthy.

The neurotic capitalizes this fact by playing sick. This is no conscious, malicious malingering. The neurotic really believes he is ill, suffers his symptoms as much as, or more than, a really sick individual, and can usually point to very good evidences of his incapacity. He must deceive himself before he can deceive others. The leitmotiv or theme-song of every neurosis is to be found in the words 'if' and 'but'. I would gladly play the piano in public but I suffer from stage fright' says the neurotic artist, thus saving his face and demonstrating not only his good intentions but the existence of some accidental, unhappy, undesirable disability which prevents him from performing. The reader will have guessed the sixth commandment in the neurotic decalogue: *Thou shalt, in the face of problems and perplexities, establish thy good intentions and demonstrate conclusively the weakness of thy flesh to perform thy obligations.*

(7) In the seventh place we find that, in every true neurosis, some scapegoat is established. The neurotic believes that his failures are not due to his deplorable lack of courage or knowledge, or to his defective sense of humour or to his lack of social responsibility, but to the existence of this scapegoat. The scapegoat is always chosen unconsciously with an eye to its effectiveness in attaining the neurotic goal. The neurotic who seeks a unique sense of power, and finds that he is about to fail, establishes some physical ailment as the cause of his failure, and thus demonstrates his helplessness to achieve his conscious goal.

Thus a man who demands a fortune by the time he is forty, and finds that he has not made the first ten thousand pounds at the age of thirty-five, develops sleeplessness as a scapegoat. He trains himself to become a virtuoso in insomnia by tossing and turning all night in his bed. He wakes up tired in the morning and cannot go about his business with the necessary zest. If I did not suffer from Insomnia (and no drugs can cure me, because when I take drugs I sleep all night but cannot rouse myself in the morning), I should easily have made a fortune" Minor physical ailments are favourite scapegoats. But the badness and inconsiderateness of other human beings, or the actual persecution of hostile and envious competitors, compulsive habits, misunderstood character traits such as a bad temper, laziness, or impatience may also be chosen as the scapegoats. The seventh commandment runs: *Thou shalt not assume responsibility for any failure so long as thou canst find a scapegoat for thy shortcomings.*

The discovery of a scapegoat and the process of unloading all guilt and blame on its unsuspecting back, leads to the eighth tenet of the neurotic credo, personal irresponsibility and passive resistance to the obligations of the social life. Cain's query, 'Am I my brother's keeper?' serves to illustrate this point. We hear modern echoes of Cain's famous retort in the words of the hypochondriac who excuses his idleness with the words 'Can I help the fact that I was born with migraine and get headaches the minute I sit in an office?' One of my patients, when urged to go out and do a day's work, replied in shocked tones, 'But, Doctor, I've had an inferiority complex f or twenty years', as if this fact excused anyone from working.

Examine the life pattern of any neurotic and you will find that it leads by a broad highway to the limbo of irresponsibility. Obstinate lack of cooperation, in the face of an intellectual understanding of the problem, the attitude of *laissez-faire* and *laissez-aller* and, in its final form, passive

passive resistance and non-cooperation, and punishes him for his bad manners. The less society countenances the neurotic's behaviour, the more he feels justified in resisting the common-sense laws of cooperation and participation in the world's work. The consequent restriction of his mental horizon finally robs him of the very opportunities for ego-expansion which alone could vouchsafe him an objective sense of superiority.

This is the vicious circle of every neurosis. Ignorance produces fear, and fear leads the neurotic to whittle his cosmos to the dimensions of his oyster-shell. The more he restricts his horizon, the fewer his opportunities for growth and strength. In turn, this abets his ignorance and exaggerates his fear. Frantically he builds his walls about him and retreats into his self-made castle, while his subjectivity grows apace and his futility increases inversely as the radius of his activity is lessened. The ultimate limits of this process lie in the slow disintegration of insanity or in the more dramatic annihilation of suicide. The final commandment of the neurotic decalogue is: *Thou shalt isolate thyself from thy fellow-men and their problems and perplexities and thus shalt restrict thy sphere of activity to the least possible radius consonant with life.*

Types of Neuroses

After this description of neurotic patterns and their essential elements we may well proceed to the discussion of the various types of neurosis and attempt to understand why one man chooses one neurosis and his neighbour another. Neuroses have been known and described for a long time, and many Writers have attempted to explain them. The failure of all but a few modern psychiatrists to understand the neurosis is due largely to the fact that most human thinking in modern times has been under the tyrannic thumb of a causal philosophy and a mechanistic point of view. The attempt to explain the neuroses from a mechanistic angle was doomed to failure, a priori because the neuroses are purposive and must be interpreted in terms of conation, not causation.

Modern science has been frankly afraid of the conative, hot- mic, or teleological explanations of human phenomena because of their superficial resemblance to the outworn teleology of the theologians and the Book of Genesis. The difference between theological teleology and scientific teleology is very simple. The theologians say, 'an egg is smaller at one end than at the other because it is part of God's will and plan for the universe'. Scientific teleology teaches that the shape of the egg is part of its indwelling purpose - the best possible way of safely hatching young birds. Theological teleology is extrinsic: scientific teleology is intrinsic. Dead matter permits of a mechanistic explanation; but living matter, which has an indwelling purpose - to keep alive - must be judged from a teleological point of view.

The purposiveness or hormic drift of the neuroses has not been understood until very recent times, and is still not understood by many physicians. In ancient times the aberrations of human conduct were laid at the door of evil spirits, demons, or Satan himself - a purely mechanistic explanation. The treatment of neuroses, until fairly recent times, therefore, was directed chiefly to the exorcism of the evil spirits whose presence caused the unfortunate victim to err from the path of human rectitude. The unspeakable tortures that were inflicted on the victims of nervous and mental disease in the old days are common knowledge.

In due time the demonic school of thought fortunately gave way to the more modern method of describing the neuroses according to the symptoms they present, and thus attempting to understand them. Thus one set of neuroses were called anxiety neuroses because the emotion of fear together with the frantic and irresponsible activity of spiritual panic were the most noticeable characteristics of the neurotic's behaviour.

Others were called psydiasthenia, because the individual seemed actually to have a spirit too weak for the problems of this world. Aboulia, an apparent absence of will, was considered a cardinal symptom of some neuroses, and compulsive doubt the characteristic of others.

The syndrome which we know as dementia praecox was characterized as schizophrenia because the personality seemed to be split into two or more distinct personalities; another clinical syndrome was known as manic-depressive psychosis, because of the wide variation in the patient's emotional attitudes, and because of his sudden changes from exaltation to profound despair. Some neuroses were characterized primarily by aberrations in the sexual sphere, others in the social or vocational spheres. Many of our old misconceptions are hallowed in the names we still give to certain mental states: the name hysteria is due to the fact that this neurosis was believed to be due to the wanderings of the uterus, and the name melancholia is due to the ancient belief that despair was caused by an excess of black bile in the system. Valerian and asafoetida are still occasionally given to nervous patients in large doses, probably in the belief that the medicine, being more foul than the disease, may cure the patient. These are examples of the pious nonsense to which mechanistic interpretations have driven the neurologists of days gone by.

Fallacies of Freudian Psychoanalysis

Modern psychiatric concepts date from the work of Janet, Freud, and Breuer, and there is no doubt that psychoanalytic concepts were a vast improvement upon the old descriptive psychiatric classifications of Kraepelin and the German school. Although the entire Freudian theory is based on mechanistic interpretations, it has the great merit of being a dynamic, not a static interpretation of human conduct. The tragedy of Freud is comparable to the tragedy of Columbus, of a man who sets out to discover a far country with a preconceived notion of what he will find, only to discover an entirely new continent. Astonishment is mingled with disappointment, and the daring explorer dies unreconciled with his own discoveries and unaware of their extent.

The Freudian school of psychoanalysis has failed rather dismally because it fell back into the old demonic ideas despite the fact that it was the first to see the promised land. Instead of having bad little devils causing frank neuroses by their presence, the Freudians dressed up the little devils with pseudoscientific names, and called them libido, id, super-ego, censor, repression, polymorphous perverse sexuality, death-drive, narcissism, Oedipus complex, feelings of guilt, and the like.

Although Freud claims that his is a scientific method, that is, a mechanistic cause and effect method, comparable to that used in the physical sciences, no one has ever seen or demonstrated a libido, nor has anyone ever discovered or charted the limits of the unconscious, the fore-conscious, or the subconscious. Freudian psychoanalysis has degenerated into a system of demonology. Any objections to the Freudian method made by other serious investigators are promptly anathematized by Freud and his school. If you accept the teachings of Freud as gospel - and it is a very contradictory gospel - you understand them and are accepted into the orthodox fold. If you criticize, or if you refuse to accept the gospel, or point out its inconsistencies, you are told that your criticism is 'unconscious resistance'.

This device of excluding all objective evaluations of the theory and practice of psychoanalysis on the grounds of heterodoxy, leaves the structure of Freudian psychoanalysis intact against scientific assaults on its infallibility. But psychoanalysis forfeits its right to consideration as a science because by this same device it becomes a religion and a cult. What will happen to the cult when the high priest is dead, only the brave may conjecture. Even to-day no two Freudians can agree in their interpretations, but all unite in savage denunciation of the contributions of non-Freudian workers in the field.

Adler and the Hormic Point of View

Despite his mistakes, his obstinacy, his high-handedness, and his inability to accept criticism, Freud must be heralded as a great pioneer of the science of mental health, and a courageous explorer of the unknown mysteries of the human soul. But it has remained for his unorthodox co-worker, Alfred Adler, also a Viennese psychiatrist, to give us a working understanding of the neuroses, and a key to their meaning. Alfred Adler has called his science Individual Psychology. Individual Psychology bears the same relation to older psychiatric theories that Einstein's theory of relativity bears to Newtonian physics.

All modern psychiatric theories prefer the dynamic point of view to the old static classification of neuroses according to their symptoms. Adler has pointed out that the important thing to know about any neurosis is its goal or purpose, in contradistinction to older psychiatrists, including Freud, who focused their attention on its cause or origin. The word "hormic"[2], like its synonyms conation, intrinsic teleology, or Adler's own term Immanent', or in-dwelling, teleology, is applied in modern psychiatry to dynamics of human behaviour, both normal and neurotic.

To quote MacDougall[3], "those of our activities which we can at all adequately describe are unmistakably and undeniably teleological... we undertake them in the pursuit of some goal, for the sake of some result which we foresee and desire to achieve. And it holds that such activities are the true type of all mental activities, and of all truly vital activities, and that, when we seek to interpret more obscure instances of human activity, and when we observe activities on the part of animals that clearly are goal-seeking, we are well justified in regarding them as of the same order as our own explicitly teleological or purposive actions.' Adler was the first of the great modern psychiatrists to apply this hormic point of view to the understanding of the neuroses. We shall take the key Adler and other exponents of the hormic philosophy of human behaviour have given us, and apply it to the various forms of neurotic behaviour.

We may consider the neurosis as the strategy of the evasion of the complete solution of the three great problems of society,

---

[2] First used by P. I. Nunn in his Education, its Data and First Principles.
[3] William MacDougall, in The Psychologies of 1930

work, and sexual fulfilment. To understand the dynamics of this strategy we have three points to consider: the problem, the method of evasion, and the individual. From a purely dynamic point of view there are five chief neurotic patterns: the first, an assault on some special sector of the battle-front with full forces; the second, hesitation at a distance from the front; the third, a detour around the chief arenas of human endeavour; the fourth, a frank retreat from the fighting front; and the fifth, the preliminary admission of defeat, and the destruction, in part or entirely, of the self.

The reader should remember that a neurotic individual need not confine himself to any single type of these strategies to the exclusion of the others. It frequently happens that one strategy is preferred until its usefulness is exhausted or the conditions change. The neurotic then suddenly seems to change his entire character, and he emerges in an entirely different role. If we apply the hormic principle of purposive goal-seeking we can easily understand this change of front, because the goal has really not changed in essence although the means may have been modified. If the behaviour is really neurotic, we shall be able to discover that reality and its problems are evaded as much by the second strategy as by the first.

The neurotic can be likened to a gambler on the stock exchange. His steadfast goal is to make money. When there is a 'bull, market he is to be found on the side of the 'bulls'. When the market is depressed, he will be found on the side of the 'bears'. In either case his operations swell his exchequer, although his strategy seems antithetical. Let us examine the various patterns of neurosis now, in order better to realize the unity of all neurotic behaviour.

Fundamental Dynamics of Neurotic Behaviour

(1) *Evasion of reality by assault on a single sector of the battle front.* This aggressive form of neurotic behaviour is so common that it is hardly considered a neurosis any longer. It lies close to genius, because the genius differs only from the 'assault neurotic' in the fact that he approaches a useful problem in the same intense, single-track fashion. The superiority complex, so-called, is to be considered an example of the assault neurosis. The typical business man who focuses his entire energy on his job, neglecting his social and sexual responsibilities, fits into this category, as does the Don Juan who emphasizes sex to the exclusion of all else.

The super-enthusiasts, the over-ambitious aggressive go- getters, adopt this strategy as the most appropriate to their ends. We may well imagine that the assault neurotic wastes little friendliness on his fellow-men. He is too intense in his. approach to his goal. Hurry is the keynote of the assault neurosis, while suspicion, avarice, the will-to-power, the desire for great riches, for leadership, no matter of what, are its common attributes. The assault neurotic must be at the head of the line. He must be unique by being at the top, by being always the first, the best, the most famous.

If he fails in his neurosis, and cannot reconcile himself to his failure, the nervous breakdown, and that form of insanity known as paranoia, in which systematized delusions of persecution, suspicion, and misanthropy are the common symptoms, are likely to follow in his wake. The greatest proportion of 'nervous breakdowns' that occur in previously successful business men are the results of failure of this 'shock-troop' assault on a single problem of life. Underlying this neurosis is the fear of not being noticed, of being left behind, of arriving too late. Assault neurotics dream of flying or of performing herculean feats. They are the little Napoleons of daily life. Not infrequently they actually accomplish something of value, but as a rule they leave a trail of unhappiness in the wake of their successes.

(2) Hesitation at a distance from the battle-front. In this, the commonest form of neurotic behaviour, the man who has been carried along during the early part of his life by the applause and help of his parents and environment, coming face to face with reality for the first time, shrinks from the assumption of mature obligations and responsibilities, and seeks to project the inevitable solution of these problems into the indefinite future by indecision, doubt, procrastination, hesitation, time-killing, worry, solicitude over details, the cult of perfection in details, conflict, and similar devices. Conflict, indeed, is the keynote of the hesitation neuroses. The conflict is always a conflict between "good, and 'bad', between the desire to remain an infantile irresponsible egoist and the desire to taste the fruit of maturity by assuming the obligations of adult life. Conflict, however, is a psychological paradox. It cannot exist unless we assume that human beings are not unitary organisms, but vague colonies of good and bad demons. If this were the truth, we could never predict the conduct of any human being by understanding the pattern of his life. But human conduct is predictable, as dramatists, poets, prophets, philosophers, business men, and generals have known since time immemorial. It remains that conflict, real as it may seem to the hesitation neurotic, is a symptom of a neurosis and not an objective but a subjective reality.

In this type of neurosis, the individual demands excessive guarantees of safety. His principle is 'Safety first', and because he refuses to risk anything, he gains nothing. The anxiety neurosis is an excellent example of this dilatory strategy. Spoiled and dependent younger children are likely to be found in this group. The hesitation neurotic hopes that if he waits long enough, the obstacle will disappear or some *deus ex machina* will appear to solve it for him as his problems were solved for him in childhood by a fond and solicitous parent. If he procrastinates long enough it actually becomes too late to do anything. He trains himself by dreaming of the world as if it were some terrifying and death-dealing holocaust. He is afraid to live, yet, being an egoist, afraid also to die. He would like to believe in a second chance after death.

Neurotics of this type are usually worshippers of immortality and often drift into spiritualism. They involve themselves in ridiculous metaphysical tangles in their hope to find the 'right' way and in their anxiety to avoid the 'wrong'. They are inclined to be perfectionists. Without exception they believe in the philosophy of 'all - or none'. Absolute truth or absolute right does not exist in this world. Reality is an approximation, and concessions must be made constantly to the factor of the unpredictable in nature. The hesitation neurotic, however, applies himself to the rigorous absolutes of theology, or to pious subscription to other cults which promise certain success in the worlds beyond this. For this reason, hesitation neurotics are inclined to be superstitious, because nothing is so intangible, and yet so absolutely satisfying, as superstitions, dogmas, and creeds.

Melancholia is frequently the end result of the hesitation neurosis. When the problems can no longer be denied, and the neurotic realizes that it is very late, that he has thrown away the greater part of his life in wasting time, he becomes depressed, "blue', deeply discouraged, and life-weary. The end result, whether a cure by clarification, or chronic mental invalidism, or suicide, depends largely on his environment, and on his willingness to make final concessions to reality.

Techniques of Evasion

(3) *Evasion of reality by a detour of the chief arenas of human endeavour.* In some ways the detour neurosis presents some of the most interesting problems of the neurosis, because the detour is frequently so clever that no one realizes that it is one, and often it is so wide that the neurotic loses sight of his first objective and becomes completely confused by his own strategy. The detour neurotics are differentiated from the hesitation neurotics by their greater activity. They are very much occupied in deceiving themselves, the better to deceive the world. Faced with a problem which they are afraid to solve, they call attention to the necessity of doing some other apparently important piece of work. This is the "red herring' principle applied to human conduct.

The detour neurotic attempts to throw the world off his true scent. He is deserting from the battle-front of life, and wants a medal for sprinting so well. In the detour neuroses we find the flower of neurotic virtuosity. Compulsion neurotics perform miracles of concentration, application, and zeal in the perfect performance of their cramped rituals. The same amount of energy devoted to a useful end would bring them lavish praise from their fellow-men and an objective basis for self-esteem.

The conversion neuroses belong to the category of the detour neuroses. Here the 'red herring' is a physical symptom. The complex host of neurotic symptoms which drive 70 per cent of patients to their physicians belong in this category. Migraine, nervous indigestion, some forms of asthma, so-called neurasthenia and psychasthenia, a great many sexual symptoms such as impotence, frigidity, the perversions, dyspareunia and dysmenorrhoea, stuttering, neurotic disturbances of circulation, palpitation of the heart and paroxysmal tachycardia, neurotic itching, constipation and kindred disorders, and a long list of physical symptoms which cannot be enumerated in a general discussion of the neuroses, are typical conversion neuroses.

The test of the neurotic character of a physical symptom can be made in the following way: ask the sufferer what he would do if he were immediately cured of his symptoms. If his answer indicates that he would proceed more courageously to solve any one of the three great problems, you may be certain that the symptom is neurotic and represents an unconsciously created obstacle to the solution of a vital problem. Were the symptom an actual organic disease, and the patient a normal individual, he would go immediately to his physician and get himself cured in the quickest and least dramatic fashion possible, disregard the symptom, or reconcile himself to it.

Conversion neurotics can cultivate a high blood pressure, a nervous stomach, sleeplessness, a vague pain, 'nervousness', fatigue, or a supersensitive paranasal sinus, until it becomes their most precious jewel. The existence of a tendency toward any physical abnormality, such as a simple curvature of the spine, the ptotic habitus, or a vasomotor lability, is a boon to a conversion neurotic, because his abnormality enables him to make himself important not only in the eyes of his family and his doctor (who is often hard pressed to remove the symptom) but also enables him to avoid with a clear conscience the performance of his human obligations.

It is a sad reflection on the psychological insight of the medical profession that so many major surgical operations, so many unnecessary physical treatments, together with so many futile hours of examination and treatment, are worse than wasted on conversion neurotics each year. For the conversion neurotic does not wish to be rid of his symptom, and goes to the physician nor for cure, but for a confirmation and legitimatization of his illness. The more the public learns about the rudiments of hygiene, the more conversion neurotics rush around from one doctor to another for unnecessary basic metabolism tests, sensitivity tests, and blood or urine analyses. The medical profession, as a whole, has not yet learned that a sick human being is not a broken-down machine, pure and simple. Few doctors investigate the possible social meaning or social value of a symptom, and many busy specialists are so blinded by their specialization that they have not the time to ask the most rudimentary questions about the mental hygiene of their patients.

So long as physicians remain ignorant of the dynamics of the conversion neuroses, these neuroses will increase and multiply. The belief that a sound mind dwells in a sound body is one of the tragic misconceptions of our age. Most of the great contributors to human welfare have inhabited sick or malformed bodies. The perfect athletes have done little to better the human race, all the eugenists to the contrary. A sound mind may capitalize the defects of an unsound body, but a sound body housing an unsound mind is a constant social menace. Modern medicine has yet to understand fully the first law of mental hygiene: physical symptoms may have a great social value. A sick patient is not only a defective machine: he may be a discouraged human being broadcasting his inability to function responsibly in terms of an "organ dialect'. Some human beings say 'no' to their obligations in so many words. The conversion neurotic says 'no' with his sinus, his heart, his stomach, his sexual organs, his skin, his blood vessels, or any other organ that happens to be the loudspeaker of his soul.

Another form of detour neurosis is found in a preoccupation with metaphysical problems beyond the province of human thought. The detour neurotic makes the solution of these insoluble problems the condition without which he cannot proceed to the solution of more usual problems. Thus, some detour neurotics will not do a day's work until they have determined why we are here, and what the purpose of life is, while others cannot find time to seek a mate until they have determined the answer to the age-old riddle of the precedence of the hen or the egg.

If you believe there is no sense in working until you have determined whether you will inhabit the body of a grasshopper in the next world - and there is no known method of proving this contention - there is no sense in working. The detour neurotic applies the principle of lying with the truth' to the conduct of his life. Stuttering is an example. The stutterer finds difficulty in making social contacts because of his disability. He blames his disability and isolates himself farther. He is lying with the truth. It is more difficult to make social contacts when you are a stutterer, but the stutterer would not stutter if he applied himself to the task of making contacts and contributions to society, instead of cultivating his disability. He does not realize that he is the victim of a self-made 'frame-up'.

In this type of neurosis, we find the best expression of what the German philosopher, Vaihinger, called the preponderance of the means over the end. A detour neurotic finds that a test performance can be avoided if he can create the physical syndrome of stage fright. He is excused once for his failure to perform. From this time, stage fright, originally a means to an end, becomes the immediate goal of his life. By the use of imagination and phantasy, he creates images of imminent failure, and thus produces the physical symptoms of stage fright anew. In the end he is involved in the little side-show of stage fright and its production. Half the energy applied in the direction of an attempt to be useful or amusing to his audience would make the detour neurotic suffering from stage fright a competent artist.

The Flight from Reality

(4) *Evasion of reality by frank retreat from the battle front.* In this form of neurosis, the individual more or less tacitly admits his inferiority to cope with the situations of life, and breaks into an open retreat. This retreat may take a variety of forms. Many retreat neurotics flee into the make-believe asylum of childhood. As they grow to maturity and realize the nature of the difficulties that face them, they turn tail, and direct all their efforts to the reproduction of childhood conditions of greater security and dependence. They simply refuse to grow up or to relinquish their belief in Santa Claus. They remain childish playboys, irresponsible, infantile, unconcerned with the problems of reality. Pleasure, comfort, ease, and security, together with irresponsibility, are their goals. Often they develop a very charming air of helplessness which definitely announces to the rest of the world: I am a helpless child. You must do something for me.' This country is cursed with a growing host of these adult infants who refuse to grow up. Films are made and magazines written for their edification. Our whole civilization abets them in their plans. They remain incurable romanticists, and, when reality touches them, they retreat with an air of surprised and injured helplessness.

A second form of retreat lies in complete isolation from the mature, work-a-day world, and a retreat into the realm of fairy tales and phantasy. The world of make-believe is a haven to the retreat neurotic. In a sense, these retreat neurotics are perfectly justified in their retreat, because in the large majority of cases they have been inadequately prepared in childhood either to assume the burdens or to reap the dividends of maturity. Occasionally these individuals get into the business world where they become phantastic bankrupts; and frequently they are bruised in their relations to the opposite sex, which they approach as if they expected their mates to be fairy princes or fairy princesses. These neurotics often remember how, in their childhood, they spurred their childish imaginations in order to experience the phantastic apotheosis they desired by "believing hard' in the powers of some magical wand or wishing gift. When they grow up they become the most ardent champions of the power of faith to work miracles.

When this retreat from reality becomes very marked we have the clinical picture of dementia praecox. In this mental disease we have a complete retreat from reality, complete non-cooperation, negativism, phantastic hallucinations, and stereotyped, childish behaviour. Fortunately, not every retreat neurotic degenerates into a dementia praecox case. Probably some still unknown constitutional abnormality must be present for this disease to develop out of a retreat neurosis. But many retreat neurotics do become so frightened of reality that they unconsciously seek to lessen their responsibility for their shortcomings by seeming to split themselves into two or more personalities. This so-called splitting of the personality gives dementia praecox its scientific name, schizophrenia.

Split Personality: A Neurotic Fiction

No actual split of the personality can ever occur. The unity of the personality is the first law of modern psychiatry. If two or more personalities could exist in the same body, we might just as well go back to the belief that human beings could be possessed by evil spirits. The split personalities are usually divided, antithetically, into a 'good', responsible personality, and a 'bad', unmoral, irresponsible personality. The 'good' personality always loses in the end, because the result of any personality split is always a diminution of the personal responsibility and effectiveness. The belief in a splitting of the personality, like the belief in the actuality of conflict, demands a belief in the possession of the body by good and bad demons. v Such a belief would set psychiatry back a thousand years.

The scientific advocates of the splitting of the personality explanation for dementia praecox seem never to have asked the question why the splitting never results in an extension of the personality. This must be possible, theoretically, for if 'good' personality A can be submerged by 'bad' personality B when Mr X. develops dementia praecox, the more powerful, bad personality B has been held in check by the weaker personality A of every-day life during the period that Mr X. was normal.

A split of the personality, therefore, ought to result in a better personality *in some instances* according to the laws of mathematical probability, but so far as the writer knows, there is no record in psychiatric literature of such an occurrence. We must, consequently, accept the fact that a real splitting of the personality is impossible, and understand the phenomena of splitting as an unconscious fiction.

The neurotic only acts 'as if' he were a split personality in order to escape the responsibility demanded of an integrated personality. We can understand the usefulness of a seeming split in the personality when we consider that a split personality is completely irresponsible for its actions, and that irresponsibility, in the last analysis, is the purpose and meaning of every neurosis. If it were not for the fact that we can trace all the events leading up to the actual split in the personality and predict that it will occur in one form or another, and if it were not for the fact that we can see the growth of irresponsibility throughout the entire history of the dementia praecox sufferer's life, the phenomenological data might lead us to believe that such a splitting was actual and real.

The hermits and the wasters, the childish dreamer, the phantastic psychotics who believe in their own deity, the false Messiahs and the false Christs are examples of the tendency to withdraw from reality and substitute a world of phantastic ideas which offer no risk and impose no real test of the personality. It stands to reason that a man who isolates himself and retreats from the battle-front of life finally stands alone. The symbol of that aloneness is Jesus Christ or the Messiah. The truth of this contention is attested by the fact that the men and women who are facing the problems of life, who cooperate and contribute to the commonweal, are individual and unique because of the character of their contributions. But those who run away from life can run in only one direction. For this reason, all the men and women in the dementia praecox ward of a great asylum look and act alike, whereas the men on the firing-front of the world, the Einsteins, the Pasteurs, the Ivreislers, differ vastly in their appearance and their behaviour. In severe cases of dementia praecox there is a progressive deterioration of the personality leading to pitiful dilapidation. These people become veritable human vegetables, the least common denominators of human life.

Suicide

(5) Evasion of reality by the destruction of the self. The fifth strategy of the neurosis is suicide. This is the last emergency exit open to those who lack the courage to live and to face reality. The philosophy of the suicide is never a brave one. When a human being commits suicide he does so because this seems the best way out of his difficulties. That suicide solves no problems must be apparent to any normal human being, but perhaps every human being has been so discouraged at one time or another in his life that suicide has seemed justifiable. Normal men and women who are faced with problems and losses that seem to excuse suicide seldom choose this method of escape. The suicide usually betrays his real motive in the notes he leaves behind. Many a suicide does away with himself to revenge himself on the world, his parents, or the sweetheart who did not take him at his own extravagant evaluation.

A minor form of suicide is that form of neurosis which I have called self-sabotage. In this neurosis the individual cuts off his nose to spite his neighbour's face. Shell shock and the paralyses of hysteria are classic examples. Hysterical blindness, deafness, and self-mutilation are further examples. Rather than cooperate, these neurotics damage themselves to such an extent that cooperation becomes really impossible. Self sabotage closely resembles suicide in its psychological value. This last form of the neurosis is perhaps the most discouraged expression of life that exists, for it is based on the assumption that every other human being is a superman, while the discouraged neurotic considers himself the lowliest and most insignificant worm, completely incapable of success.

While the neurotic announces his hopelessness by committing suicide or mutilating himself so that he can no longer participate in the common tasks of life, he exhibits his antisocial nature by taking a Parthian shot at those he leaves behind him. If he commits suicide, he knows that the disgrace will become a permanent heritage to those affected by his demise. And the self-mutilating neurotic knows very well that society will continue to support him, and thus achieves not only an excuse for his failures, but a sense of superiority over those who are not so clever as he and must continue to work hard to give him his daily bread.

In this discussion of the psycho dynamics of neurotic behaviour we have barely touched upon a complex problem, a full description of which would require a book much larger than this volume. The reader may well ask, why, if the neurosis is always purposive and effective toward its ends, we should not let neurotics continue in their way without hindrance? We allow a man who has a wart on the end of his nose to reconcile himself to his blemish without always wanting to do something about it, even though we know that the wart could be painlessly removed and so he could be made much more presentable. Why should anyone want to be normal? Are there any normal people? And can a neurosis be cured if it is the expression of a life-long pattern? These questions must be answered satisfactorily before we can proceed to the discussion of the cure of neuroses.

The High Cost of Neuroses

We have intimated that every neurosis is a profession, but few neurotics realize the extent of the training and effort required to maintain their neurosis. We can describe the cost of the neuroses in the words of a famous advertising slogan: It isn't the first cost, it's the upkeep.' The upkeep of any neurosis is a very expensive matter. Let us take an example to illustrate the point. Mr Q., who was exceptionally small as a child, believed, in his childish ignorance, that he would never grow up to be as tall as other people. This belief troubled him greatly during his childhood and gave him an inferiority complex. He spent most of his youth comparing his height with that of his fellows, always to his own humiliation. Then, one fine day, a boy showed him how to walk on stilts, with the result that he suddenly found himself in possession of a device which would not only compensate him for his short stature but actually allow him to look down on people.

Having found this device effective in removing his sense of inferiority and raising his self-esteem, both mentally and physically, Mr Q. has persisted in the use of stilts long after his period of childhood has passed. Although Mr Q. is no longer conspicuously short, the use of stilts continues to bolster up his self-esteem. His need of this additional prop is a psychic hang-over from childhood. While he is on stilts he feels perfectly at ease, and indeed enjoys the admiration and comments of the passers-by who cannot understand his peculiar behaviour. Little by little the stilts have become an integral part of his life. They are the symbol of his security and superiority, and he cultivates them as if he were eternally committed to their use.

The stilts, however, despite their effectiveness in bolstering up his self-esteem, are very inconvenient at times. Instead of riding in the tube to his work, he finds he must pay a great deal more to ride in a taxicab, as he cannot enter the train on his stilts. He has enormous difficulties with lifts, and wastes a great deal of time walking up endless flights of stairs because some lifts cannot accommodate him. At the theatre, which he enjoys, he is annoyed by the comments and jibes of some of the audience who ridicule his appearance as he walks into the foyer on his sticks.

Certain very attractive jobs are closed to Mr Q, because his stilts interfere with the conduct of his business. Finally, Mr Q., who has tolerated the ridicule of his fellows because of the inner satisfaction that his stilts vouchsafe him, meets a girl he would like to marry, but she refuses to marry him on stilts, and he feels he cannot dismount without becoming a prey to his old inferiority feeling. Complication follows complication in his life, and eventually Mr Q. must isolate himself, eke out a bare and joyless existence, and depend largely on the mercies of his family.

Although the case of Mr Q. is a phantastic hypothetical case, the analogy fits all neurotics. Mr Q. has chosen the device of stilts because he is afraid of the responsibility of competing with colleagues who are taller. One of his basic fallacies is that short stature is inconsistent with social usefulness. The stilts become a symbol of his physical and psychic apotheosis. Their continued use becomes a point of pride, and although he no longer knows why he uses them, he cannot relinquish them. He set certain artificial conditions to life, and refuses to meet his problems in a responsible or objective fashion. But he excuses himself by saying: 'You must not expect too much of me. You see, I have to go about on stilts all the time"

This excuse satisfies some of his opponents some of the time, but eventually others appear who refuse to believe in the inexorable nature of Mr Q's compulsion, because it is perfectly evident that Mr Q. can walk on the ground like anybody else if he wishes. This leads to conflicts with society and a further discouragement of Mr Q., who bears his cross very cheerfully so long as it absolves him from competition.

In order that Mr Q's stilts-neurosis shall work, he must wear stilts at all times, for otherwise people might accuse him of bad manners or malingering, and, if they could prove their contention that Mr Q. could walk as well as they, and was really entitled to no special privileges, he would be compelled to retire discomfited from the scene. Therefore, when Mr Q. met the girl he would have liked to marry, his stilts were a great annoyance. When, moreover, he was offered a much better position in an office situated at the top of a building, whose small lifts would not accommodate his stilts, the subjective solace of his stilts became very costly. In other words, Mr Q., who chose his stilts to avoid the chance of failure in competition, and the responsibility of meeting the world on ordinary terms, suddenly finds that he is responsible to his neurosis, and that in the last analysis the responsibility to his stilts is more burdensome and oppressive than the risk of open competition.

The point in describing this bizarre neurosis is that no neurosis works for ever. You cannot fool yourself and the whole world all the time. While it is true that any neurosis effectively absolves a neurotic from certain obligations and responsibilities, it is equally true that it entails its own obligations and responsibilities which are more onerous than those which the neurotic is attempting to evade. There are only four possible ends which the neurosis can serve: (1) temporary excuse for failure; (2) protection of the ego in a psychic vault; (3) the indefinite projection of the final test of ego-value, and (4) the exaggeration of the importance of make-believe triumphs. None of these ends is permanently valuable or permanently attainable, because the neurosis is an attempt to get something for nothing. And no one has ever succeeded in getting something for nothing, or creating something out of nothing. The neurosis, therefore, is doomed to failure, a priori because it runs counter to the logic of the universe.

Psychological 'Rackets' and the 'Cure' of Neuroses

Certain neuroses, however, are more or less temporary devices of individuals who have suddenly found themselves momentarily involved in a situation which exceeds their powers of adjustment. With time, the situation becomes less dangerous, or the individual finds a better technique of meeting it. In these circumstances the neurosis suddenly becomes a useless crutch, and the neurotic searches for an opportunity to relieve himself of his encumbrance, because nothing is so annoying as a neurosis that has outgrown its purpose.

The famous healing shrines of Lourdes, the alluring blandishments of the latest fashionable health cult, whether injections of pluriglandular extracts, diet, exercise, chiropractic, yoga philosophy, or Christian Science, are all eminently suited to the needs of thousands of neurotics who require a dumping ground for their discarded neuroses. Not only Christian Scientists, but many reputable physicians and psychiatrists, gain their reputation for miraculous healing because the neurotic who has outgrown his neurosis and is ready to relinquish it because it is no longer useful, is quickly cured and inclined to be grateful. It is for this reason that psychologists without the least understanding of the meaning of neuroses obtain excellent cures by philosophically and psychiatrically unsound methods of treatment.

The patient in these cases is already cured when he consults the physician. He consults the healer because he needs an official sanction for the removal of his symptoms, and he is willing to credit the most phantastic and nonsensical procedure with his cure. The patient, moreover, is morally obliged to credit the healer with supernatural abilities in ridding him of his formerly intractable neurosis. The neurotic noblesse oblige requires miracles. This accounts for the glamorous reputations of charlatans and faith-healers of all kinds, because no patient is so grateful as a neurotic who has 'dumped' his neurosis.

Of all the false procedures for treating neuroses, Christian Science is the most widespread and the most dangerous. The working principle of Christian Science is the distraction of the neurotic's interest from his symptoms by emphasis on the non-existence of disease, accompanied by a certain measure of encouragement. The opportunity of attaining social significance at testimony meetings by the recital of one's miraculous conquest of the forces of evil and sin is not without a certain therapeutic value. The cures ascribed to Christian Science are almost without exception examples of the cure of conversion neuroses. The 'cured' Scientist says, often not without truth, that he was 'given up by all the doctors', only to be cured by reading Science and Health. Like all health cults Christian Science permits no objective examination of its 'cures' by thoroughly qualified physicians.

Christian Science is a psychological 'racket'. If it is not a 'racket' and if Christian Science is actually capable of accomplishing its avowed results by prayer and absent treatment, then the Christian Science Church stands convicted of heinous and criminal negligence for not applying its doctrines in a wholesale fashion to the over-crowded wards of our city hospitals and curing all the patients whom doctors have really despaired of helping. Instead of demonstrating its therapeutic powers in open competition with the disciples of recognized medicine, the Christian Science practitioners content themselves with infantile invectives against medical practice as if the medical profession was a colossal junta of conspirators organized to keep patients sick and suffering.

The germ of truth that exists in Christian Science is that conversion neurosis symptoms referable to almost any organ may be dispelled by encouragement. Many conversion neurotics are spoiled, pampered, and dependent children who need someone to do something for them all the time, and Christian Science fits admirably into their scheme of things. The mother Church pampers them as their own mothers used to do in childhood, and rewards them with blessings as their own mothers rewarded them with lollypops when they did not cry about a barked shin or a bruised thumb.

The Christian Science Church and the Christian Science practitioner might still have a useful place in the cosmos, were it not for the fact that the

Church makes the egregious mistake of believing and acting 'as if' all diseases and affections of the human body were conversion neuroses. Because the Church belligerently maintains that all sickness is sin and bad thinking, thousands of gullible believers go as cheerfully to their deaths as the Indian fanatics who throw themselves under the wheels of the Juggernaut. Safely ensconced behind the constitutional freedom of religious belief, the Christian Science Church invades the field of medicine and foists its lethal doctrines on ignorant parents and helpless children. Its popularity can be ascribed solely to the widespread extent of neuroses in modern life. No truly courageous, socially minded man or woman can subscribe to theories which demand, virtually, that the believer shall check all his critical faculties with his hat and coat in the ante-room of the church.

The reader will understand the necessity for attempting to cure neuroses if he understands the vicious influence of such a widespread neurosis as Christian Science. A neurosis is never a private matter, as innocuous as the wart on the end of a man's nose. The neurosis is the most contagious disease of modern society because neurotics are constantly making converts to their neuroses. In their desire to win approbation for their own desertion from the battle-front of life, they often write most attractive dissertations on the delights of running away. Tolstoy's play, The Living Corpse, is an excellent example of neurotic proselytizing. In this masterly drama, irresponsibility is so convincingly lauded that the play maybe described as one of the most subversive ever written. The contagious nature of the neurosis demands that every human being shall take an attitude against its extension. The cure of the neuroses is as much a public health problem as the disposal of garbage or the vaccination of children against smallpox.

If the reader has understood the discussion of the dynamics of the neuroses, he must be able to answer the next question: Can a neurosis be cured despite the fact that it is a habit of many years standing? The great majority of neuroses can be cured, although there are some which tax the energies and capabilities of the most qualified psychiatrist to the utmost. We must remember that the neurotic is busy with his neurosis and nothing else, day in and day out, whereas there is hardly a psychiatrist who can devote his entire energy to a single neurotic. The physical limitations of time, money, education, and health sometimes prevent the cure of a neurosis in a patient whose neurosis is still successful. If we could have three or four psychiatrists, a corps of psychiatric social workers, teachers, companions, together with a cheering section of interested onlookers, every neurosis could probably be cured. That this is manifestly impossible under existing conditions goes without saying, and accounts for the increasing prevalence of the neurosis.

All investigators agree that neuroses begin in childhood. Trained observers can detect the prototypes of adult neuroses in young infants. For this reason, the hope of the future lies in the education of parents and teachers to recognize neurotic or problem traits in children and in their cure while they are still in the plastic stage. Mental hygiene must begin with the nursing bottle. The pre-school kindergarten and the child guidance clinic are the bulwarks of the society of the future.

How a Neurosis is Cured

The last question, 'How can we cure a neurosis once it is established?' is more difficult to answer. There is no certain and guaranteed method. Some neurotics cure themselves by suddenly realizing, quite of their own insight, that the neurosis does not pay, and they then assume a normal expressive life. Others, as we have seen, 'dump' their neuroses when they are no longer useful, without ever actually curing themselves of them. Some neurotics actually outgrow their neuroses in the course of a delayed maturation. Others relinquish neurotic behaviour in the course of business or marital experiences which demand greater objectivity. Some disappear with greater economic security. Some neuroses are dispelled by insight gained through reading or study, and it is our belief in the efficacy of this method which has prompted the writing of this book. But most neuroses get progressively worse, and lead to greater and greater isolation and conflict unless some trained outsider can clarify the picture for the neurotic, redirect his energies and re-educate his point of view.

Let us compare the average neurosis with the following situation. A foreigner sets out from Paris with the avowed intention of driving to Athens. His goal may or may not be within the powers of his endurance or the dependability of his motor-car. Let us suppose that, early in the course of his journey, he misreads a number of road signs because of his ignorance of the language or of the map. On the sixth day of his journey, when he should be in Yugoslavia, he finds himself lost in the Carpathians. He tours around vainly, attempting to find a landmark which will bring him back to the road he now feels he has lost. His ignorance of the language and customs of the Carpathian mountaineers (comparable to the child's ignorance of the mature world) leads him to misinterpret as hostility the surprise and astonishment of those he asks for instructions. He becomes more and more discouraged, more and more entangled in the web of his own ignorance. This confusion and conflict is the actual situation of his resistance to common sense and logic are constant characteristics of every neurosis no matter what its individual form. The eighth commandment of the neurotic creed runs: *Cultivate an attitude of irresponsibility. Resist all attempts of thy fellow-men to foist their common sense upon thee passively if possible, actively if need be.*

(9) We are not surprised, therefore, to find that the ninth fundamental characteristic of the neurosis is its futility. No bridge was ever built, no discovery made, no human being made truly happy, no work of genuine art created, as part of a neurosis. In this respect the neurosis is like the spurious psychic phenomena of table-tapping and tambourine-tapping beloved by spiritualists - very interesting, but completely useless, Neurotics frequently become virtuosos in the art of being futile.

Thus one neurotic woman, by practice in swallowing air, created a phantom abdominal tumour, which deceived her husband and three obstetricians into believing she was pregnant - surely a futile victory. Another neurotic cultivated her imagination to the extent that she broke into a cold sweat and vomited copiously whenever she saw a cat. A third neurotic with leanings toward yoga philosophies cultivated an hysterical anaesthesia of the skin as a result of long training. He enjoyed nothing so much as allowing people to stick darning needles through his flesh and his tongue, thus attaining a subjective sense of being different at the cost of his integrity as a human being.

We have seen many claustrophobics, people who have been afraid of being shut up in a room or buried alive, but we have never seen one of them who has invented a device for getting out of a burning building or for extricating oneself from the inside of a locked vault. While the neurosis is always extremely useful to the neurotic it is universally useless to the rest of the world. *Thou shalt be futile, Let thy neurosis be graceful if possible, clever and unusual if you can make it so, but keep it thy own, and allow none to enjoy its usufructs! is the ninth neurotic commandment.*

(10) The inevitable consequences of a neurotic pattern of life are social isolation and the constriction or distortion of human horizons. The neurotic's cult of uniqueness is not countenanced graciously by his fellow-men, but social isolation plays an extremely useful role in the neurotic scheme of things. Not only does it lessen the risk, but it precludes all tests of personal validity and simultaneously heightens the neurotic's sense of self-esteem.

After one has practised seclusion and isolation for a considerable length of time, the neurotic premise, that the world is a bad place to live in, becomes true. The world very quickly discovers the neurotic's attitude of neurosis. How should we help such a man? Ten steps are necessary to clarify his way, and put him on his road again.

If we would cure anyone of a neurosis, we must pursue the following plan: (1) The establishment of the stranger's confidence in our good will. (2) The clarification of his present situation (showing him his present whereabouts on the map). (3) The analysis of his faulty technique (tracing back his course from Paris, and explanation of his mistakes early in his trip). (4) The re-establishment of the stranger's confidence in his ability to proceed (showing him that his mistake has not been fatal, and demonstrating that nothing has been lost but a little time and effort). (5) Effecting a reconciliation between the stranger and the inhabitants of the strange country in which he finds himself, and encouraging him to make adjustments to other strangers he will meet on the way (explaining the seeming hostility as a result of his own ignorance of the country's customs). (6) The planning of a new route to his destination (where necessary this may include a change of destination when the destination lies beyond his powers or the capacity of his car). (7) Instruction in the art of reading maps in order to make him more independent and to preclude the repetition of mistakes. (8) Encouragement to proceed undismayed by his former failures. (9) Encouragement to share his trip with some other traveller who has a similar destination. (10) Instruction in the nature of some of the beauties that lie off the direct path, and encouragement to visit scenes that the stranger did not realize existed (development of artistic or creative abilities, and the extension of horizons).

Who Shall Treat the Neurotic?

Those who would direct strangers require a certain constellation of qualifications. They ought to know men and machines, they ought to know the map, they should have had the experience of being lost themselves, they should be good teachers, friendly and happy human beings themselves, and, above all, they should have learned patience and humility in the face of obstacles and resistances. The best guides, therefore, would be men and women who were physicians, men and women who had themselves made mistakes, who had been lost and found their way back to normality. They should possess the maximum possible knowledge of human affairs and human history. To be effective, they should know something about all the arts and be well grounded in all the sciences. They should be good teachers, patient, courageous, open-minded. Above all they should be secure in their own adjustment to reality. The ideal person to cure a neurosis is a physician who has cured his own neurosis, a scientist who is an artist in his science, a happy man who has been unhappy, % courageous man who has been perplexed and disheartened. A great deal of mischief has been done by misguided individuals who approach their neurotic patients in the same spirit as the undergraduate, who, having been tagged himself, and graduated from freshman humiliation, wreaks his sadistic impulses on the freshman. Psychiatrists can be classified in two groups: those who have been in trouble, and are finding their way out at the expense of their patients, and those who, having been in trouble, have found a technique of extricating themselves, and are happy to share their knowledge with others who still find themselves in the neurotic morasses.

The better psychiatrists discount their own apparent authority and their own apparent security. They seek to minimize the differences between themselves and their patients. Their attitude is: 'Under the same circumstances, I should have done exactly the same thing. How can I clarify this man's position for him and help him out of his difficulties?' The good psychiatrist, seeing a neurotic patient, says, 'There, but for the grace of a little courage, go I.J Indeed the ideal attitude for those who would cure neuroses is not so much one of doctor and patient as that of a friendly teacher and his pupil.

This chapter should not be closed without a friendly warning. There is no human being who does not have this or that neurotic trait. We are all neurotics, for normality does not exist except as an ideal limit of human behaviour. The reader is urged not to label himself a neurotic because he finds one neurotic mechanism in his life. It is not the function of mental hygiene to make angels, but to prevent flesh-and-blood human beings from crippling their activities and plunging themselves into wholly unnecessary unhappiness. Our purpose in this book is solely to demonstrate the art of transforming major mistakes into minor aberrations, of avoiding useless pitfalls, of minimizing tendencies which if unchecked lead to the asylum and the mortuary.

Anyone who understands the dynamics of the neurosis must realize that the cure of any neurosis consists in education, the extension of mental horizons, the development of greater human sympathies, and the encouragement to face obstacles in reality. No neurosis is inexorable. There is no cause for any neurosis except the cause the neurotic chooses to blame for his shortcomings. Given an understanding of the neurosis, the desire to find a better way, and the encouragement of one other human being (even if indirectly through the written word), and anyone can modify or minimize his neurosis. There is no situation, either in the heredity or the environment of any individual, which can compel him to be neurotic. These hereditary factors and these vicious environmental conditions can explain the genesis of a neurosis, but they cannot maintain it in the face of the desire to get well. Anyone who is human can attain a degree of normality consistent with happiness.

CHAPTER ELEVEN.
Patterns of Cooperation: Love and Marriage

Some Causes of Marital Infelicity - Ignorance as a Cause of Marital Disaster - Marriage as a Task - The Socialisation of Sex - The Vital Role of Contraception - The Curse of Sexual Competition - Historic Origins of Our Sexual Morality - Syzygiology v. the Old Psychology - Androtropism and Gynetropism - Sex Appeal and the Dangerous Age - Tragedies of Sexual Competition - The Cancer of Romantic Infantilism - The Romantic Fallacy - Romantic Hocus-Pocus: Falling in Lope-The Aftermath of Love at First Sight - Mature Lope v. Romantic Love - Practical Suggestions.

The finest expression of the art of creative self-sculpture is exemplified in love and in marriage. Love fosters not only the expansion of the ego, but also the fulfilment of that precious feeling, inherent in all human beings, toward a member of the opposite sex. Love's responsibilities and obligations are concomitant with love's unique opportunities for personal development. Just as the fulfilment of the ego is a fundamental ingredient of a happy love life, so also the altruistic conduct, implicit in a relation which requires a maximum of self- confidence, objectivity, social responsibility, and above all, a well-developed sense of humour, is indispensable for the consummation of true love. It is no wonder therefore that more human mistakes are found in the realm of love than in any other sphere of human activity, and no wonder that the neurotic most commonly shipwrecks his life on the reefs of matrimony and the shoals of Eros.

Mistaken conduct in love and marriage is so common that it is a rare , human being who knows ten completely happily married couples, while the man or woman can hardly be found who does not know intimately some unhappy and mis-mated couple, who has not been compelled to listen to recriminations and incriminations from those who find love not a path toward peace and harmony and the development of the spirit, but an intolerable cross which not only burdens the flesh but cripples and distorts the spirit. To be sure, all happily married couples take their sexual happiness as a matter of course, just as those who have good digestions do not announce with a fanfare of trumpets the fact that they have just been able to digest their supper. As soon as there is an unhappy marriage, there are two human beings who wish to justify and excuse themselves for the failure of their cooperation. While our newspapers shriek the unhappiness of love to us from their headlines, there are, nevertheless, many human beings who find the most innate satisfaction of their lives in their love relations and in the institution of marriage, no matter in what form nor in what social stratum it exists. While the ratio of unhappy love affairs and loveless marriages to successful and happy marriages cannot be computed, the existence of good marriages and happy love cannot be doubted.

And of the unhappy love lives this may be said: the great majority are due to avoidable causes. To the discussion of these avoidable causes of sexual discontent we must give our attention, and we propose the novel method of analysing the unhappy marriages and the broken love lives, not according to any moral or traditional criteria, but as if they were unsuccessful experiments in the living laboratory found in the mental hygiene clinic and the psychiatric consultation room. From the examination of these failures we shall attempt to deduce certain general laws of conduct which may be of use to those who feel their own love fading, or those who are about to embark upon this most thrilling of all human cooperative ventures.

To begin with, we should sketch the essentials of a happy love life in order to orientate ourselves in the evaluation of the unhappy and unsatisfactory marriages we find in every social group. But we are immediately faced with an insuperable problem. There is no definite norm of happiness in

marriage, nor any absolute law which governs human relations in this most artistic of human enterprises. There are men and women who are happy in a love life that would appal and dishearten other men and women. Some couples are completely happy without children, others are dejected and depressed because children are denied them. Some married couples thrive on poverty, while others' loves are destroyed by purely economic factors. Physical opposites often lead to happy sexual unions, and as often to unhappy ones. Not infrequently, factors which are recognized but minimized in the beginning of a love relation become increasingly important with the passage of time. Many a couple that is profoundly happy in the beginning becomes unhappy eventually simply because human beings grow and develop, spiritually and mentally, at varying rates.

There are certain fundamental prerequisites to a happy marriage: both partners in a happy love relation should possess an objective sense of self-esteem, a well-defined social feeling, and both should be completely free of any neurotic striving for prestige at the expense of the opposite sex. Mental maturity, physical health, and psychological independence in outlook, a knowledge of the art of love and the practice of contraception are important premises of a normal sexual life. A mature sense of social responsibility, the willingness to make concessions to reality, freedom from neurotic traits (including any tendency toward romantic idealism), a wide and catholic range of human interests, and the willingness to grow, to cooperate, to suffer sometimes, and to share always the disappointments and the joys of life - these are the foundations of success in the solution of the love problems of every-day life. The willingness to encourage, the ability to identify oneself with the situation of the sexual partner, help one over the usual obstacles, especially when these qualities supplement the possession of some socially valuable occupation, and, if possible, of some common avocations. Financial independence, religious accord, social equality, and freedom from neurotic relatives, while not essentials, help immeasurably to cement the ideal sexual union. Some Causes of Marital Infelicity

There are manifestly very few human beings who can approach the love relationship with any such ideal equipment. When two human beings love each other they love not only each other but also the imponderable facts of their entire backgrounds and traditions. The absence of some of these desirable fundamental prerequisites is not in itself a bar to a happy marriage, because love and marriage are not fixed but movable patterns. Like the human body, the sexual community of two lovers is elastic in its possibilities of compensation. Many a couple that one might expect to be completely unhappy because of the absence of some fundamental prerequisite has managed to carry on for years of average happiness because of the mutual interest of both lovers in their children, or because of their cooperation in some social problem, ambition, or avocation. We have seen couples who seemed at first sight doomed to complete failure as lovers, held together by the bonds of music, a love of horses, or a devotion to a particular cause.

An amazing number of men and women choose their sexual partners as a road-maker would choose rocks to fill up a temporary hole in a road. Men expect their wives to be the complete compensation for their own defects and inferiorities, and women choose their husbands for similar false reasons. For this reason, we find apparently insane matches between brutal men and 'clinging vine' women, between aggressive, masculinized women and effeminized gigolos, between independent and courageous men and helpless and stupid women, between athletic, physically vigorous women and dried-up bookworms, and so on. There are men and women who seek marriage with a certain mate because such a marriage offers an opportunity for quickly filling in gaps in their own personalities which they have been too cowardly to develop for themselves by adequate training, as if marrying an individual who has the desired qualities ready-made were a magic device designed for the quick acquisition of the goals they had failed to attain.

The love relation can never be more than an opportunity for mutual service and encouragement. Far from being a magical panacea, the marriage relation is a task to be fulfilled during the course of years, a task not to be accomplished by any magical flourishes of an invisible wand, but by work and sympathetic cooperation. Men and women would be far happier if it were harder to get married, and easier to get divorced. We wish there were some test of social courage and cooperation which could indicate the willingness and ability of each partner to merge his ego for the common good of the marriage. Happy marriages result most frequently where both partners look at their love life as an opportunity for fulfilling a social contract, which, despite difficulties inherent in its very nature, it is possible in the majority of instances to carry out effectively and well, and to the mutual benefit of the contracting parties.

All too often, men and women who would be careful and discriminating, nay, hard and matter of fact about the purchase of a car or the choice of a week-end excursion, marry for thoroughly inconsequential and childish reasons. There is hardly a reader of this page who does not know a woman who, while willing to spend an entire day in the choice of the material for a dress that may last a season, is perfectly willing, to marry a man because he 'dances divinely and mixes such good cocktails'. We have seen men who would stalk a business adversary for weeks and lie awake night after night planning to make a profit of a single halfpenny, marrying a girl because of her well-turned ankle or her good complexion. It is not at all uncommon for a girl to marry a man out of spite, because she has failed to wrest a proposal from the first man of her choice, while otherwise intelligent and rational men have married their typists or chambermaids for no better reason than those of convenience or contiguity.

The natives of Thuringia in the Black Forest of Germany have an excellent device for testing the mutual cooperation of two people who desire to marry. The prospective bride and groom are escorted by their friends to a large fallen tree in the forest, given a huge double-handled saw, and told to saw through the tree trunk. Differences in strength and size must be nicely adjusted in this communal activity, and the friends of the betrothed pair prophesy their happiness according to the speed, despatch, and ease with which the lovers accomplish their task. There is no such simple device for city dwellers, unless it be the packing of a trunk or the unravelling of a tangled and knotted cord. We can judge of the success of any marriage solely by the examination of the past performances of the contracting individuals, with respect to their cooperativeness and social responsibility.

But, when we examine the broken marriages and the unhappy loves, we learn very definitely that most of the avoidable unhappiness in marriage is due to three great causes: (1) ignorance of the physiology and art of love; (2) competition for prestige between the sexes; and (3) infantile romanticism in the approach to the problem of choosing and living with a mate. One of these factors is almost certain to be present in any unsuccessful marriage, and frequently more than one is an active determinant of the marital disaster. We shall do well to examine in greater detail these three great groups of vicious determinants of sexual maladjustment.

Ignorance as it Cause of Marital Disaster

Let us consider ignorance of the physiology and the art of love first, because it is the least excusable of the three. Sexual ignorance, bred of the Puritan tradition under which we still labour, is one of the chief factors in the production of unhappy marriages. This patriarchal tradition is very insidious, because it poisons official as -well as unofficial sources of information, and effects its nefarious influences very early in our lives. Our whole system of education is permeated with the underlying fallacy that sex is something vaguely sinful and bestial, concerning which we should be decently mysterious and silent.

Even in the best circumstances there is an air of solemn pedantry about telling young children the so-called facts of life. Parents who are objective in nearly every other way hesitate to explain the simple mechanics of love and reproduction to their children, and teachers who could fulfil this function are constrained from being objective by fear of hurting the parents' feelings, while doctors, who are perhaps the best suited, after parents, to enlighten the young as to the nature of sex and love, are either too busy or too inarticulate to do so.

We are taught how to walk, speak, shake hands, dress ourselves properly, from the beginning of life. Soon we complete the first stage in our school education and are taught social graces, manners, the art of driving a car or playing golf. Technical information in the complicated business of earning a living is given us without stint, and usually with a great deal of skill. But there is hardly a man or a woman to be found who has ever been taught how to be a good lover, a good husband, an effective wife, or an amorous sweetheart by an expert teacher.

The paradox of our modern life is that we swamp our children with sexual misinformation, with a veritable torrent •of pseudo-sexual novels, pornographic newspaper articles, and more or less lascivious films and plays, which serve only to stimulate normal sexuality to an exaggeratedly high pitch. At the same time, we withhold really valuable information on sexual subjects from young and old alike by investing the whole theme of sex with a cloak of mystery, secrecy, and filth.

At the time a girl is led to believe that her only salvation in life is to be found in marriage and the building of a home, most useful information about sex is withheld from her and all experimental preparation for this task is made taboo. Ancient and outworn concepts still obtain a stranglehold on the mental processes of the average man. The great majority of 'nice' girls still value an intact hymen more highly than the courageous solution of their love problems. The majority of men believe that their masculinity is jeopardized if they are not the sole breadwinners in their homes. The average man still believes that woman's place is in the home, and harbours a lurking suspicion that women are second-rate men.

Ignorance of sexual and personal hygiene is still widespread. Men and women who think nothing of taking lessons in bridge, golf, or lampshade making, are content to leave love to nature despite the fact that literature is full of instances of unhappiness because of ignorance in the art of lovemaking. Because of the prevailing taboo against sexual intercourse with girls of one's own class, young men are forced by the traditions of a patriarchal civilization to find sexual solace with prostitutes. When they marry a 'nice, respectable' girl they know only the furtive and obscene technique of the brothel, with the result that their own impotence or the inexcusable humiliation of their wives results.

Other men and women who take the taboos of society seriously, wait until they have attained the age of thirty or thirty-five, and then marry without any previous sexual experience, often ruin their married lives by their own clumsiness, self-consciousness, and ignorance of the simple mechanics of sexual intercourse.

Marriage as a Task

The situation in our civilization is as if a man were told from the earliest days of his youth that if he wished ever to attain social significance he would some day have to build a bridge across the Mersey, only to have all information about bridges, materials, engineering, and architecture hidden from him until the day that he was to begin building his bridge. We may well understand the perplexed quandary of young people who are either forced into marriage by their parents, or assume marriage voluntarily in complete ignorance of its implications. Misuse of marriage as an institution is simply another aspect of mankind's ignorance of its meanings. There are many young men who mistakenly marry because of the opportune licence to indulge in sexual relations without let or hindrance, while as many young women mistakenly marry as if marriage in itself were the complete solution of all their problems.

Marriage is both a task and a contract whose solution and fulfilment require long and assiduous preparation. Tackling a major problem can never be the solution of a minor problem. You cannot cure neurotic traits by marriage, because love does not grow well in neurotic soil, and if the contracting parties are neurotic, marriage intensifies rather than minimizes their difficulties. Women who marry simply to make sure of someone to provide their meals for them generally get just what they have bargained for, but, in the great majority of instances, bitter bread is their fare. Men who marry in order to have a convenient and inexpensive substitute for a combination nurse and housekeeper, get just what they want - at best a faithful slave, at worst a nagging kitchenmaid who makes their lives unbearable because of her insistence on the importance of trivialities. Some women marry the first attachable male simply because they desire freedom from the solicitude of parents, only to find, in a day or a year, that they have married a man and not a pair of wings, a human being and not a mode of escape from their difficulties.

Similar cases of ignorance of the meaning of marriage could be duplicated without end. In all of them the same basic fallacy, that marriage is a cure or an escape from this or that intolerable situation, can be found at the bottom of the subsequent failure. It is in marriages in which the true nature of the marriage contract has never been understood that we find the conversion neuroses of dyspareunia, sexual incompatibility, frigidity, and impotence growing like rank weeds. But so long as we learn about love from the sentimental novels written by frustrated spinsters or amorous but impotent bachelors, and so long as we educate our children to believe that they must wait for the fairy princess or the fairy prince to arrive at the psychological moment and make everything happy on earth as it is supposed to be in heaven, we shall be faced with an increasing percentage of unhappy marriages.

One of the greatest sources of unhappiness in marriage is ignorance of contraception and contraceptive techniques. The love relation between civilized men and women is not the simple biological affair that it is among animals. Every love affair has not only biological but also social, intellectual, economic, educational, civic, political, and occasionally religious ramifications. If marriage were simply a biological problem, and if human beings mated, like animals, simply for the purpose of carrying out a vague biological urge to procreate - a belief still held by certain religious sects in contravention of all common sense and scientific facts - its solution would be as objective and simple as it is among rabbits and guinea pigs.

The Socialisation of Sex

But there are certain fundamental differences between men and other mammals. For one thing, the human female is the only mammalian female that will countenance sexual intercourse at any other period than the rut or menstrual period. This single biological fact is the origin of many human sexual problems, because it alone takes marriage and love between men and women out of the realm of the purely biological and puts them definitely in the realm of the social.

Like many another simple biological urge or reflex, sex has been taken out of the sphere of the biological and diverted into the realm of the purely social. We have repeatedly demonstrated man's fundamental need for a social life, and this fundamental need has changed the meaning of many primitive biological urges or instincts. This process of redirecting biological drives into social channels has been variously called hormic reconstellation, conative reconstellation, or emergent evolution. The hormic reconstellation of so primitive a need as the urge to eat in order to keep alive, has been reconstellated by the necessity of closer social bonds into such purely social manifestations as tables, knives, forks, and spoons, glasses, table decorations, table manners, and the like. Eating in civilized society is as much an occasion for social intercourse as for the nutrition of the body.

Similarly, clothes, at first a compensation for man's nakedness and the means of effecting a purely biological attempt to protect the body, have become instruments of social defence and offence, of social intercourse. Surely a lady's lace evening gown and a gentleman's white tie and silk hat have little to do with man's primitive need for bodily protection. They have suffered a hormic reconstellation under the influence of the social need. The need for closer social relations has similarly given us art and literature as hormic reconstellations of the original need for communication, while plumbing, skyscrapers, newspapers, life insurance, sports, and a host of other everyday activities can be analysed as hormic reconstellations of biological activities instinctively carried out by our anthropoid ancestors.

The complexity of modern civilization with its tendency toward specialization, decentralization, and depersonalization of all human effort, has effected a radical change in the meaning of sexual activity in the economy of man's life. We can imagine primitive man mating in blind obedience to a primitive and unconscious biological urge to procreate. In early savage societies the communal activities of hunting, hut building, warfare, dancing, and other social activities gave the savage a sense of meaning and value in life. In the early civilizations, with their emphasis on individualism, opportunities for finding social significance were even more plentiful.

But with the increase of power, machinery and the depersonalization of human labour, the rise of mass dwelling-places in our large cities, a tremendous need arose for a more immediate circle of human beings toward whom a man could feel his personal obligations and from whom he could reap the rewards of his personal labours. A tendency to find social values in the sexual union, the only profound human relation that may really be said to exist for the average man of to-day, has consequently grown in civilized society.

The exceptionally civilized human beings whose social connectedness has grown with the complexity of their civilization, do not sense this need so poignantly as the worker who finds but little value in his daily job, and surely no glory or significance in filing reports or in selling underlinen. As this need for more intimate social relations has grown, the tendency to reconstellate sexual intercourse from a purely biological hormic pattern into a personal hormic pattern is so universal that in our present-day civilization it is far more common for men and women to practise sexual congress for their personal satisfaction and for the establishment of a closer social accord, than for the primitive biological need of procreating children for the maintenance of the race.

The biological consequences of sex, however, are just as important as ever in the history of mankind. Sexual union leads to impregnation and childbirth to-day just as surely as in the days of the cave-man. These reproductive consequences of sexual congress must be avoided in the majority of the instances in which civilized human beings cohabit sexually for purely social ends, rather than as animals for purely biological ends. If the personal hormic pattern is to be carried out successfully the biological consequences of sexual cohabitation must be avoided.

The Vital Role of Contraception

No woman can afford to be ignorant of modern contraceptive methods if she is to lead a civilized life. The price of this ignorance is tragedy multiplied by tragedy, as the records of any society for the spread of birth-control information can eloquently attest. The modern woman does not practise sexual congress merely for the procreation of children, and she is not in a position to deny herself to her husband except in those circumstances where children are desired. The economic difficulties of our age militate against the large families of yesteryear. That children cannot be brought into this world at random by responsible parents goes without saying.

The more oppressive the economic problem and the more complicated our civilization, the greater is the necessity for a volitional control of offspring. Civilized human beings have children when they desire them, not accidentally, as a result of wild and irresponsible sexual congress. But the very factors that make the limitation of offspring to children of choice desirable, make the sexual relation, as a means of social congress, revivification, and relaxation, more indispensable. Hence the importance of contraceptive knowledge to every adult human being.

Ignorance of contraceptive methods is a potent cause of sexual unhappiness, love tragedies, and broken homes. Because this ignorance leads to psychic reservations and to psychic inhibitions, it spoils those very moments when men and women are capable of experiencing the most profound of human sympathies and the most encouraging of human experiences.

In countries that depend on warriors for their power, any limitation in the number of children is not only a limitation of cannon-fodder but also a threat against the hierarchy of masculine prerogatives, and therefore taboo. But in a country that depends for its security on the happiness of its inhabitants and on international cooperation and peace, whose population is one of choice, conceived in love and nurtured in responsibility, the limitation of offspring by the conscious control of conception is as self-understood and self-explanatory as plague control and public hygiene.

No individual, moreover, can expect any great happiness in his love life if his acts are likely at any time to cripple his economic situation, or oppress his mate or his community with intolerable burdens. The psychological effects of being an unwanted child we have already described in our chapter on the growth of fear. The tragedy of ignorance in-sex and sexual relations is that it affects not only the ignorant but all those in their environment. Like the neurosis, ignorance is a contagious disease, nowhere so fatal in its consequence as in the realm of sex.

The Curse of Sexual Competition

The second great cause for sexual maladjustment is competition between the sexes for prestige and power. This competition exists in a very marked form to-day, and is in part the outgrowth of the movement for the emancipation of women from the tyranny of a dominant male sex. Whatever value may be ascribed to competition as a life-giving force in the business conduct of an individualistic society, competition is the death of love, and the hidden reef on which many a marriage has foundered.

We have good reason to believe that this competition is a matter of considerable historical antiquity, and is coeval with the rise of private property and the coincident rise of a patriarchal society based on the dominance of the male sex. We are still living in an age in which the male sex rules and makes rules for the conduct of the female sex. Until most recent times certain professions and vocations were open only to males, and, even to-day, important positions in the government and in private business enterprises are openly or tacitly denied to women, and far greater obstacles are placed in the way of women's efforts than are placed in the way of men who desire the same goals.

It is characteristic of any society in which one sex Is dominant and the other subordinate, that all the useful virtues are arrogated to the dominant sex, and the vices usually ascribed to the subordinate sex. Thus, virility, courage, intelligence, responsibility, resourcefulness, honesty, are the virtues which men consider more, or less their prerogatives in our society, whereas women have to content themselves with the petty virtues of chastity, modesty, gracefulness, sensitivity, intuition, and the like which are palpably designed to set off the virtues of the dominant male to the highest degree.

A woman should be chaste so that her male may appear as a deliverer and saviour; she must be modest so that his courage may stand out to better advantage; she must be home-loving so that his occupational exploits may appear the nobler, and so on. Furthermore, such traits as gossip, irresponsibility, dependency, impracticality, nagging,' treachery, infidelity, and the like are considered in many circles the prerogatives and constant characteristics of the female sex. The adjective 'masculine, has a universally good connotation, whereas the adjective 'feminine' as it is usually applied implies weakness and inferiority. When a man fails, it is because he has unfortunately acquired womanly attributes, but when a woman makes a signal success it is because of the existence of 'masculine' or 'virile' qualities, i.e. she is no proper woman, but a man in woman's body.

The extent to which the female sex has been maligned throughout history by the dominant male can be conceived only when we recall the Biblical legend that the fall of man, and his expulsion from the Garden of Eden, were due to the wickedness and weakness of woman. The age-old depreciation of woman is to be found, moreover, in the fact that woman was supposed to have been created secondarily, to ease Adam's loneliness (as if she were an afterthought of God), out of an unimportant part of Adam's anatomy. St Paul, with his famous dictum that 'it is better to marry than to burn', expresses the typical patriarchal view that woman is a necessary evil.

The Church has been the worst enemy of womankind throughout the ages. Women who rose above the universal slavery of their sex, and developed any wit or sagacity, were immediately branded as witches and persecuted as if they were possessed of devils. The philosophy underlying the centuries of witch-hunting and witch-burning was manifestly: how can a woman show any signs of intelligence unless she is possessed of the Devil?

Perhaps a majority of adults still believe in the fiction of the inferiority of women, and the great majority of children are impregnated with this falsehood in the early years of their lives. Few men know that large sections of the earth's crust are inhabited by people who regard women as the dominant sex, and fewer people are aware that, only a few thousand years ago in the highly developed agricultural civilization of early Greece and Egypt, matriarchy was in force, and women ruled the world much as men rule the world to-day.

Few people realize that, in ancient Egypt, the child derived its name from its mother rather than from its father, that older women married younger men, that men had to be chaste before marriage, whereas women were allowed a double standard; that a man had to bring a dowry to a marriage, and a woman had to swear to support her aged parents and those of her husband; that men used cosmetics, changed their fashions every season, and remained at home to watch the pots and pans, while their women-folk were out running the business of the day, wearing the same tunic year in and year out, abjuring cosmetics as inferior, and even laughing at their husbands for their gossip and pettiness.

This proves that there is no such thing as a masculine trait or a feminine trait, as such, because the roles have been completely reversed in historical times, and are reversed in every purely agricultural culture even to-day. What we call 'masculine' really signifies 'belonging to the dominant sex', and what we term 'feminine' means 'belonging to the submerged sex'. That the present prejudice is not natural is to be deduced not only from history and archaeology, but also from the fact that if the inferiority of women were a natural truth, no laws would be needed to keep women in their place, and no age-old conspiracy would be required to prevent women from ever regaining their former high position. We do not need laws to prevent idiots and imbeciles from becoming judges, and we need no legal devices to prevent a feeble-minded child from becoming Prime Minister.

Historic Origins of our Sexual Morality

How the change from matriarchy to patriarchy came about we do not know exactly. One thing we do know, and that is that the change was coincident with the rise of private property, and the change from an agricultural, communal civilization to a herding, individualistic civilization based on private property. When the first man took a mountain goat and domesticated it; when the first horse, cow, camel, or sheep was tamed to man's uses; and when the first man built a fence around a piece of grazing acreage for his own flocks, private property was born. Men and women can participate equally in agriculture, but the superior strength of men is an advantage in the control of herds and flocks. And these flocks gave man his superiority, because it is a sociological law that the sex which is predominantly concerned with obtaining the means of subsistence, becomes the dominant sex, and rules the other sex to its own purposes.

While it was of little import to know your own father in matriarchal civilizations, with the rise of private property every father needed to know his own son so that he might be certain that his own flesh and blood would inherit his hard-won flocks and hard-kept acres. With this change, that unimportant piece of tissue, the female hymen, attained a sociological value. A man must marry a virgin to know that the result of his first intercourse with his wife would be his own child.

Thus began the exaggeration of the value of chastity and modesty – obviously of no advantage to women, but of great advantage to men who desired to retain their patrimony intact. Thus also began the over-valuation of the male heir, and the under-valuation of the girl child. Thus began the concept that women were chattels, like so many heifers, to be used by men in bargaining for greater docks and more grazing ground for them.

At various times in the history of human culture, women have rebelled with greater or less success against the imposition of a man-made slavery. But so long as the essential economic situation remained unchanged; so long as women were not equal to men in the production of the world's goods, women had little chance of real emancipation. True, the microscope, that first great emancipator of women, proved conclusively that women were the equivalent of men, that nature had divided their toll, that neither male nor female was more important in nature's scheme, that both contributed equally to the production of the new-born child.

But it was the machine that initiated the final emancipation of women, because the more complicated the machine, the more women were capable of competing with men in the production of the world's goods. We can really date the emancipation of women from the nineteenth century, therefore, and despite the obstacles placed in the way of this emancipation by men desiring to retain their age-old prerogatives, that emancipation marches on, until to-day only a few fastnesses in the fortress of man's ego remain to be conquered by women.

When we look at our animal neighbours we find their sexual life highly cooperative. Such a thing as a conflict between stag and doe is unknown, however much two stags may compete for a doe's favours. Competition between the sexes is definitely a product of the overgrowth and over-function of man's brain. Sexual competition is a distinctly human vice, a product of man's mistaken interpretation of his place in nature, a result of a profound inferiority complex which leads him to seek a scapegoat for his own shortcomings. Historians of the future will no doubt refer to the present age as the epoch of the death struggle between patriarchy and some new form of marriage based on sexual cooperation. Our age will be known as the age of the disintegration of the patriarchal family, as it exists to-day.

Syzygiology v. the Old Psychology

It is not astonishing, therefore, that this sexual epoch of change and reform is characterized by many sexual neuroses whose origins may be traced directly to the attempt of women not only to prove their social and sexual validity, but, in many cases, their superiority. Nor can we be astonished that neuroses result from the desire of men to retain their artificial and time-honoured prestige, dominance, and prerogatives. It is impossible to isolate human conduct from its network of connections with economic, climatic, technical, and political environments, and the relativity of all human conduct is nowhere demonstrated so beautifully as in the sphere of sex psychology. Indeed, it is high time to discard the term psychology, based on the old daemonic belief in the separate entity of the psyche or soul, and speak of the science of human conduct as syzygiology the science of the social relativity of human behaviour.

It is difficult to consider the effects of the growing economic emancipation of women upon the psychology of sexual relations as fully as the subject deserves. We must content ourselves with the bald statement that the unnatural imposition of masculine dominance on the life-patterns of women has given rise to two distinct types of feminine psychology: slave psychology, and protest or rebel psychology. The repercussion of these feminine psychologies on men has been two-fold. Where we find slaves, we find masters, and where we find successful revolt we may look for defeated lords. In the case of men, the appropriate psychologies are: master-psychology, with all the bluster of the professional he-man, and defeatist psychology, the psychology of the homosexual man who can no longer stand the onslaughts of emancipation-intoxicated women. It is this sexual competition which transforms the love life into an arena in which discouraged men and women stage their sexual conflicts in an attempt to establish their general validity by demonstrating a spurious superiority over their partner of the opposite sex.

For one woman who believes that she is the equivalent of a man in every sense, and lives her life as if she enjoyed all the prerogatives of womanhood to the fullest, we can find a dozen women who are discouraged by the prevailing patriarchal tradition, and stimulated by that discouragement either to imitate men and masculinity to the limits of their physiological capacity, or to demonstrate their weakness and dependence, thus enslaving men by their weakness and winning a sense of superiority by undermining the dominant male, rather than by an active attack on his prerogatives. In both cases, the masculine woman and the 'cringing-vine' woman over-rate masculinity and under-rate femininity, the one by the flattery of imitation, the other by the indirect flattery of helplessness based on the alleged greater independence and resourcefulness of the male.

Androtropism and Gynetropism

Adler has called woman's dissatisfaction with her feminine role the 'masculine protest', but this term is confusing, and we propose to substitute the term androtropism, the turning toward the masculine sex, to designate that symptom-complex of psychological behaviour of a woman dissatisfied with being a woman and attempting to act 'as If' she could become a man. Gynetropism is the parallel term used to describe the over-valuation of the feminine principle by the male, as we find it in certain male homosexuals.

It is manifest that the love relationship and the marriage bed are the logical arenas for the 'play-off' of this age-old sexual competition. We may state it as a psychological law: happiness in a love relation is impossible if the sexual partner is being prostituted as a means of proving one's own superiority. The sexual athletes we have described in a previous chapter, who enjoy their sexual relations only in proportion to the difficulty of the conquest of their sexual partner, do not experience the normal enjoyment of the companionship of love because their belligerent and aggressive drive for personal prestige distorts, disfigures, or paralyses their relations to the opposite sex.

Fear and ignorance not only spoil the art of living; they also preclude adequate relations between the sexes. It is impossible for a woman who has been trained to believe that men are just out for what they can get to surrender herself to her husband without believing that she has also surrendered the best of her personality, and has become a slave. It is impossible for a man who has been trained from early childhood to believe that all women are false and untrustworthy to be unprejudiced in his relations with his wife, no matter how sincerely he protests he is in love with her.

One of the most common manifestations of the competitive spirit in love is that phenomenon called 'sex appeal, or 'It'. In animal communities every normal male has an appeal for every normal female, and vice versa. But in our civilization of sexual competition, it is apparent that any man or woman who can heighten his sexual attractiveness by an intuitive exaggeration of all sex-stimulating behaviour, is better armed for the sexual fray, and enjoys a certain prestige because members of the opposite sex 'fall, for these charms. The very words we employ to describe sexual relations clearly indicate the power motive behind much of our sexual behaviour.

Men fall (that is, they tumble from the heights of their masculine prestige) for a woman's charms. Women 'succumb' to a man's 'line' (that is, their natural cunning is overcome). Children go to the picture houses to learn the wiles of the vampire, and go home with the steadfast resolve that no woman shall 'get' them! Women boast of their ability to arouse a man's sexual passion without gratifying it. The woman with the most provocative 'it' is usually envied by her sisters. This belligerent 'it' is no more than an attempt to batter the male out of the stronghold of his domination by the use of sex as a weapon of offence and defence.

Sex Appeal and the Dangerous Age

Sexual competition leads to restlessness and neurosis because there is no natural satisfaction to teasing beyond the temporary experience of power. The woman who uses her natural 'it' only to make men fall for her, sooner or later herself falls for a neurosis. It is common to see women who have been very beautiful and eminently successful in the exploitation of their sexual charms as a means of attaining significance and power, becoming melancholic and depressed when nature robs them of their charms, and they have no more permanent tools with which to make their old age interesting and worthwhile.

Occasionally we see the most perverse behaviour on the part of older women who wish, just once more, to prove that they have not lost their 'it' Usually they seduce some young boy, and although the youngster's attention in the beginning is an immense satisfaction to them, they soon become cramped in their relations and seek to hold the boy against his natural inclination to find a sexual mate of his own age. The tragedy of the deserted woman follows this fallacious technique.

The multiplicity of neuroses which occur at the time when men and women are passing through the period of sexual senescence has given rise to the term 'dangerous age' to describe this period. Men who have fixed all their hope of personal significance in the continued expression of their sexual potency have a dangerous age when potency wanes, just as women do. When a couple who harboured a feeling that sex is the only real expression of power, approach the dangerous age, tension and conflict within their private lives, and dissatisfaction and restlessness in their outer relations are certain to follow. Many divorces occur at this time, where a little patience and the re-estimation of values would pave the way for a happy and mature old age.

The problem of adultery is almost exclusively a problem of sexual competition. There are, no doubt, cases in which 'polite adultery' is the most desirable solution of a vicious marital problem, but these cases are a negligible minority. In most cases of adultery, whether committed by husband or wife, the partner who breaks his vows is punishing his mate and simultaneously expressing his sexual superiority. If a man is unfaithful to his wife, or impotent with his wife and potent with his mistress, as is so often the case, the psychological meaning is: "You are insufficient for me. I must seek sexual satisfaction elsewhere"

When a wife commits adultery she is usually expressing her rebellion against the imposition of her husband's false masculine authority. Her adultery expresses not only her rebellion, but also her superiority. In her eyes her husband is degraded as a cuckold when he is deceived. When a husband deceives his wife he is usually exonerated as "just one of the boys', whereas a man who is deceived by his wife is just as generally regarded as an inferior and inadequate husband. Even in adultery we find evidence of the existence of masculine dominance.

Tragedies of Sexual Competition

Were we to remove the discussion of the various forms of sexual competition from our' newspapers, novels, and films, there would hardly be a theme left for these purveyors of current moods in sexual ethics. So long as we have had a written word, there have been descriptions of the struggle for supremacy between the sexes. Some readers may be led to believe that psychologists are advocating a very drab world in which all forms of sexual competition are removed, with a consequent minimizing of the stimulus to much of the aesthetic gratification of modern life. Nothing could be farther from the truth. We believe in competition as a natural stimulus to human growth, but most of the sexual competition of our day is not only unnecessary, but so damaging to mental health that the competitors come out of the struggle to establish their sexual prestige so battered in body and distorted in mind that they form a public health problem.

Anyone who has seen a homosexual haunt in which hundreds of men, some dressed as women, dance with one another; anyone who has observed those parodies of 'queer women' whose Lesbian tendencies compel them to disfigure their bodies and cramp their minds, will understand something of the damage wrought by false competition in sex. If you know any of the host of dried-up women whose fear of sexual competition has led them to seek 'sublimation', so-called, in painting lamp shades, running tea rooms, or becoming Christian Scientists, nuns, or prostitutes, you will agree with us that the products of this competition form an unsavoury excrescence upon our society. Any husband who has been nagged, any lover whose beloved ruins his life by the poison of her possessive jealousy, any man whose life has been blighted because a wife, mother, or sister could not feel herself secure unless she had the last word, any man who has been libelled and maligned by a woman whose sexual frustration could be expressed in no other form of revenge, will understand very well why we find sexual competition one of the commonest causes of human unhappiness.

No woman who has been beaten by a husband who could find no other means of assuring himself of his masculine dominance ; no woman who has been denied a job for which she was perfectly qualified with the words 'No women wanted'; no woman who has been paid less than her male neighbour at a factory bench simply because that neighbour was a man; no woman who has had to bear children because a dominant husband would not spoil his sexual pleasure by thinking of contraception, or refused to allow her to care for herself; no woman who has had to drudge at menial household tasks because her husband's vanity would not permit her competition in the business world; no woman who has been denied access to a coveted professional appointment simply because no women were allowed, will fail to understand the wreckage caused by the persistence of patriarchal ideals and traditions in our culture, or fail to deplore the existence of a conflict between the sexes.

We do not speak of the charwomen, the 'slaveys', the underpaid factory workers, the unmarried mothers victimized by our patriarchal society, the 'kept' women enslaved in luxurious chains, the unnumbered little typists and clerks who do the world's dirty work, because they are women, and because they must slave for the dominant male to keep body and soul together. It is our purpose to draw attention to the variegated manifestations of sexual competition and to indicate the terrific cost not only to society, but to victor and victim alike. For it may be written as a psychological commandment: *Whosoever humiliates and deprecates his partner of the opposite sex will be denied the happiness of love.*

The Cancer of Romantic Infantilism

We come to the third great cause of unhappiness in love relations, emotional infantilism and romantic idealism. That romantic infantilism must be a potent cause for sexual dissatisfaction will be evident to anyone who understands that sexual happiness can result only from mature sexual relations. It is a psychological truism that a mentally mature adult is a rarity. Most of the human beings we meet in the street are still emotional infants, afraid of responsibilities, dreamers, and fantastic believers in fairy tales, socially unadjusted, and mentally subjective souls groping in ignorance for the moon.

Look at the films, those living Bibles of the mentally immature, read the sensational newspapers and the popular magazines, and you will realize the extent of the blight of adult infantilism in our civilization. The causes of this adult infantilism are chiefly the pampering of our children, the maternal over-solicitude of murderous mothers who insulate their children from reality with thick layers of emotional cotton wool. Our film magnates grow fat on their excellent psychological insight into the desires of the immature, emotionally over- protected adults who crowd our country; our most successful politicians attain their success because they can gather the votes of emotional morons with the sounding shibboleths of outworn ideas. Our advertising agencies fill their coffers because they pander to the vanity, the egoism, the snobbery, and the inferiority complexes of all grown-up children.

Of all causes of sexual unhappiness, romantic infantilism is the most common. Where it exists, it strikes at the very basis of reality, and permits very few adjustments. A woman who believes that women are unjustly oppressed and rebels against masculine domination, may still lead a useful life and conclude a stormy, but finally successful marriage, because she makes certain concessions to reality. A man who spends his youth being a Don Juan, in order to prove his masculinity, and then awakens to his responsibilities with age and maturity, may become a model husband and father and a veritable pillar of society, despite the trail of broken hearts he has left behind him.

But the girl who believes she is a princess, and expects the world to sit at her feet and stand at attention to serve her every whim, and the boy who believes he is the favoured of the gods and considers the adulation of every woman he meets not only his privilege but his birth-right, seldom alter their chronic belief in this, that, or the other Santa Claus unless they undergo a drastic psychological re-education. Divorce courts are crowded with their loud complaints, novels are filled with their romantic passions and irresponsible and uselessly tragic lives, and lunatic asylums are filled with their vegetating remains.

The Romantic Fallacy

It is surely easier for a camel to pass through a needle's eye than for a spoiled child to be happy in the cooperative venture of marriage. No matter how many untoward experiences they have, romantic idealists continue unmoved by adversity in an obstinate belief in the validity of their own magical formulas. They make their experiences to suit their own magical beliefs. They distort reality to suit their own ends, and come out smiling, with their belief in their own magical fetish as vigorous as before. Their lives are devoted to the recapture of the lost happiness of a childhood paradise.

Often these pampered boys and girls are 'good' sons and daughters, good because they obey blindly, accept no responsibilities and remain close to their pampering parents. Their sphere of activity is constructed on a radius the length of which is determined by their maternal apron-strings. If they marry, and succeed, as is not infrequently the case, in getting a mate who will continue to pamper them in the fashion they would like to become accustomed to, they stifle their children with a cloying over-solicitude and thus spread the contagion of their neuroses into the next generation.

There is no psychiatrist who has not at some time or other had one of these unfortunate children of romantic idealists in his care, who has not been stopped in his cure by the interference of parents whose vanity and egoism knew bounds neither of reason, time, nor of space. There is no business man who has not wanted to take some young man and give him a good spanking, no teacher who has not been impelled to bring the reality principle closer to some maliciously pampered little girl with the help of a well-applied birch switch.

And yet we must sympathize with these unfortunates, who are the unwitting victims of generations and generations of false educational ideas. We must admit that they act rationally and justly according to the plan they have been led to expect the world is constructed on. We must not lose patience with them, but we cannot afford to be ensnared by their charming personalities or their flattering helplessness. It is criminal not to awaken them from their romantic dreams in order to make useful human beings of them.

The romantic idealists fall into several groups. There are the girls whose parents have so convinced them of their special virtues that they can find no man to suit them. They fall in love with far-away heroes of the stage and screen, with married men, with great characters in story-books and fairy tales. Theirs is the quest for the ineluctable prince charming. Concessions to reality they never make. In time they become critical and crabbed, and when they are forced into marriage by social conventions or the necessity of finding someone to provide for them - they cannot work for a living and soil their princess hands - they revenge themselves on the poor man they marry because he fails to come up to their fantastic standards. The man of their choice is a composite of Croesus, Apollo, Adonis, the handy-man from the garage, their favourite brother, an image of their father in his prime, Lindbergh, Dempsey, Keats, Santa Claus, and perhaps the white-whiskered family physician thrown in for good measure.

The romantic idealists are the people who are for ever falling in and out of love, and dramatizing their lives with the false sentimentality of a bad play. The psychological nature of 'falling in love' deserves more minute consideration because it is so common and so generally a mistaken technique of life. It is highly improbable that people who Tall in love at first sight' in the accepted sense of the word, ever attain a happy love life. The vast majority of people believe that they must fall in love or be in love before they can be happy in a sexual relation. Nothing could be farther from the truth. Occasionally a man and a woman see each other for the first time, and sense a feeling of complete kinship which they call falling in love; and, on the premise that, because love is present, all else can be attained, they marry and live happily ever after according to the time-honoured formula of the story-books.

But this probably occurs with great rarity. For, as we have explained, love is the result of years of cooperation, of mutual enjoyment, and mutual suffering. It cannot then, except in the most unusual cases, be the *premise* of happy sexual relations. 'Falling in love' is the happy *reward* of a correctly and normally lived life *à deux*, not the foundation of a sexual relation. If this simple psychological truth were more commonly recognized, much of the romantic twaddle of our neurotic drama and literature would disappear, as would many of the post-marital tragedies now all too commonly found in divorce court and clinic.

Romantic Hocus-pocus: Falling in Love

The psychological process of falling in love may best be likened to the operation of those electrical robots which are actuated to the performance of the most complicated functions by the application of the appropriate stimulus. As soon as the proper word is uttered, the entire complicated mechanism is set in motion and no prayer will stop it from the performance of its mechanical task. The romantic idealist is like such an electrical robot. His psychological antennae are attuned to a certain stimulus predetermined by the experiences of his early childhood. For instance, a girl who throughout her childhood was pampered only by an indulgent father, a robust grey-haired man with a deep bass voice and a hearty booming laugh (while her four brothers, all slight in build, were always cruel to her), goes through life with her psychic antennae 'set' by her early childhood conditioning for the favourable reception of just such another big man with a booming laugh and grey hair. It is her unconscious hope that the recapitulation of the physical background will bring the same players and the same drama to the stage of her life. Of the thousands of men she meets in the course of her thirty-five years of life, no one quite fits the pattern, and she manages to find objections to all other men because her psychic antennae have never 'tuned in' on exactly the right stimuli.

Then, on a steamer going to America, the young lady meets Mr G., who presents just the right stimulus. He happens to be the purser of the ship, a married man with two children in New York, and a wife he loves very dearly. Our young lady immediately abandons her critical faculties and surrenders herself to the imaginary enjoyment of her life's dream. She leaves out of account the fact that the purser is a man of little education and a social background dissimilar to hers, that he is already married, and that he is only very mildly interested in her.

She distorts every pleasant word he utters, into a confession of love, and fully expects him to leave his ship and return to Europe to marry her at the first possible opportunity. She has 'fallen in love'. There is no doubt of the sincerity of her feelings, of her genuine regard. She seems hypnotized by the man's personality. She can dream only of the recapitulation of her childhood paradise in the company of this man who seemingly fits into her pattern exactly. To an outside observer who sees the manifest incongruities of the situation, her attitude and her apparent inability to recognize or weigh the obvious obstacles to her scheme appear insane.

'Falling in love' may be considered a form of temporary insanity. Like the electrical robot, tuned to open a door when the password 'Kismet I' is uttered, our young lady has set the entire machinery of her emotional life into its irreversible, complicated courses, because a psychological password, this time in the form of a certain physical human type, has touched her. She feels that she is the victim of some ineluctable and ineffable passion, completely beyond the control of her personality, When the disinterested bystander objects to her marriage, saying that the man is already married, has children, cannot support her in the style in which she lives, that he would be a poor mate because he is committed to his ship most of the time, that he would refuse to live in England, that he is ten years too old to be her mate - she answers simply, 'But I love him. He must leave his wife and come to me, I love him, I tell you"

The Aftermath of Love at First Sight

Thousands upon thousands of otherwise intelligent young people fall in love for similarly inconsequential reasons, equally romantic, equally quixotic, equally inauspicious for the happy conduct of a marital relation. If our young lady were to induce the ship's officer to follow the course she had decided upon, and if he were to marry her after a brief but furious courtship, the great probability is that she would wake up one fine morning to realize with horror that she had a stranger in bed with her. She would find that, despite the physical similarity to her beloved father, the purser was a hard-drinking, rather brutal, and inconsiderate man, perfectly incapable of talking to her about art and literature, her two greatest interests in life, and completely incapable of meeting her friends socially. Then another love tragedy would begin. And another broken heart and two broken lives could be chalked up to the credit of romantic infantilism.

It is quite probable that our young woman would not give up with the first flush of chagrin. She would carry out that second time-honoured formula of the romantic idealists: 'Because I love you, you must do what I say!' The ship's officer would then be nagged to give up chewing tobacco, drinking grog, and the like. We do not believe that these are the most admirable traits of human conduct, but they are G.'s traits. Our young lady could have noticed them from the very beginning if she had not been hypnotized by 'falling in love' to leave all her intellectual faculties at home.

She has received her just deserts. No one can marry a person for some single fetishism, such as grey hair, a booming laugh, a good complexion, tall stature, or beautiful feet, and expect that the rest of the personality will somehow fit in!

English people look with horror at the arranged marriages of certain foreign peoples, in which the love of the young people for one another is considered a wholly secondary matter, the social, economic, intellectual, political, or religious factors being considered more important. We are not in favour of arranged marriages because they are usually arranged for the benefit of the parents and not for the happiness of the married couple. But we do firmly believe that 'being in love' is not the condition a priori without which marriage and love are inconceivable.

A great many marriages would turn out more happily if the contracting parties gave less thought to love, and more to the matter of financial budgets, the pedagogic principles according to which the children were to be educated, the mutual use of leisure, the past performances in social cooperation, the willingness of each to share responsibility, and the like. When a man goes into a business venture or partnership for no better reason than that he likes the look of the office furniture, he is put down as a fool by his associates, but the same man, entering into marriage with a girl because she has a pretty figure, plays bridge well, and likes to go to cocktail parties, is congratulated by his friends.

Ten years later he is having an affair with his secretary; his wife is a chronic alcoholic, both are extremely unhappy, and remain together solely for the sake of their child, the neglected football which is kicked between the goal-posts of their antithetical egoisms. This is a common result of falling in love without considering more mundane prerequisites for marital cooperation before marrying. The expected marital happiness expressed in the phrase 'and they lived happily ever after' is seldom the result of such flimsy and stupid bungling in the choice of a mate. Mature Love v. Romantic Love

Mem and women would be far happier if they planned their marital relationships according to the deep compatibilities of social, intellectual, and occupational interests, responsibilities toward children and State, mutual helpfulness, and acted 'as if' love might be the reward of five or ten years of successful cooperation. The commonly misused word love in whose name so many crimes are committed by the emotionally immature, the romantically idealistic, and the psychologically infantile, should have its connotations changed. It is usually believed that love belongs to a special category of human emotions and feelings, but, as a matter of fact, it is no more than a special form of the social feeling, the communal consciousness on which all human relations are based.

Love is friendship plus the element of heterosexual cooperation. Love equals friendship plus sex. The romantically infantile may be mature physically and go through the motions of sexual intercourse, but it is as improbable that they will experience mature love, psychologically, as that a road-sweeper will appreciate the beauties of the original Greek text of the Odyssey,

No one suffers so much from love as a romantic idealist. Although it is true that some of these romantic idealists have given us our best poetry, a few excellent plays, several stirring novels, and not a little splendid music, they might have lived a more complete love life and still written equally excellent poetry and music. Let no reader believe that one must be a romantic idealist to produce good literature or music. 'Artiness' is just another form of romantic idealism. It requires no more 'artistic temperament', no more romantic idealism to write a symphony than to excise a gall-bladder or build a sky-scraper.

More has been written about the erotic antics of the emotionally immature than about any other single subject in the world's literature. Every romantic idealist remains steadfast in the belief of his rightness. It is because he believes that his problem and his tragedy are unique, that his shredded modesty fails to prevent his airing, in some artistic form or other, the soiled linen of his erotic misadventures, that all may see, sympathize, and make excuses for him.

It is hardly astonishing that the romantic tradition is so deeply ingrained in the lay mind. The epics of romantic love are written daily by adolescent minds for the avid consumption of other adolescent minds. They are engulfed without criticism and without perspective by school-girls and schoolboys, who proceed to pattern their love-lives in the romantic tradition unless some friendly and objective adult either explains the facts of life to them verbally, or by example. Many, like the late Isadora Duncan, carry their romanticism to the grave and beyond.

What, then, are the real prerequisites for a happy love life, whether before marriage or after? To the reader who has understood the meaning of the three cardinal sins against love -ignorance, competition, and romantic infantilism - it is sufficient to answer: avoid these obvious errors, and with the use of a little effort and a modicum of a sense of humour you can make a success of any marriage or any love affair. Vanity, a struggle for prestige, a desire to dominate at the expense of your sexual partner, the inability to identify yourself with your partner's problems and situations, the desire to be perfect, or right, or superior, will spoil any human relations - and their evil effects are most noticeable in the love relation. The love relationship is a creative and artistic activity, as much as living itself. Let only those who have made progress in their own self-sculpture attempt to join forces and essay the creation of new worlds in the cooperation of sexual 'two-ness'.

'Practical Suggestions

The fact that the family, as a patriarchal institution, is in process of disintegration, and the fact that economic factors frequently complicate the proper solution of the love problem, compel us to admit that there is no single ideal solution of the problems of love and marriage. In view of the fact that every individual must solve this problem in the way he finds best, our only counsel must be: know the facts, and cooperate to the best of your ability with the best standards of the social group in which you live. If you feel you are not in full possession of the facts, a conference with a reputable psychiatrist, or a successfully and happily married couple, when no expert aid is available, may often serve to throw valuable light on a problem which at first glance seems insuperable.

The correct solution of any individual sex problem is often complicated by the petty annoyances of daily life. Love affairs have been wrecked because of the too close proximity of the contracting parties for too long a time. We believe in the prophylactic value of an occasional separation of married couples, in which each partner plans a little holiday for himself, and carries out his plans without interference from the other partner. In normal people this separation should lead to a renewal of interests, and a strengthening of affections. Where it leads to jealousies, worries, suspicions, and the like, it is a sign of an unhappy possessiveness on the part of one partner or the other. Possessiveness, jealousy, sexual envy, sexual over-solicitude are further signs of romantic infantilism. The jealous man exposes his own sense of inferiority, just as the possessive mate broadcasts his own sense of insecurity by attempting to chain his beloved.

Love may be shared, love may be bestowed, but it can never be demanded. I have known wives complain bitterly that their husbands did not love them any more, as if this were a sign of some defect in their husbands. More likely such a failure of love is an indication that the wives have not made it sufficiently interesting for their husbands to continue the affection of the honeymoon. I have known parents complain bitterly that their children no longer respected or loved them, as if the transient sexual collaboration which is the sole requirement of procreation were a guarantee that the child of any sexual union was bound for life to love his progenitors. I have known husbands, romantically infantile in their vanity, sigh and weep because of their wives' lack of interest in them, as if ceasing to show all the pleasantries, the little favours, the unimportant concessions, and the insignificant gestures of esteem that were the rule during courtship, were not in itself evidence of a lack of human understanding and a perfectly legitimate excuse for sexual frigidity.

Happiness in love, like freedom, is to be bought only at the cost of unflagging watchfulness and assiduous mutual adjustment. No love is happy in which one partner does all the adjusting and the other remains an unbending rock, complete in his self-assurance of perfection and immovability. Nagging and criticism are the easiest ways to undermine love. Sentimentality and a cloying display of public affection are likewise well designed to spoil the even tenor of love, just as the belief that all expressions of love and affection are childish and silly, robs love and loving of its spontaneity, its playfulness, its very beauty. Somewhere between cool, objective matter-of-factness in sex, and the dripping marshmallow of romantic passion, lies the golden mean of human love. Like happiness, love may be achieved only where each partner is not only confident of his value to his mate but also to humanity at large, and is willing to assume that his mate, likewise, is well adjusted and useful not only to him but to humanity.

No two human beings are perfect. It is more than likely that even in the best arranged matches, one or both of the partners have some vestige of childish, romantic behaviour. There is hardly a man who does not like to play God in some respect, though he may be largely normal and objective about the great issues of life, and there is hardly a woman to be found who does not at some moment or other wish to be considered a princess in her own realm. The intelligent mate will allow her partner his little God-game, especially where it concerns un- essentials.

I know of marriages which have remained happy despite the fact that the wife had an utterly unobjective belief in the impeccability of her cooking, which her husband allowed her to maintain despite the evidence of tongue and stomach to the contrary. I know of another marriage in which a wise wife has allowed her husband to believe he was responsible for all important decisions, although she knew very well that she had made the decision for him weeks ago, and waited confidently for her husband to announce her opinion with the air of a God-like and spontaneous discovery. And I have seen other marriages wrecked because the wife objected to her husband's technique at bridge, or insisted that he did not know how to mix cocktails, hang pictures, or choose the proper ties to match his shirts.

Examples of this type of mental unhappiness could be multiplied indefinitely, but they lead to no general rules of conduct beyond those we have already outlined. The best counsel is: try to know your mate before you marry him, but once having married him, take him for what he is, and make the best of it. Men who marry prostitutes to make good women of them, and women who marry drunkards, morphine addicts, inveterate golfers, or gamblers with the intention of reforming them, get just what they deserve - insults to their vanity. For them marriage becomes a veritable hotbed of neuroses.

Marriages and love affairs will continue to be unhappy until we remove the fallacies of the omnipotence of romantic passion from the thought vocabulary of our children, and until we institute objective training in the art of love, and teach men and women that they must be responsible for their emotions and their erotic passions just as they are responsible for curbing other anti-social tendencies in their behaviour.

Much of the difficulty of our love-life is directly due to the fact that the vast majority of our young people cannot make love in decent surroundings. We continue to blind our eyes to the immense social value of love, and treat it as if it were a foul sin, instead of the highest form of human cooperation. We need never fear that there will be too much love. The world suffers only from too little love.

CHAPTER TWELVE.
Of Techniques: The Triumph of Maturity

The Technique of "Empathy - The Dynamics of Friendship - How to Start a Friendship - Hints on Social Success - The Fine Art of Making Presents - Flow to Widen Your Social Horizons - The Vital Need for Hobbies – 'Either... or' v. 'Both... and' - Some Useful Hints on Controversy - Of Deferred Living - How to Grow Old Gracefully - The Uses of Leisure and Adversity – L'envoi

In the foregoing chapters it has been my purpose to outline the fine art of creative self-sculpture which leads to human happiness. I have sketched, briefly, not only the problems which beset each human being who faces the task of taking the rough clay of his human heritage and making a meaningful design of his life, but also the opportunities that present themselves for the compensation of the difficulties. I have, moreover, attempted to explain how fear and ignorance, originating in early childhood misconceptions of life and its meanings, divert many a valuable human being from the path of happiness, and I have mapped some of the pathways of unhappy living. Finally, I have explained some of the individual goals of living, some of the tools and techniques of creative self-sculpture, and described possible sources of failure and disappointment.

We have not blinded ourselves to the difficulties that face every human being, but, despite the existence of countless obstacles in the external world, we have discovered that the vital elasticity of the human body and the human spirit is capable of transmuting these obstacles into assets. If follows, therefore, that much of the unhappiness in the world is preventable, and the way to the creation of a full, vital, and meaningful life lies open to all who know and understand themselves, to those who have clarified their insight into the dynamics of human conduct The more completely we understand life the greater our courage to go on with the task of living.

We come, finally, to the discussion of those practical devices and techniques which may help the reader over temporary difficulties, once he has understood the grand strategy of living fully and completely, and devoted his energies to the pursuit of the good life. These practical suggestions cannot, in and of themselves, make anyone happy, but they may help in the solution of a number of problems, once you have understood that most problems can be solved. In the first chapter, in which I stated certain psychological laws that govern all human beings in their conduct, I pointed out that the way to happiness must, of necessity, lie along the channels of two great movements: the art of living with other people and the art of living with oneself. Social adjustment itself is not enough for the good life, because there are periods in everyone's life when isolation may be arbitrarily enforced, when human contacts are practically precluded. It is in these periods that each of us must be able to make good company of himself, in order that life may be rich and tolerable, and in order that we may prepare the foundations of future bonds with our fellow-men, once out social contacts have been re-established.

It is apparent that the first and most important device in the art of living with other people is the art of making friends. Unfortunately, the men and women who need friends most are the least schooled in the business of making acquaintances, or, if they can make casual contacts with more or less ease, they have not learned the art of holding their friends. The 'follow through' of social contacts is the most difficult part of this art because it assumes the ability to identify yourself with your friends, to fit yourself into their patterns, and aid them on their way. This quality or faculty of emphasising, or identifying ourselves, must be learned, and can be learned. Socially well- adjusted individuals do it as a matter of course, but to those who are not socially well-adjusted, and need an additional training, the following technique may prove valuable.

It may be stated almost as a psychological law that every human being, no matter how great or powerful, is discouraged in some degree, or in some special facet of his life. The neurotic, however, believes that his discouragement and his distress are unique. He acts as if everyone else in the world were a superman, and he alone an impotent worm, incapable of meeting people without qualms of conscience and self-consciousness. As a matter of fact, some of the people whom the isolated neurotic most envies because of their ready ease in social situations, are themselves the most discouraged, and, like the small boy who whistles in the dark to keep himself from trembling with fear, they over-act their courage in order to hide their own perplexity from their fellows.

We have already learned that the pattern of every individual's life is a stream from an imagined 'minus' situation to an imagined 'plus' situation. What we must do, if we wish to make a new acquaintance, is to guess his goal from his actions - with a little practice this is not at all difficult - and tell him something that will encourage him along the path which he is taking, to show that we appreciate his ends and are aware of his success. To those who are expert in this art it is not difficult to divert an individual from a false pattern into a good one, and this is the essence of psychotherapy. In other words, when we wish to teach someone a new behaviour pattern, we must make our suggestions seem to fit into his pattern, although we know all the time that if he takes our suggestions he will drift imperceptibly into a new and better pattern.

The Technique of Empathy

The technique of empathy is best illustrated by the story of the town fool and the lost donkey. In a small Russian town which boasted but a single donkey, great consternation was caused by the donkey's sudden and mysterious disappearance. A conclave of the village elders was called, and for three days and three nights they sat solemnly discussing the theoretical motives and causes of the donkey's disappearance and the possible chances of finding him again. In the midst of one of these solemn conferences a knock was heard on the door and the town fool entered with the news that he had found the lost donkey. When asked how he had been able to succeed in his quest, where all the elders, despite their wisdom, had failed, the fool replied, 'When I heard that the donkey was lost, I went to the donkey's stall, faced the wall as the donkey did, imagined that I was the donkey, and thought where I would go if I were to wander from the stall. Then I went to this place, and there the donkey was.'

If you would learn to make friends and keep them, observe closely, find some good point about the friend you wish to make and compliment him thereon. There is no art in finding defects in people - anyone can spot and criticize a character defect, a foolish habit, or a stupid custom. It is much more difficult to find something good about a neighbour and to mention it in approbation without becoming sentimental or maudlin in the act. No woman wishes to be told she has grey hair, but every woman wishes to know that the colour scheme she has chosen for her dress, probably with great care and forethought, is appreciated by the onlooker.

If you have learned in advance that a man has a particular hobby, make it a point to ask a question about that hobby that will draw him out, thus enabling him to feel superior and more knowing, and giving him an easy opportunity to expand his ego. There is no human being, who, if given the opportunity, does not like to find an audience. The art of making friends consists in large measure in shrewdly guessing the particular subject your dinner party would like to expand upon. Once you have learned to look sharply, and judge from the general ensemble of a man what his probable interests are, it is not difficult to get that dinner partner to speak.

Each man and woman we meet, therefore, offers us an opportunity for constructive social behaviour. Do not imagine that it bores the man who has just built a fine bridge, written a best-seller, or composed a great symphony, to hear your appreciation, even though your opinion is not expert. Do not imagine that success in the eyes of the world is in itself a complete satisfaction to the individual who has attained it. Even the most successful crave iteration and reiteration of social approval. Nor is the ordinary layman who has achieved no world success at all beyond encouragement. It may be the colour of his tie, the quality of his laughter, or the fact that he knows the batting averages that gives you an opportunity to praise, to understand, and to find happiness by encouraging a fellow human being.

The beneficent results of this technique are twofold. It gives the prospective friend the necessary encouragement and the necessary sense of social appreciation which move him to be natural and expressive. Secondly it is likely to colour his attitude toward you and make him want to approve of you. Consequently, he will search your personality for some facet worthy of approbation in order to make your approval of his conduct or ideas the more valuable.

The Dynamics of Friendship

After a series of such searches, a friendship will germinate under the warm sun of mutual admiration. Your friend will feel a certain sense of noblesse, oblige to inquire about your interests, and you, in turn, will have the opportunity to air your views and expand your ego. And, if you are a good human being, you will always see to it that the other fellow has the greater say. You will minimise your own interests and accomplishments, no matter how great they actually are, and emphasize the interest you have in the other fellow's situation. This is the way of true friendship.

We must, in all fairness, admit that you may occasionally be taken advantage of by the egoistic neurotic who seizes upon your good nature as an opportunity of venting his little neurosis on your all too willing ears. When your partner becomes too neurotically voluble, discretion and retreat are the better part of valour. But one friend made is worth a dozen neurotics who bore you with their egoism. Even these neurotics can be used as parables in the understanding of human nature, and of what not to do if you would be happy in the friendship of your fellows.

There are always certain men and women who indulge in the sport of soul catching. They are usually pampered neurotics who put their best foot forward in order to catch you in the net of their affability, with the ulterior, unconscious purpose of exploiting your friendship later. Everyone knows people who know a host of acquaintances, but have no single friend. Soul catching is their profession, a profession in which they develop a considerable virtuosity. Soul catching is another of the side-shows of the social life, characterised, like begging, confidence games, charity rackets, and the like, by a misuse of the social feeling of the victim. It is impossible completely to avoid entanglements in the nets of an occasional soul catcher, but if you wish to rid yourself of the company of such a neurotic it is only necessary to ask him to do you a favour. The soul catcher retreats from the social responsibilities of friendship with incredible celerity.

As a matter of fact, two willing ears are among the most valuable of all social assets. Learn to listen intelligently and to identify yourself with the speaker while you listen. Many a man who has no special gifts or talents has gone through life with a host of friends, happy in the security of the good will of every neighbour, because he has been willing to listen to the recital of the exploits of a neighbour's baby son or pet terrier. Because most people are lonely and have no one to talk to, they are for ever seeking a willing listener; and a sympathetic listener is a rare find.

I once asked a patient how he explained the sudden cure of an anxiety neurosis of eight years' standing, and he answered, 'Doctor, you are the first person I have met for ten years who made a noise like a human being.' I knew that this patient had not listened very hard and asked him to explain more fully. He answered, 'Well, you're the first man I have met who could listen to a man's story for an hour without trying to pin a label on him or hurl a sermon at him.'

This brings us to the consideration of the tendency of most human beings to secure themselves in their judgement and in their own self-esteem by making snap judgements of their fellows, and thinking that, because they have labelled another a snob, or a cad, a good fellow, or a bounder, they have understood him. Everyone runs across other people who seem to be acting in an inconsequential or even insane fashion. The first impulse is to damn that which we cannot understand, and this impulse is probably at the basis of many of the persecutions, wars, and abuses of human rights we read about in history.

It seems far better to reserve and suspend judgement on any questionable case until we are in possession of more facts. And, in any case, the happy human being identifies himself so far as he is able with any freak he meets and says, 'Now, in what circumstances, and to what end, should I be doing exactly the same thing?' We must realize that everyone is trying to be a superman according to his own interpretation of the facts. It does not help either our understanding, or our influence on these people if we rashly put them in this, that, or the other fixed category, and believe that, because we have labelled them, we have understood and mastered their personalities.

A great many people go through life with the firm conviction that men are dishonest and bad, and that, when you find a person who is ostensibly good, he is being good for some ulterior motive. However true this may be in individual cases, from a practical point of view this philosophic attitude of misanthropy and mistrust is false and dangerous. That there are cheats and crooks goes without saying, but the great majority of human beings are essentially honest and decent. We would far rather be deceived a dozen times by a scoundrel than allow a really worthy individual to go once without our help. Somehow the rewards of helping a fellow human being in distress outweigh the chagrin of being duped and deceived by a smooth social parasite.

On the other hand, there are a great many people, notably professional beggars and the like, who make a profession of preying on the sympathies of their more socially minded neighbours. It is a mistake to give aid to these people. Charity should always be given where you know that your charity is being effectively administered by organizations which make it their business to help the needy and the sick. When you help a social parasite you rob three people - yourself, the really needy who could have been helped by your contribution, and the parasite who is encouraged to a useless way of life.

How to Start a Friendship

Our traditional codes of social conduct are so stultifying that the average man. or woman looks at any stranger as if he were a potential enemy. I have often suggested to my patients that they should begin a conversation with their neighbour in the bus or at the theatre simply for the purpose of initiating a conversation, only to have the patient shrink in horror from the suggestion of such forwardness. If we use a little common sense in such contacts, there can be no harm in them. If you speak to another human being at an art gallery or a concert, the likelihood is that his goals and aims will be somewhat similar to your own. Most of the individuals who make up a crowd waiting in line at a railway station, at a steamship pier, or at a theatre, are just as lonely as you are and just as afraid to make contacts. No one says a word, and everyone is bored and distressed. Someone must be more intelligent and more courageous and make the first step toward establishing a social rapport. Be that more intelligent person.

In my experience, a courteous or a kindly word of greeting or interest is almost never rebuffed. And let anyone who is rebuffed remember this: any human being who rebuffs a cordial greeting or an expression of human interest is likely to be a severely neurotic man or woman, too prejudiced in his egoistic self-approbation to make fresh human contacts. Great minds are the most cordial and the most friendly. I have known neurotic, ill-bred, spoiled, and socially maladjusted adults insulted by the greeting of a stranger, but I have never known a really big human being to be so insulted. On the contrary, I have seen one of the world's most eminent surgeons spend half an hour discussing the plight of a sick horse with a superannuated, hack-driver, and I have seen an admiral stop an important; interview to explain the mysteries of a battleship turret to a twelve-year-old boy.

Part of the technique of making friends, therefore, consists la breaking the ice. It is for this reason, primarily, that weather, football, and politics exist as topics of small talk. I have known super-serious neurotics who spurned conversation because they could not immediately discuss Kantian metaphysics or the Einsteinian theory of relativity with a casual acquaintance, but it is obvious that this type of intellectual snobbery is merely an artificial defence mechanism.

Let no one who would make friends forego these small topics of conversation. They serve as the lubricating oil of human communal life, and are as important as good manners, cleanliness, and being well-dressed. To those who are incapable of making these contacts, I suggest the following: go up to several strangers every day and inquire the time, or the best way to reach a certain address, regardless of the absolute value of such information. This is the first step in training yourself to talk to strangers. Carry this on until it no longer makes you self-conscious to make a 'cold' contact.

The second step in the art of making friends is the 'follow through' of making yourself valuable to the people you have contacted. It is a very good technique to begin with people who are overlooked by the average egoistic men and women we see madly searching for their own advantage in life. It is always valuable to be pleasant to elderly people, to cripples, to shy and timid souls who seem to shrink from social contacts, to children, to 'wallflowers', and to animals. It is tremendously encouraging to any elderly individual if a young man or woman comes up to talk with them when younger, more attractive individuals are in the same gathering.

Hints on Social Success

Success in the social life lies in the path of the man who can make himself valuable to those who are all too frequently overlooked in the mad rush of the machine age. Being attentive to the overlooked minority is doubly valuable because it gives you the best possible opportunity of immediately proving your social-mindedness: it not only enriches the timid or overlooked and adds to the store of human happiness, but also immediately gives you the feeling of being indispensable to another's happiness. And this feeling is the basis of objective self-esteem.

I know of a young architect struggling for his first job, who, in a spirit of levity, offered to design a kennel in Georgian style for an old lady. The lady was pleased with the idea of having her kennel in harmony with her country home, gave the young architect the commission, and was so satisfied with his work that she later commissioned him to do a large job in the modernization of her town house, which marked the beginning of this architect's successful career. Similarly, a young doctor who was called into a home to take care of a minor emergency, endeared himself to the family by his solicitude in the care of a sick cat. Subsequently, he became the family physician and was enthusiastically recommended to an important clientele of patients simply because he had taken the time and the interest to do more than his required work.

I can hear the objections of social and moral purists who consider these methods of establishing social contacts crude and hypocritical. It is all very well for those who are socially well-established to allow themselves the luxury of formal introductions, but, for those who are isolated, the traditional means of meeting new people are totally inadequate. So long as the average community makes no conscious effort to make the social adjustment of its constituents its immediate concern by establishing clubs, recreational facilities, community dancing, singing, or athletic activities, we must fall back upon these primitive devices. And so far as the seemingly coldblooded hypocrisy of these techniques is concerned, we must add that sincerity and formality are social luxuries beyond the means of the isolated, timid, and self-conscious. Nothing is insincere nor hypocritical if it extends and enriches human relations.

It is highly important to begin by mastering the philosophy of friendship, and understanding the value of a constructive social life. But once you have set yourself on the path of increasing your social horizons, it is equally important to 'follow up' and 'follow through' to make those friendships vital and lasting. It is in this secondary sphere that most neurotic and isolated individuals fall short. Yet the technique of social 'follow up' is very simple. A few minutes a day devoted to telephoning old friends and expressing concern and interest in their activities will quickly result in the reinforcement of friendships which would otherwise fall into desuetude.

It is a good idea not to enter a friend's home without bringing some little gift. This does not entail great investments, because the value of this good old custom inheres in the thoughtfulness, not in the gift itself. Sometimes a single rose is richer in its indication of friendship than a precious stone. It is wise to keep a record of anniversaries and birthdays, and to recall one's interest in a friend or relative by remembering these occasions if only by a card or a telephone call. Human relations are built around a structural framework of philanthropy, sympathy, honesty, and helpfulness, but the single bricks which give the house of friendship its unique facade are cemented by trivial favours and inconsequential affirmations of regard.

A patient once came to my office crying bitterly because her husband had neglected her on her birthday. The husband had, she admitted, handed her a package containing £20,000 worth of stock in his company, but he had neglected to send her the yellow roses which had always been the sign of his love and affection on previous anniversaries. Objectively we may agree with the husband that her demands were somewhat unreasonable, in the light of his more valuable gift, but we know that many marriages go on the rocks of unhappiness just because a husband or a wife neglects the little things that count.

The Fine Art of Making Presents

This brings us to the very practical consideration of gifts. There are two kinds of gifts. You either give something you like and value highly, or you go out of your way to give something that will be valuable to the person you desire to honour. Many people choose the former, or projective type of giving, which includes that useless prostitution of giving, the giving of gifts for reasons of duty, custom, or the like. This is the easiest - and the worst - way to make a present. When you give a small boy who is aching to have a new tennis racket, a copy of Marcus Aurelius' Meditations because of some vague hope that it may do him good, you practise a subjective-projective giving. You might just as well never give anything as make an inappropriate, casual, or inconsidered gift. The only- proper giving is giving which represents the donor's active identification with the presentee's pattern of life. Such empathy takes more time, but it enriches both him who gives and him who receives, and this mutual enrichment is, after all, the only valid reason for ever giving anything.

How to Widen your Social Horizons

As no one can be happy in work which is centred entirely about his own person and deals exclusively with the satisfaction of his own immediate needs, so no one can be entirely happy in social relations which focus only in himself and his immediate and narrow sphere of influence. To find happiness we must seek it in a focus outside ourselves. To do this in the social world it is desirable that everyone should commit himself definitely to a programme of social awareness, social expansion, and social concern. There is little merit in deploring social injustice, civic corruption, political chicanery, or international chauvinism, but if you get into some social movement that appeals to you and devote your interest, attention, and activity to it, you are likely to reap a valuable dividend therefrom.

If you live only for yourself, you are always in immediate danger of being bored to death by the repetition of your own views and interests. If your centre of gravity is in some extra- personal social movement you profit by the vitality and the objectivity of that movement. It matters little for psychological purposes whether you interest yourself in making your city cleaner, or enlist in the international campaign to rid the world of the illicit opium traffic, whether you go in for Birth Control or become a crusader against the vicious influence of prudery and superstition. Choose a movement that presents a distinct trend towards greater human happiness and align yourself with it. No one has learned the meaning of living until he has surrendered his ego to the service of his fellow-men.

Wide social horizons are the more worth cultivation because no single social group is completely objective in its scope. Read conservative and radical papers at the same time, and learn to draw your own conclusions from the evidence that is presented by both. Try to make your social contacts and interests complement your occupational or professional interests. If you are a school teacher, you may well afford to interest yourself in international politics or some artistic movement. If you are a physician, it cannot hurt you to interest yourself in artists and business men. If you are a lawyer, it will extend your usefulness to know the latest pedagogical theories.

Groups which devote themselves to cultural and social ends exist in every town, and those who are cut off from the greater; urban centres are no longer entirely isolated because of the pervasive influence of wireless. It is well to remember that the - more, languages you know, the more times you multiply your humanity, and those who are really constrained by force, of circumstance from making further human contacts can always make new contacts with foreign cultures and past ages by learning a new language.

There may be some readers to whom even these elementary steps seem difficult. We urge them to spend their sleepless nights in thinking about giving someone - not a member of their immediate families - some little pleasure. After some thought they will, in all probability, find ways and means to carry some of their thoughts into practice. I once advised a successful and very egoistic business man who could find no time to concern himself with the affairs and woes of his fellow- men during his business day to go down to the main waiting room of a great railway terminus and look for someone to help, someone to carry a heavy valise for, someone to encourage with a smile or a cheery word. I forbade him to leave the station until he had found an opportunity to be of some service to another human being. Largely in a spirit of supercilious condescension and patronage he obeyed, and his opportunity for social service came on the very first evening he made the experiment.

A poor woman from the country had come to Town to meet her daughter. She had lost the slip with her daughter's address, and was too shy and too timid to ask a porter. She sat weeping silently in a corner of the waiting room, a picture of forlorn perplexity. My patient managed to find her daughter's address in the telephone directory, took the old lady and her bags and put her in a taxicab, and accompanied her to an obscure street. On the way he stopped and bought the old lady a few roses - the first that had ever been given her.

He deposited her, smiling between her tears, in her daughter's house, and rushed to a telephone. 'My God, Doctor, I feel like a human being at last!' he blurted as he told us the story. Thereafter, he became a figure haunting the waiting room at the station, a sort of modern Haroun-al-Raschid. Every Christmas he sends the old lady of his first adventure in constructive humanity a dozen of the finest roses he can buy. Since then he has become one of the directors of a boys' club, and a member of various child welfare and civic organizations.

The Vital Need for Hobbies

We should expand our occupational interests at the same time we attempt to extend our social horizons. The business of being busy is one of the most important in the life of a human being. Those sad human beings who do not have to work are to be pitied if they do not find some avocation to divert their energies into a useful channel. A great many agencies and individuals set themselves up nowadays as vocational guidance experts, and after elaborate tests they direct their clients to this, that, or the other occupation. In most cases they lose sight of the essential fact that the well-adjusted person finds work a source of salvation, and therefore has already found the proper vocation for himself.

Most of the people who seek vocational guidance really need to have the psychological reasons for work explained to them, so that, seeing work as a veritable source of personal expansion and self-esteem, they find the nearest and best occupation available, and devote themselves to it. The choice is really one between working and not working, never of an actual choice of occupation. The man who for a good reason is dissatisfied with his job, usually has the courage to get out of it, and into another occupation that gives him greater satisfaction.

The best work in the world, as I suggested in a previous chapter, is that occupation which represents training in the compensation for some organic or other inferiority feeling in terms of social usefulness. Not everyone can find the best job for himself. A great many are forced by the unfortunate economic structure of modern society to busy themselves with the necessary chores and hackwork of the world, in order to earn a living. For them the focus of values must be not in work itself but in their other human relations, whether in society, sex, their own family, or some avocation. While it is true that the economic structure forces many people into work which is neither interesting nor satisfaction-giving, nothing can prevent anyone from assuming an avocation which does offer that satisfaction.

There is a certain quantum of creative energy in every human being which is not absorbed by the business of a work-a-day world. Even people who are engaged in some eminently satisfactory occupation have some creative energy left over. This is the essential godliness in man. We must all create something - or class ourselves as human vegetables. No one can be happy who does not find some channel for this creative energy.

When we suggest creative or artistic activities to neurotics, we are usually met with the objection that they have no artistic talent, no time, or no inclination. I have never done anything like that" Often they call attention to the fact that there are already so many experts that they cannot compete. Herein lies their psychological difficulty. It is not necessary to compete with the greatest sculptors of all time. It is quite possible to get a great deal of pleasure and recreation simply from attempting to model your wife's head in plasticine. It is not necessary to be a Rembrandt to get fun in drawing the types in the tube or in your office.

Hobbies there are without end. They are one of the most effective forms of insurance against the boredom of old age or the heavy artillery of adversity. No man can afford to be without a hobby, and so long as his hobbies are subordinate to his life work, the more hobbies the better. There is hardly a device which is such an effective prophylaxis against subjectivity or melancholia as a hobby, it matters not whether you cultivate dahlias or raise goldfish. The wise man has a variety of avocations - outdoor hobbies and indoor, summer and winter ones, social and solitary forms of amusing himself in his leisure moments. No one with a good hobby is ever lonely for a long time. A good hobby is one of the best possible bridges between the social and the vocational worlds.

'Either... or' v. 'Both... and'

One of the essential differences between the mentally immature and the emotionally adult lies in their attitude toward perfection. Perfection is a curse, and the cult of perfection, that is, living according to the motto of 'one hundred per cent or nothing' restricts men and women to the narrowest spheres of isolation. Perfectionism is the blinker that keeps many a man on the path of failure. Only in the child's world, or in the cosmology of the savage and the neurotic, do the finalities of 'all or none', of 'either - or', of 'large or small', 'right or wrong', exist as veritable entities.

In the world of mature men there are no finalities. Everything is relative. The emotionally mature adult lives according to the law of 'Both...and'. For the romantically infantile, fixed and absolute standards of right and wrong exist, but the completely adult individual realizes that right and wrong are elastic conventions, variable with time and place and circumstance. He seeks to understand rather than to label. He seeks to join together in creative inventiveness rather than to disjoin in romantic idealism.

This realisation leads to important conclusions with regard to the technique of living. There are people who cannot bear to be in the wrong. They must have the last word at all costs. Their insistence either intimidates their adversaries into submission or arouses their natural resistance. We see the most bitter and unnecessary controversies arising from the attempts of neurotics to prove their point at all costs. It is almost universally true that the more noise a man makes in an argument or discussion, the greater the likelihood that he is in the wrong and that he has to bolster up the weakness of his arguments by the loudness of his protestations.

Peaceful social intercourse can exist only in a society of mentally mature individuals. You can achieve a great deal of happiness and gain an enormous host of friends if you will incorporate the wisdom of social relativity not only into your major vital activities but also into your most unimportant conversations. Remember that your neighbour is likely to be just as discouraged as you are. If you wish to convince him of a point, or teach him a new technique, minimize the distance between your superior position of knowledge and his inferior position of ignorance. No one likes to be inferior; no one enjoys ignorance. You will find the greatest souls among the most modest men, the best teachers among those who get down on the floor with their pupils. Conscious modesty in attitude, quietness in gesture, combined with firmness of purpose and decision, mark the well-adjusted adult.

Some Useful Hints on Controversy

To this end it is wise to eschew all words of finality and superiority. The words 'absolutely', 'certainly', 'always', 'never', and the like have little place in the vocabulary of the happy man. If after mature thought and consideration you really believe in the truth of a certain proposition, and wish to convey it to another, it is always best to put it in such a form that your listener can accept your word without losing his self-esteem. To this end it is sometimes the part of wisdom to wink at the truth. If a belligerent neurotic shakes his fist in your face and tells you that horses have three legs, and you know from experience that horses have four legs, it will not help your argument to shout back at him and tell him he is irrevocably wrong. It is better to say: I agree with you and your excellent experience. In the great majority of cases horses do have three legs, but to my mind, in this particular instance, this chestnut mare has four legs. In nine cases out of ten you will gain your point and win a friend.

Trivial quibbles about right and wrong are most apt to occur between parents and children, between husbands and wives, and between business partners, and in our experience nothing is so well calculated to upset good social relations as a useless argument. If these arguments cannot be entirely avoided, we caution those who would be happy, to allow their opponents to have their say, agree with them completely, and then proceed to do what they think right without further comment. Usually controversial actions are not nearly so soul- destroying as the conversations that accompany, precede, or follow them.

If you are dealing with a man with an exaggerated Jehovah complex, let him play Jehovah to his heart's content, and bend your energies to the more objective task of getting out of his environment. Usually the Jehovah complex is manifested in minor matters, because few men can carry their ideas of omniscience or infallibility into the major spheres of human activity. It is better to concede, to smile, and to run away. Here, surely, discretion is the equivalent of social valour.

Remember that in twenty-five years it will make very little difference whether you smoked only ten cigarettes a day as your father desired or forty as you wished, that no one will remember whether you drove your golf ball into the bunker at the fifth hole or laid it up to the green, whether you should have spent only two guineas for a pair of dancing pumps, or whether you were wrong to kiss Mrs Smith in her husband's presence. Develop a stoic disregard for trifles, and extend your horizons to such a degree that trifles can never affect the even tenor of your pursuit of goals that are worth while.

Of Deferred Living

One important source of unhappiness is the habit of putting off living to some fictional date in the future. Men and women are constantly making themselves unhappy because in deferring their lives to the future they lose sight of the present and its golden opportunities for rich living. 'When' I have a thousand pounds in the bank I'll go to Egypt.' Why not go to Egypt as inexpensively as possible now, and enjoy life while you are young? 'When I am thirty-five years old I will marry.' Why not marry now, and have the fun of struggling for some common objective in comradely cooperation with your wife? 'When I am married, I'll settle down and do some serious reading.' Why not one good book a month during your celibate days? 'If I had more time I'd study interior decoration.' Why not go to fewer films and play less bridge and spend two nights a week studying?

If we defer living too long, unfortunate events frequently spoil our plans and change our aims. Sometimes we grow so old that our former goals lose their glamour, with the result that we are left high and dry *sans objectives*, and sans the joy of living. We have often heard disconsolate adults complain, 'Oh, if I had only learned to play the piano when I was young.' While it is my belief that it is never too late to begin anything - and we have ample evidence to prove that we really learn better when we are mature - witness John Stuart Mill beginning the study of Greek at the age of seventy- most of the excuses people make during their maturity really mask their fear of not reaching a high stage of perfection. And perfection is death.

For those who would be happy while they are alive, the importance of developing their curiosity and their sense of adventure while their faculties are sharp should be apparent. Hunger, love, and curiosity are probably the most irresistible of human urges, and life without adventure is a pallid life indeed. Take a chance. Buy a new picture for your room, enrol in a new course, take that trip you have so long planned, even though you cannot do it as you desired. Buy that car even though it is a second-hand Austin Seven. Sit in the gallery and see that play, or listen to that concert. Do not defer life. The dividends of too much caution and security are boredom and smugness. It is better to have adventured in life and made mistakes, than to have petrified in mind and body in the secure depths of an easy chair, with an horizon bounded by your office, the daily paper, and the four walls of your home. **Only the dead know complete security.**

One of the chief differences between the life pattern of the child and that of the adult is the element of planfulness. The mentally mature man develops a plan of conduct, a grand strategy of living which consists not only in an immediate plan of attack on the problems of the present, but a secondary scheme for maintaining the position gained in maturity throughout old age. The child (whether in age or in mental immaturity) lives a planless life. His strategy consists either in muddling through or dreaming through life.

How to Grow Old Gracefully

It must be apparent that the chances of happiness are much greater when an individual makes provision for his old age during his maturity. The socially responsible, mature individual cannot bear the thought of reverting to the helplessness of childhood when the relatively greater helplessness of old age will affect him, whereas the grasshopper characters among men, never having outgrown their childhood, place their faith in God, in society, or in luck, and make no responsible provision for their last years. Happiness is impossible for the adult- in-body-child-in-mind man because his whole character is an anachronism. Just as precocious children miss the fruits of childhood, so the mentally immature forego the usufructs of adult life. The planlessness of their lives is evidence of their lack of self-confidence and self-respect, and an indication of their disbelief in their own ability to meet the obstacles of life and conquer them.

The quest of happiness is not conceivable without a definite plan both for the present and the future. Everyone should develop activities in his youth and early maturity which will carry over into the period of old age. The tragedies of men and women who have outlived their usefulness, and are tolerated by their children or other workers about them who grudgingly support them, can never be understood by any except the old. Many of these old men and women who have grown to ripe years but have retained their childish concepts of the world because they have not grown and developed with the world about them, assiduously devote themselves to the mischief of pampering their grandchildren or injecting discord into the lives of their children. You need not fear old age if you have invested sufficiently in the social graces and avocations. When these investments mature they continue to bring dividends of happiness and satisfaction even when your physical powers have begun to wane.

The best insurance against melancholia, depression, and a sense of futility in old age is the development of wide horizons and the cultivation of mental elasticity and interest in the world. Unlike the flesh, the spirit does not decay with the years. Many of the happiest people in the world are men and women in their sixties, seventies, or eighties, who have contributed richly to the world's work during their maturity, and at the same time have cultivated sufficient awareness and interest in undying cultural activities to make their leisure a delight. By contrast, those tragi-comic figures of men and women who are trying to keep young at all costs, seem pitiful. We have seen women of fifty and sixty torturing their flesh in order to fool themselves into the belief that they are still young. Others go through obscene and vulgar sexual or social contortions to prove vainly that they have not lost their youth. We have seen seventy-year-old men with arteries like pipestems trying to compete with boys in tennis until they dropped dead of apoplexy, simply because they could not look the reality of old age in the face.

Millions of pounds are spent annually by women who, when they should be enjoying a happy old age, rush around from masseur to beauty expert and back again in a panicky attempt to prove that they are still young. Neither face-lifting, flashy clothes, heavy drinking, sexual orgies, nor social overactivity can dupe nature. These temporary devices, in the end, do not even deceive the faded and jaded women who use them. The more hectic the attempt to prove youth in the face of sagging tissues and hardened arteries, the more tragic the spectacle, the more intolerable the situation, the greater the danger of a complete mental and physical breakdown of the personality. The reckless quest for speed, power, youth, or vitality leads first to the open arms of the charlatan, to the embrace of the sneering gigolo, and eventually to the grave.

It is as if youth were a beautiful house in which we have been invited to sojourn temporarily. Delightful as our weekend may have been, it is both tactful and right that we should pack our things and be on our way and off to our work before our host becomes restless and is compelled to make false excuses to speed our parting. Maturation and senescence of body and mind are inexorable laws of nature. We cannot escape from the final truth that we all grow old and die. It is better, therefore, to be philosophic about this fact, and to prepare to make the long reaches of maturity interesting and peaceful. To do this we must learn the fine art of growing old gracefully.

To grow old gracefully requires a maximum of that form of objectivity we call 'a sense of humour'. The man or woman who has found his focus of satisfaction within himself during the whole of his youth and early maturity finds it very difficult to face the problems of old age and death with equanimity. This is one of the facts that no neurotic dares to face. Every egoist, moreover, hopes that some extraordinary Providence will look out for the exigencies of his old age.

Clinical practice indicates that this hope is unfounded. The only really happy old people are those who have tasted the satisfactions of a good job well done in the past, while they exhibit a lively interest in some avocation as a means of making their time of lessened activity rich and meaningful in the future. The older men grow, the more they realize that it is only by putting the focus of their activities upon some movement or activity greater than their individual ego that they can attain peace and security in old age.

This truth is especially applicable to the woman who is inclined to make the important work of raising her children her only profession, only to find that these children, too, mature and grow out of their dependence, leaving their over-solicitous and over-protective mother a mere shadow of a human being without a good reason for living. The necessity for interesting herself in some extra-familial activities should be apparent to every woman who does not consciously desire to raise a brood of neurotic and dependent children for the express purpose of being a martyr to their adult infantilisms at a time when she should be secure in the friendships and activities of her contemporaries. Many women unconsciously keep their children infantile because they themselves are afraid to look at a future in which they have no cogent activities either to fill their leisure or to occupy their energies.

Growing old gracefully should begin with youth. No one who intends to lead a happy old age should neglect the adventure of books, of music, of dancing and the other arts, and above all, the art of social intercourse. The last of life, as Browning has so well put it, is the goal of youth. How can one be happy, then, looking always at the lost paradise of youth and denying the reality for which we were created? This problem is the more pressing because *more and more people grow to a ripe old age nowadays than ever before.*

The Uses of Leisure and Adversity

Modern medicine has increased the span of life, and the economic structure of society has lessened the number of working hours and increased the number of enforced holidays. If we do not simultaneously increase our interest in living, it would really be better to scrap our public health activities and let men and women die in the height of their maturity. Too many people live as if their lives were to be snuffed out at fifty. And while they may make certain provisions for their animal care by taking out insurance policies when they are young, they seldom take out mental insurance in the form of a lively investment in the cultural and artistic activities which give life its fullest meaning. The problem of making adequate use of leisure no longer affects only the plutocrat. The machine age has made it every man's problem.

The dim realization that we live longer and have more leisure has stimulated that excellent movement known as adult education. In the old paternalistic and authoritarian cultures, school was an unpleasant period of stupid preparations to take examinations and get a diploma. As soon as the diploma was properly framed, education ceased. But the artist in living must never stop learning. The man who would grow old gracefully must be constantly fortifying himself with new ideas and new interests. You cannot coast through life on the momentum of a school or college education.

Life teaches us much, but we must learn and learn and learn. To stop, even for a moment, in the pursuit of knowledge and in the search for new and greater awareness is to bring mental death closer. We petrify all too soon. We can at least protract our personal usefulness and our individual interest in life by searching for ever for new worlds to conquer. Those who live in the larger towns will find many opportunities for adult education. And men and women who live in places deprived of all cultural advantages can become the pioneers of adult education in their own communities and thus find a valuable social activity helpful not only to themselves but to their neighbours.

Despite the obvious neuroticizing tendencies of modern life, we can console ourselves with the thought that never before in the history of the world has life been so eminently worth living, and never before so thrilling. The morning newspaper and the monthly magazine are veritable storehouses of challenges and stimuli. Never before has the opportunity for living life at a high conscious and intellectual level been so apparent. Never before have there been so many profoundly important causes crying for intelligent social cooperation from adult men and women. Never before has the challenge of living fully been so clear. You can hardly name a sphere of human activity, be it transport or international peace, be it economics or sociology, be it commerce or medicine, politics or philosophy, in which old values are not tumbling, in which there is not a cry for leaders and for soldiers in a good cause.

One could almost close his eyes and put his finger on the morning paper at random, or open the encyclopaedia at a chance page and immediately find a good cause. The world is sick of its mistakes; it is hungry for peace and brotherhood. We stand at the crossroads as never before in the written history of the world. One road leads definitely toward that brotherhood of man which has been the goal of every religious and philosophic movement of the past. One road leads to the destruction of mankind by war and competition. We can choose consciously. Mankind must make civilization work for mankind if we are not to be destroyed by the Frankenstein monster we have created. No one need ever be unhappy who sees this task clearly, who looks to his resources, who goes forward, singing, to the accomplishment of the greatest task of all, the establishment of a practical brotherhood of man.

What shall we say of adversity, of the 'slings and arrows of outrageous fortune" that beset us in the course of our studies in the art of living? Two schools of thought exist with reference to misfortune. Many pray nightly that life's difficulties may be kept from their path. 'Lead us not into temptation" runs their prayer. It seems highly problematical whether any secure happiness can be attained by running away from temptation, discord, pain, disappointment. Since these things exist in the life of everyone, it seems wiser to counsel a stoic philosophy.

Not freedom from temptation, but a serene fortitude in the face of disappointment and chagrin, should be our goal. If you have evaded all unpleasantness in life, your happiness is placed in unstable equilibrium by the constant dread that some unavoidable disappointment is just around the corner. If you have faced pain and disappointment, you not only value your happiness more highly, but you are prepared for unpredictable exigencies. Just as we can immunize ourselves against certain bodily diseases by stimulating our reserves to over-activity by taking graduated doses of toxin into our bodies, so we can immunize ourselves against adversity by meeting and facing the unavoidable chagrins of life, as they occur. There may be happy human vegetables who have succeeded in avoiding unhappiness and pain, but they cannot call themselves men.

L'Envoi

I have come to the end of my book, but before I reach the last page, let me make a plea for leniency. I am fully aware of the limitations of my outline of the fine art of being human, and I take this occasion to remind readers that in my very first pages I stated my purpose in writing this book: to prepare a catalogue of investigations to stimulate the reader's further study and further labour. I shall feel that my purpose has been accomplished if the reader has found a crystallization of knowledge which he has already sensed and understood, in these pages, and if, here and there, he finds an occasional practical suggestion applicable to his own case. The reader is reminded that I set out to describe an art, the fine art of living, not to prepare panaceas and formulas; and although I have attempted to describe the processes, the ends, and goals of the art of living richly, I can at best make only some hints and suggestions which the reader must apply in the course of his own individual creativeness.

The reader himself will have to practise his art. The fine art of living is to be learned only by living, never by thinking or talking about it, alone. There are countless omissions in any textbook of art. Some are due to the ignorance of the writer, some are due to the exigencies of space, but many are due to the ineluctable and mysterious characteristics of life and art themselves. Some readers will find my descriptions over-simplified, others over-complicated. These flaws are inherent in any guide-book, whether to a foreign city or to the soul of man. It has been my sole purpose to awaken an interest in the most thrilling of all arts, the art of being happy, to describe the material of that art, and to stimulate and encourage the reader to see and to do for himself.

It is inevitable that a book of this sort will be read by certain timid individuals who have lost their courage and mistaken their way, and it is just as inevitable that these men and women will identify themselves with some of the cases cited in the previous pages, choosing here a symptom and there a characteristic, thus making out a case against themselves. These readers will misuse the book to discourage themselves further, saying, 'You see, I am a hopeless neurotic, and no good can ever come of me. How can you expect me to begin all over again when I have been making mistakes all my life?" For these readers I must add a special postscript.

Even though this book may not have led them to that inner clarification that comes of knowing the truth, and though they do not choose to practise any of the suggestions I have outlined, I believe they will have gained a certain measure of tolerance and understanding of their fellow-men and their struggles, and, in this way, my book will not be without a certain value. It has been my hope, it is true, that the previous pages will have helped readers to assume the responsibility for the self-education of their characters and personalities. So wise a man as Socrates maintained that virtue could be learned. But if I have not succeeded in stimulating the reader to tackle the task of broadening his mental horizons and enlarging the scope of his pattern of life, to the end of attaining a larger and surer happiness in being human, I at least have succeeded in showing the over-timid and over-cautious reader that he is not alone in the world, that others, too, suffer from fear and isolation. And this may be of some solace and consolation.

If you have really understood the meaning of my book, I feel almost certain you will realize that almost everything is possible. No man, no woman, is damned to live an ineffectual, unhappy life either by the facts of heredity or the defects of environment. Almost every human being can be happier than he is, and nearly every human being can either master the fine art of living richly or at least contribute to the general happiness of humanity by cheerfully helping those who are more adept or more experienced. No one need be useless, no one need be isolated, no one, knowing the truth, need be unhappy.

There may also be readers of this book who have realized in the reading that they have completely lost their way, and have no certain maps and no fixed stars to aid them in charting their course. To these readers and to those others whose specific problems have not been satisfactorily illumined, together with those readers whose problems are too complicated or individualized to have been touched in these pages, I counsel seeking the advice of a recognized psychiatrist or mental hygiene clinic. The time is happily gone when it was a disgrace to ask the advice of an expert in mental hygiene. Help exists for those who would be helped. When in doubt, it is more intelligent to seek advice from those whose training fits them to understand quickly and to help surely. Neither ignorance nor fear is a disgrace. The only sin is to remain ignorant and afraid when knowledge and encouragement are within reach.

I have reached the end of my book, but to living there is no end. Life begins where books end. Let us begin to live.

THE END.

Printed in Great Britain
by Amazon